Globalization and Public Sector Reform in China

This book analyses public sector reform comprehensively in all parts of China's public sector—government bureaucracy, public service units and state-owned enterprises. It argues that reform of the public sector has become an issue of great concern to the Chinese leaders, who realize that efficient public administration is key to securing the regime's governing capacity and its future survival. The book shows how thinking about public sector reform has shifted in recent decades from a quantitative emphasis on 'small government', which involved the reduction in size of what was perceived as a bloated bureaucracy, to an emphasis on the quality of governance, which may result in an increase in public sector personnel. The book shows how, although Western ideas about public sector reform have had an impact, Chinese government continues to be best characterized as 'state capitalism', with the large state-owned enterprises continuing to play an important—and increasing—role in the economy and in business. However, state-owned enterprises no longer provide care for large numbers of people from the cradle to the grave—finding an alternative, efficient way of delivering basic welfare and health care is the big challenge facing China's public sector.

Kjeld Erik Brødsgaard is Professor and Director of the Asia Research Centre at Copenhagen Business School, Denmark.

Routledge contemporary China series

Globalization and Public Sector Reform in China

Edited by Kjeld Erik Brødsgaard

Routledge
Taylor & Francis Group

LONDON AND NEW YORK

First published 2014
by Routledge
2 Park Square, Milton Park, Abingdon, Oxfordshire OX14 4RN

and by Routledge
711 Third Avenue, New York, NY 10017

First issued in paperback 2016

Routledge is an imprint of the Taylor & Francis Group, an informa business

British Library Cataloguing in Publication Data
A catalogue record for this book is available from the British Library

Library of Congress Cataloging in Publication Data
Globalization and public sector reform in China / edited by Kjeld Erik
Brødsgaard.
    pages cm. – (Routledge contemporary china series; 118)
    Includes bibliographical references and index.
    1. China–Economic policy–2000–2. Public administration–China.
    3. Government ownership–China. 4. Globalization–China. I.
    Brødsgaard, Kjeld Erik.
    HC427.95.G5596 2014
    352.3′670951–dc23

                                                            2013040222

ISBN 13: 978-0-415-78806-9 (pbk)
ISBN 13: 978-0-415-72359-6 (hbk)

Typeset in Times New Roman
by Wearset Ltd, Boldon, Tyne and Wear

Contents

Figures

Tables

Contributors

Kjeld Erik Brødsgaard is Professor and Director, Asia Research Centre, Copenhagen Business School.

Daniele Brombal is Assistant Professor, Department of Asian and North African Studies, Ca' Foscari University of Venice.

John P. Burns is Professor of Political Science and Dean of Social Science at Hong Kong University.

Chen Gang is Research Fellow, East Asian Institute, National University of Singapore.

Manoranjan Mohanty is Chairperson and Honorary Fellow, Institute of Chinese Studies, Delhi and former Professor of Political Science, University of Delhi.

Jean C. Oi is the William Haas Professor in Chinese Politics; Director, Stanford China Program, and the Lee Shau Kee Director, Stanford Center at Peking University.

Dragan Pavlićević is a PhD candidate at the China Policy Institute, University of Nottingham.

Jesper Schlæger is Associate Professor, School of Public Administration, Sichuan University.

Jayan Jose Thomas is Assistant Professor, Humanities and Social Sciences Department, Indian Institute of Technology, Delhi.

Andrew G. Walder is Professor of Sociology, Stanford University.

Zhengxu Wang is Associate Professor, School of Contemporary Chinese Studies, and Senior Fellow, China Policy Institute, University of Nottingham.

Zhang Xiaowen is Senior Research Fellow and Director of the Division of Enterprise System Research, Institute of Economic Systems and Management, National Development and Reform Commission of China.

Huang Yanjie is Research Assistant, East Asian Institute, National University of Singapore.

Zheng Yongnian is Professor and Director of the East Asian Institute, National University of Singapore.

Acknowledgements

This book is based on selected and updated papers originally presented at a conference on 'Globalization and Public Sector Reform in China and India', held at the Asia Research Centre, Copenhagen Business School, September 23–24 2011 and co-sponsored by the Danish Foreign Ministry. I am grateful to David Strand (Dickinson College) for his meticulous comments on the draft manuscript. I am grateful to Peter Sowden (Routledge) for accepting the manuscript for publication at Routledge. I also wish to thank the East Asian Institute at National University of Singapore and especially the institute's director, Zheng Yongnian, for hosting me during the final stages of manuscript preparation.

Abbreviations

ASI	Annual Survey of Industries (India)
CASS	Chinese Academy of Social Sciences
CCP	Chinese Communist Party
CCTV	closed-circuit television
CHIMA	Chinese Hospital Information Management Association
CMS	Cooperative Medical Scheme
CNPC	China National Petroleum Corporation
CPS	Central Party School
DRC	Development Research Center of the State Council
DRG	Diagnosis Related Groups
GAPP	General Administration of Press and Publication
GDP	gross domestic product
GIS	geographic information system
GPS	global positioning system
GVA	gross value added
HIS	hospital information systems
ICT	information and communication technologies
IMF	International Monetary Fund
IP	inpatient
IT	information technology
LIS	Labour Insurance Scheme
MCA	Ministry of Civil Affairs
MHRSS	Ministry of Human Resources and Social Security
MNCs	multinational corporations
MNREGA	Mahatma Gandhi National Rural Employment Guarantee Act
MoC	Ministry of Commerce
MoF	Ministry of Finance
MoH	Ministry of Health
NDA	National Democratic Alliance (India)
NDRC	National Development and Reform Commission
NGO	non-governmental organizations
NPC	National People's Congress
NRCMS	New Rural Cooperative Medical Scheme

NSS	National Sample Survey (India)
OP	outpatient
PDA	personal digital assistant
PSEs	public sector enterprises
PSUs	public service units
R&D	research and development
RTE	Right to Free and Compulsory Education Act (India)
SARS	Severe Acute Respiratory Syndrome
SASAC	State-owned Assets Supervision and Administration Commission
SEZs	Special Economic Zones
SFDA	State Food and Drug Administration
SOEs	state-owned enterprises
SRC	Securities Regulatory Commission
THE	total health expenditure
TVEs	township and village enterprises
UNDP	United Nations Development Programme
UNICEF	United Nations Children's Fund
UPA	United Progressive Alliance (India)
URBMI	Urban Residents Basic Medical Insurance
UWBMI	Urban Workers Basic Medical Insurance
WHO	World Health Organization

1 Globalization and public sector reform in China

Kjeld Erik Brødsgaard

Introduction

Reform of the public sector has become an issue of great concern to the Chinese leaders as they realize that efficient public administration is a key to securing the regime's governing capacity and ultimately long-term survival in a globalized world. The public sector in China is large, comprising 65.5 million people and efforts to reform the system as well as to change the work habits and routines of the personnel staffing of the administrative organs are of an enormous nature. Reform in this area is also constrained by the complexity of the Chinese public sector. At one level the public sector in China is not a unitary system. It can in fact be divided into three institutions: Party and state organizations (*dangzheng jiguan*) comprising twelve million people; public service units (PSUs or *shiye danwei*) with 27 million employees; and state-owned enterprises (SOEs or *qiye danwei*) employing 26 million staff and workers. Each component has its own personnel management system and personnel and budget allocations. But behind this division and fragmentation, the Chinese Communist Party remains in ultimate control. Some studies have been done on reform of Party and state organizations and public service units, but very little is available on reform of state-owned enterprises in the overarching context of public sector reform. There are also no scholarly attempts to discuss the linkages between the various components of the public sector in China. Our book aims to remedy this lacuna in extant research.

Clearly, how China conducts this reform will have an important bearing on the political and social development and stability of the country. It will also provide interesting comparative perspectives for public sector reform in other major emerging economies, including India. The following chapters are based on papers presented at a conference on "Globalization and Public Sector Reform in China and India," held at the Copenhagen Business School, September 23–24, 2011. The papers pertaining to China have subsequently been revised and updated in the fall of 2012. They provide an overview analysis of the character of the Chinese public sector as well as a number of case studies of the issues at stake in reforming the three main components of the public sector. They show that the Party-state has different and at times conflicting reform goals. There is no doubt that the civil service system will continue to form the core of the bureaucracy. Reform in this area aims to strengthen the professional capacity of civil servants while maintaining their political loyalty. Civil servants will be subjected to streamlining and institutional merger, but there is no intention of reducing their status and their key role in government at central and local levels. Public sector units, on the other hand, will be subject to a reform which will transfer a large number of them to enterprise status leaving their employees without their former tenured job security and associated pension and social security benefits. Finally, the state-owned economy has been subject to an ambitious corporatization process. However, the result of this has not been comprehensive privatization. In fact the strategic sectors of the economy, such as steel, telecom, aerospace, power generation, oil and gas, are still dominated by a group of huge state-owned enterprises. Thus the reform process seems to have resulted in consolidation of state dominance in certain sectors, whereas other sectors have been exposed to market forces, and less favorable supply of state benefits. This disparity has not made it easier to implement reform.

In most of the world the public sector expanded after World War Two until the early 1980s. As economies grew and societies became more differentiated and complex, the state's functions of regulation, allocation, and redistribution grew correspondingly (Bertucci and Jemiai 2013). This was clearly the case in the US and in Western Europe and in particular in the Scandinavian countries. In East Asian countries such as South Korea, Japan and Singapore economic development was stimulated by an interventionist developmental state (Brødsgaard and Young 2000). In communist countries central planning necessitated the existence of a strong state that could take care of resource mobilization and allocation. In China the state also grew in terms of scope and task. This was especially the case after the Cultural Revolution during Hua Guofeng's interregnum and the first few years of the reform period, when large numbers of cadres were rehabilitated.

During the 1980s and 1990s the critique of big government and big spending was the dominant theme of public policy and debate throughout most of the developed world, providing the intellectual framework for the emergence of the New Public Management Agenda of reducing direct state intervention. The Thatcher and Reagan regimes and the ascendancy of neo-liberalism further strengthened the idea of downsizing government personnel and functions in order to reduce fiscal deficits and create more efficient public management.[1] In addition, many European countries tried to fulfill the criteria for membership in the European Monetary Union in the 1990s. An important criterion was the ratio of total government debt to GDP and government borrowing to GDP. Therefore these governments were pressed to initiate various public cost containment programs (Bender and Elliott 2003). Moreover, international financial institutions such as the International Monetary Fund (IMF) and the World Bank advocated measures to reduce state intervention in economic affairs in the developing world (Fukuyama 2004). In essence this was the prescription the IMF suggested to solve the Asian Financial Crisis in 1997–98.

During the 1980s and 1990s, Chinese leaders also perceived reform of the public sector in quantitative terms. It was thought that the main problem was big government and that streamlining and reducing the bureaucracy in terms of personnel and agencies would create favorable conditions for a more efficient public sector.

In 1981 the first of a series of post-cultural revolutionary administrative reforms was launched in an attempt to downsize the state bureaucracy. Government ministries and agencies had multiplied so that there were 100 ministerial-level working departments, of which no fewer than 65 were responsible for economic management (Brødsgaard 2002). There were for example no less than eight machine-building industries as well as a number of ministries within the power and energy sector, such as the Ministry of Coal-mining, the Ministry of Petroleum, the Ministry of Electricity and the Ministry of Metallurgy. In addition there were a number of commissions dealing with overall as well as sectoral planning such as the State Economic Commission, the State Commission of Science and Technology, the State Planning Commission and the State Capital Construction Commission. The proliferation of ministries and commissions were symptomatic of a centralized planning system that had grown out of proportion and did not harmonize with the reformers' goal of creating a more market-friendly economic environment. In order to address the problems of overbureaucratization, the reformers took two initiatives. The first initiative was to introduce an ambitious administrative streamlining program which reduced the number of central-level ministerial organs by more than one-third to 61. The second initiative was to shift functions that previously had been handled by central ministries to newly created enterprises. Thus abolishing the Ministry of Petroleum resulted in the creation of three new companies: China National Offshore Oil Corporation (established 1982), China Petrochemical Corporation (established 1983) and China National Petroleum Corporation (established 1988). These were all carved out of the assets and functions of the former Ministry of Petroleum. In other sectors of the economy similar restructurings took place. These developments became the start of the corporatization process that created a number of huge business groups and transformed the state's control and management of an important part of the public sector in China (Brødsgaard 2012b).

The 1981 reform was only the beginning of a series of administrative reforms during the 1980s and 1990s, i.e., in 1988, 1993 and 1998. The reform launched by Premier Zhu Rongji in 1998 deserves special mentioning. It involved reducing 41 ministerial-level working departments to 29 and downsizing central-level administrative staff by 50 percent. Zhu Rongji also initiated an economic restructuring that left two or three dominant business groups in each sector. The role of the large business groups was further strengthened by reorganizing a number of ministries such as the Ministry of Coal Industry, Ministry of Metal-lurgic Industry, Ministry of Power, Ministry of Chemical Industry and the remaining Ministry of Machine-Building Industry into bureaus and placing them under the management of the State Economic and Trade Commission. By dismantling these old branch ministries associated with the Soviet administrative model and heavy-industrial development strategy, the autonomy of the business groups was considerably strengthened (Brødsgaard 2012b: 629).

In the 2000s there have been three major administrative reform attempts—in 2003, 2008 and 2013. The 2008 plan was particularly ambitious and was launched under the rubric of "super ministry reform" (*dabuzhi gaige*) ("Guowuyuan jigou gaige fang'an (caoan)" 2008). The plan involved the establishment of five new super ministries: the Ministry of Industry and Information; the Ministry of Human Resources and Social Security; the Ministry of Transportation; the Ministry of Housing and Urban-Rural Construction; and the Ministry of Environmental Protection. They were formed by reorganizing, merging and expanding existing ministries. However, some of the original reform ideas had to be given up because of vested interests and political opposition within affected ministries. For example, it had not been possible to merge the Ministry of Railways with the new Ministry of Transportation. Powerful interests were against the merger since it would appear to downgrade the importance of the railways in China's transportation system. Moreover, the idea of creating a super ministry within the area of energy also had to be abandoned due to heavy resistance from powerful entrenched interests in the big business sector. The big SOEs within the energy sector were against the establishment of a ministry that might interfere with their activities. In 2013, it finally became possible to close down the Ministry of Railways by moving the administrative functions to the Ministry of Transportation and by turning the commercial operations of the railways into a large state-owned company. The ministry had been severely weakened by a serious high speed train accident in July 2011, near Wenzhou, Zhejiang province. The move against the ministry was further facilitated by a huge corruption case involving the powerful railway minister Liu Zhijun. However, it was still not possible to establish a Ministry of Energy (Brødsgaard and Grünberg 2013; Gore 2013). In Chapter 4 of this volume Jesper Schlæger shows that at the local level there can also be heavy resistance to consolidation and mergers of institutions. He mentions how an attempt at consolidation at the local level in Chengdu through service centers set off "fierce bureaucratic turf-wars."

In general, although downsizing and streamlining still are important objectives of administrative reform, in recent years the discussion in China has shifted towards a more qualitative-based discourse. The question is no longer whether to downsize the bureaucracy, but how to define which essential functions the state must take care of and to identify how this should be done in the most efficient way. On this basis a determination would be made as to the number of personnel and administrative organs to take care of key functions. The process is called the three fixes (*san ding*) in Chinese administrative terminology. There is also a renewed focus on the abilities and competences of civil servants in government agencies as well as officials and personnel in public service units (*shiye danwei*). There is a growing realization that public sector reform cannot be reduced to administrative reform and downsizing alone. Moreover, the corporatization process has resulted in the formation of huge state-owned enterprises, which do not signify a retrenchment of the state, but in fact only has resulted in transferring resources and power from one part of the state (the central planning apparatus) to another (the SOE sector).

Civil servants

The civil service system was conceived in the mid-1980s as a way of professionalizing the administrative work in state agencies and reducing the role of the Party in public sector management.[2] Due to the political fallout from the Tiananmen debacle, plans were put on hold until 1993, when regulations for a new civil service system were decided on and published. During the 1990s and early 2000s a number of additional regulations detailing issues such as appointment and removal, employment appraisals, training, rotation, resignations and dismissals, retirement, management and supervision as well as remuneration were published, and in January 2006 a set of revised regulations were adopted in the form of a Civil Service Law.

The various regulations all aimed at creating a civil service system characterized by ability and professionalism. They also aimed to create a younger and better-educated state bureaucracy. A look at available statistics seems to show that formal qualifications did improve. We do not have detailed information on the composition of the civil service corps. However, available information on the composition of the cadre corps can be used as a yardstick. Although the main part of the 41 million strong cadre corps are not civil servants, all of the ten million civil servants manning the state and Party bureaucracy are considered cadres. Moreover almost all leading cadres are civil servants. Therefore changes in the composition and qualifications of the cadre corps is indicative of similar changes among civil servants.

In 1979 only 29 percent of Chinese cadres were below 35 years of age. This percentage has now risen to more than 50 percent. The share of cadres between 36 and 54 years of age has fallen from 65 percent in 1979 to 45 percent today. Thus the Chinese cadre corps is now considerably younger than at the end of the Mao era (Brødsgaard 2011).

The educational level of cadres has improved dramatically since the beginning of the reform period in 1979. The share of cadres with junior middle school education or less was almost 50 percent in 1979, now this share of less educated cadres is below 8 percent. Among leading cadres, the share of people with a university degree has increased from 16 percent in 1979 to more than 80 percent. Now more than 95 percent of the Central Committee have a college degree and an increasing number of top leaders even hold a PhD.

The change to a younger and better-educated cadre corps is associated with rigorous training courses for Chinese officials. The rule now is that Chinese officials must have at least three months of training within a five-year period. For many officials training and educational courses at Party schools or training centers in China and abroad is a precondition for advancing in the system.

New guidelines and regulations have been adopted with stipulations concerning open appointment and selection of cadres and filling of official positions and examination. These include a public notification system for positions below *ting*-level and experiments with multi-candidate elections for leading government and party posts; regular job rotation from section level and above; and strengthening the supervision of cadres by introducing clear measures for performance evaluations combined with public feedback on the quality of work done. There are also flexible remuneration and pecuniary rewards to high performers.

As shown by Zhengxu Wang and Dragan Pavlićević in Chapter 3, civil servants form the backbone of the Chinese bureaucracy. They are the primary instruments through which the Chinese Communist Party controls the country (Brødsgaard 2012a). It is not an easy task to determine the numerical strength of the civil servants. Estimates vary between six million and ten million. In this volume Kjeld Erik Brødsgaard and Chen Gang in Chapter 5 choose the higher estimate. This figure of ten million is based on the category of "employees in organs of the Communist Party of China, government agencies, People's Political Consultative Conference, democratic parties, and various organizations such as the trade unions" minus the number of logistical personnel.[3] It is noteworthy that the concept of civil servants is markedly different than in European countries. In Europe civil servants are bureaucrats staffing agencies, bureaus and offices at local and central levels, including positions of permanent secretary. However ministers, including the prime minister, are selected according to electoral results not as a consequence of administrative skills or seniority. In China the concept of civil servant covers all state employees from a section member (*keyuan*) to the prime minister and president. They are all remunerated according to a uniform national civil service pay system. In Western countries, leaders enter the top of the power pyramid horizontally as a result of elections. In China leadership selection takes place as a vertical process within the bureaucratic apparatus. A prospective leader starts his/her career as a section member in a Party or state organ and works his/her way up the power hierarchy as section leader, division leader, department leader, minister, and may finally become prime minister or president.

Due to China's integration into the global economy and global political governance structures there is increasing pressure on Chinese leaders to continuously upgrade their leadership capabilities. Leading officials are evaluated by their colleagues and superiors on a regular basis and subject to continuous training in Party school and various training centers. Top civil servants are even sent abroad on month-long intensive training courses in Europe, Singapore and the US, where they learn about international leadership and management practices and alternative political, economic and social models.

Shiye Danwei (PSUs)

Shiye danwei or public service units (PSUs) refer to organizations and institutes in the cultural, educational, sporting and medical care sectors providing social services and welfare to the public.[4] Thus public service units include hospitals, schools, kindergartens, universities, museums, publishing houses, etc. Traditionally these institutions received funding from the state and were regarded as non-profit enterprises. Brødsgaard and Chen Gang show that although employees in public service units are not considered civil servants they have for many years received salaries and benefits similar to civil servants. Many institutions have both civil servants and *shiye danwei* employees. This is for example the case in the Central Party School where the professors and teachers are employed according to *shiye danwei* conditions, whereas the leading personnel and Party officials are employed according to civil service regulations.

With 27 million people employed, the *shiye danwei* sector is much larger than the civil service sector in terms of number of personnel as well as in terms of administrative costs. In many localities salaries and pensions for *shiye danwei* form the main part of the local budget. The phenomenon of hiring more people than allowed by the stipulated personnel quota is especially pronounced within this sector. One example is Lingshui county in Hainan. This county of only 310,000 people had more than 5,000 people employed to teach 50,000 students. This blatant overstaffing was uncovered when the county no longer could afford to pay for the salaries and went bankrupt (Brødsgaard 2002: 369).

In order to save money and social resources, the Chinese government recently introduced reform measures which aim to delink *shiye danwei* from the civil service system in terms of salaries, pensions and other benefits. The government has also put forward a reform scheme according to which *shiye danwei* will be classified into three categories. One category will have their status changed to enterprises. As a consequence they will have to commercialize and find their own funding outside the state budget. This has already happened to many media and publishing houses. Another category will have their status changed to civil service status and receive the same salary and benefits as civil servants. This is the case for institutions such as the Development Research Center of the State Council, which in the past was regarded as a *shiye danwei*. A third category will continue to function as a *shiye danwei* with government funding. This is especially the case for institutions that provide social welfare, medical care and education. Hospitals will probably also fall into this category in order to avoid the kind of excessive profit-seeking behavior described by Daniele Brombal in Chapter 6.

Locally, experiments are ongoing, taking the *shiye danwei* reform even further. There are for example experiments in Guangdong province that aim to separate government and social service providers. The social service providers are supposed to function as social organizations which can register without having to hook up (*guahao*) with a government institution. The government is supposed to buy its services from these new providers. Services will be purchased according to contracts between the government and the service providers. Such a system is close to the ideas in the new public management model that had its heyday in the West during the 1980s and 1990s. It is unclear how the Chinese authorities will ensure the quality of the products and services they buy from these service providers. There is also the risk of hollowing out the public sector, since resources and manpower will likely be transferred from the public sector to these new service providers.

State-owned enterprises

State-owned enterprises exist at various levels.[5] The most important are the 115 so-called central enterprises (*yangqi*) managed by the State-owned Assets Supervision and Administration Commission (SASAC). They have undergone a process of corporatization where the most productive parts have been listed on stock exchanges in New York and Hong Kong as well as the domestic Chinese stock exchange. The mother companies of the listed companies still exist and have become huge business groups or conglomerates. As mentioned above, these business groups or national "champions" control the strategic sectors of the economy including oil and gas, chemicals, steel, power generation, shipbuilding, aerospace and telecommunications. They generate huge profits, which they mostly keep within the company for reinvestment or for paying high salaries to staff and company executives. The leaders of the 53 largest companies are on the central nomenklatura and therefore, similar to ministers and governors, are managed by the Central Organization Department of the Communist Party of China (Brødsgaard 2012a). This new managerial elite enjoys high salaries and special benefits. Currently, as analyzed by Jean C. Oi and Zhang Xiaowen in Chapter 8, the big state-owned enterprises are advancing and have in some instances acquired privately owned companies. Thus the current trend in China is not further industrial privatization, rather it is corporatization in which the state advances and the private sector retreats (*guo jin siying tui*).

The SOEs are part of the public sector. Their leaders are appointed by the state and, for the 53 largest, by the Party. Top business leaders are also part of a rotation system where they may be transferred to take up a government job (e.g., provincial governor or vice-governor) or they may be transferred from a government position to an executive position in big business. Even though they are not classified as civil servants they are often treated as such and are subject to similar promotion schemes and appointment policies. The result is a new generation of managers who are changing the management of the public sector, as they alternate between the corporate domain and government. Many of these new and sophisticated managers have learned about business in the world's best business schools. They have been exposed to international business practices and bring a new perspective of the world into public management. In this sense business executives form an important recruitment pool for leadership positions in the public sector and within the Party itself.

SOEs are also part of interest and power relations that form so-called vested interests. Vested interests are interests that profit from existing power and authority relations and essentially seek to maintain the status quo. They are often linked to monopolies which make it possible to gain excessive profits or to engage in rent-seeking. In the Chinese case SOEs monopolize key sectors of the economy and do not allow competitors to enter. The state nurtures and supports the central SOEs as it is interested in creating powerful "national champions." The Party is also interested in supporting and further developing the SOEs as they form a mainstay of the economy and as SOE executives are an integral part of the cadre corps at the elite level. Together Party, state and big business form an iron triangle of vested interests which is difficult to break up. The iron triangle has succeeded in creating a number of huge enterprises that increasingly function on a global scale. Seventy-three of them are now on the Global Fortune 500 list. However, as shown by Huang Yanjie and Zheng Yongnian in Chapter 7, their growth depends on state support and assistance. It is doubtful whether they would be able to compete on the global-level playing field without substantial state support.[6]

Huang Yanjie and Zheng Yongnian, in their criticism of this overprivileged state sector, also note that the large SOEs have been able to shed the extensive social welfare obligations that belonged to the old *danwei* (unit) system, where housing, schooling, medical care, pension etc. were the responsibility of the workplace. Getting rid of these obligations naturally considerably reduces the social expenses of the enterprise. However, Oi and Zhang in Chapter 8 appear to disagree, indicating that the mother company of the corporatized business group still must shoulder these responsibilities, although many have succeeded in transferring them to local governments. In reality the whole issue is probably in flux at the moment and subject to local variations. Shedding social functions has met resistance even as the logic of global competition encourages such disinvestments of pension and other obligations.

The new configuration of state, Party and business in China may be called state capitalism (Haley and Haley 2013). It has delivered record high growth rates and achieved a track record in economic development that few other economies can rival—not even Japan when it took off in the 1960s and 1970s. The immense challenge the Chinese leaders face is to combine this economic miracle with a public sector that can deliver basic welfare and healthcare. As discussed by Andrew Walder in Chapter 9, economic reform has dismantled the old system where the production unit took care of its employees from cradle to grave. Millions of workers have been laid off and the state has had to step in and alleviate the consequences of the broken rice bowls. This requires a well-functioning public sector and raises the fundamental question of whether China needs more or less government. Essays in this volume are informed by the fundamental view that in order to manage the many new tasks and functions evolving out of economic reform and modernization, China needs more, not less, government and more, not fewer, government officials. This argument can be illustrated by the fact that only 8 percent of the Chinese workforce is on state salary. In comparison, in the Scandinavian countries one-third of the workforce is employed by the state. In the US it is 16 percent.

This book details the many issues at stake in public sector reform in China. John P. Burns shows in Chapter 2 how Western practices and ideas have inspired Chinese reformers to streamline the Chinese bureaucracy and to improve the governing capacity and efficiency of government institutions. However, in recent years the large state-owned enterprises have strengthened their role and they constitute a key pillar of the public sector in China. Their leaders are intertwined with government officials in a nexus of vested interests. There are revolving doors between the large SOEs and government institutions. The forces of globalization have not resulted in the privatization of the SOEs. On the contrary, in recent years they have advanced and have taken over smaller private enterprises in many sectors of the economy, reinforcing the emergence of a particular kind of resilient state capitalism. The result is a public sector different from the one found in many Western countries. The Chinese would call it a public sector "with Chinese characteristics." Such formulations indicate the fact that Chinese policy-makers and planners are informed by public sector institutions and practices outside their own country. They realize that globalization requires China to improve, reform and perhaps even borrow from abroad. However, the borrowing is selective and adapted to Chinese conditions.

As Burns discusses in Chapter 2, in the scholarly literature on Chinese public sector reform there are two schools of thought concerning the driving forces of reform. One school argues that most of the themes of contemporary Chinese reforms are not unique, but have parallels in Western countries. Consequently, global reform theories and concepts such a New Public Management have influenced the reform agenda in China. In the case of civil service reform for example, during the 1980s there were extensive studies in China of Western civil service systems, although it was ultimately decided to reject key features such as political neutrality and the absence of political interference in core administrative functions (Chan and Suizhou 2007; Worthley and Tsao 1999; Zhang and Straussman 2003). Nonetheless, according to this school similarities in reform thinking and reform efforts in the public sector all around the world have resulted in a process of convergence. Over time, and as a consequence of globalization, Chinese characteristics will recede in the operations of the public sector.

Another school maintains that China's public sector reforms are mainly driven by internal, contextual factors rather than being stimulated by particular global reform models. Internal drivers such as the transition to the market and readjustment of the CCP's role in social and economic management in combination with unique cultural and historical legacies produce a unique context where "local solutions" are required. (Ngok and Chan 2003; Lan 2001; Cheung 1997). This school questions the globalist interpretation of contemporary public sector reform (Cheung 1997). There may be some convergence in terms of reform rhetoric, but the means and the ends of reform vary considerably depending on the history, politics and institutional feature of the countries in question. In short, there is insufficient evidence to support a convergence thesis encompassing the developed and underdeveloped world, including China.

However, there is also a third school which takes both internal and external factors into consideration. This school admits that even though the patterns and styles of reform in China and in the West during the past 30 years show similarities and parallels, there are unique Chinese features. The influence of global governance ideas and practices will, for example, be constrained by the authoritarian nature of China's Party-state polity. Moreover, various phases of public sector reform in China may have different constellations of internal and external factors. Thus the first two decades of reform seem to be more domestically based and related to internal pressures, while later reforms from 1998 onwards seem to be more externally influenced by economic globalization (Christensen *et al.* 2008; Ngok and Zhu 2007). The drive for globalization has had an influence on SOE reform in China and has strengthened arguments for nurturing and developing a group of national champions that can compete on the global-level playing field (Chan 2009). However, the structural change and adjustment of China's SOEs is not exclusively oriented towards global competitiveness. Maintaining control of the strategic sectors of the economy is also an important political consideration. So, on the one hand, the Chinese government is interested in maximizing the position of its companies in the international global order and this requires attention to market share and competitiveness. On the other hand, state economic management and vested interests in maintaining state monopoly in priority sectors counterbalances the urge to play by the rules of the international economic order (Chan 2009: 44). For business executives, political loyalty and patronage are often more important than economic performance for their career prospects.

This volume makes a case for this third interpretation. It acknowledges the impact of global reform models such as New Public Management. Chinese policy-makers and planners are well informed about global discussions and practices concerning public management. Such topics are being discussed in academic circles in think tanks and universities. High-level officials are, on a regular basis, sent abroad to learn about debates and policies in other countries. However, when translated into a Chinese context, the inspiration acquired from studying international examples are modified to suit Chinese conditions. Rarely do we see wholesale transfers of ideas, concepts and methods. In fact, as Manoranjan Mohanty points out in Chapter 11, the neo-liberal prescription of retreating the state and minimizing the public sector may not be the right prescription for the problems and challenges faced by large developing countries such as China and India.

In sum, the study of public sector reform in China is complicated by the size of its personnel and the embeddedness of its institutions in a political system dominated by the Chinese Communist Party. The institutions making up the Chinese public sector are in fact so vast and variegated that the sector seems fragmented, if not pluralistic. This helps to explain, if not justify, the adoption of different methods and measures according to which component of the public sector the government is focusing on in its reform efforts. It is obvious that the further away from the center of power, the easier it is to introduce Western experiences. In his chapter Burns shows that local leaders seem more entrepreneurial and more prone to learn from the West than central leaders. The debate on public sector reform in China illustrates that Chinese leaders are not only concerned about maintaining high economic growth. They realize that ultimately growth depends on the quality of public sector and the general business environment. They also realize that given the complexity and vastness of the public sector in China a trial-and-error process is necessary. The speed of this process varies from sector to sector and level to level, suggesting unevenness but also flexibility.

Outline of the book

Civil service reform

The first portion of the volume examines various aspects of civil service reform in China. In Chapter 2 John P. Burns analyzes the impact of Western ideas such as New Public Management and good governance on public sector reform in China. Burns introduces his paper by discussing the overarching issue of convergence versus national trajectories. He rejects the notion that China's reforms are an example of convergence towards a Western model of public administration. However, absence of convergence does not necessarily lead to a rejection of diffusion as a characteristic of China's reforms and he admits that China's public sector reformers draw considerable inspiration from Western ideas. Looking at the motives of Chinese officials, Burns argues that the so-called "climbers," who are more motivated by power, income and status and focus exclusively on promotion, are most likely to adopt Western ideas. Moreover, the incentive for promotion in a performance-oriented system especially encourages local leaders to experiment with Western reform practices. The main part of the paper is a discussion of three public-sector case studies in which Chinese leaders, in promoting administrative reform, have been influenced by Western thinking. The three cases are civil service reform, performance management reform and good governance.

According to Burns, in introducing and developing the civil service system, Chinese leaders looked to the West for inspiration. They have concluded that China could benefit from introducing some Western administrative practices and techniques such as rigorous evaluations and reviews, promotion on the basis of merit, acknowledgement of the status and ranks of civil servant, and, perhaps most importantly, recruitment of personnel through open competition. However, they clearly did not want to take over the broader political environment of Western civil service systems, characterized by multi-party competition and the political neutrality of civil servants.

Turning to the second case study, Burns maintains that in terms of performance management reform and public management techniques Chinese officials were also inspired by Western ideas and adopted new public management techniques such as contracting out, balanced score cards and performance pledges. Unlike top-down civil service reforms many of these reforms were introduced by local leaders trying to maximize their chances of promotion. However, similar to civil service reforms, the adapted public management techniques were tailored to Chinese circumstances.

The third case study concerns the issue of good governance. Burns realizes that the concept of good governance is not well defined. He chooses to focus on a number of core characteristics including accountability, participation and transparency. He argues that Chinese government agencies have become more transparent in recent years, but in his mind provincial and local governments are better at practicing transparency than the central government. Whereas civil service reform was a top-down project and the search for public management techniques a bottom-up process, China's experience of good governance came from both the top and the bottom.

Chapter 3 by Zhengxu Wang and Dragan Pavlićević focuses on the Party's efforts to build a meritocratic civil service in China. They argue that the concept of meritocracy within the Chinese Party-state differs from that of the West in that it consists of both political loyalty and professional competence dimensions. This two-dimensional notion of meritocracy is different than the Western one-dimensional notion which focuses exclusively on competence and ability. They argue that the challenges of governing an increasingly complex society puts pressure on the Party to focus more on competence and merit at the expense of the ideological purity of its rank and file. Wang and Pavlićević examine the institutions and practices in five areas of the Party-state's personnel management: regulation; recruitment; training; evaluation and assessment; and promotion. They find that the conception and practice of meritocracy still retain distinct Chinese characteristics, but are gradually transformed in response to the need to recruit, develop and promote competent officials. They predict that the ideopolitical dimension in China's meritocracy will be gradually phased out as the civil service system moves towards a one-dimensional system. They term such a trend a transitional meritocracy.

Wang and Pavlićević structure their analysis around a research platform which strives to provide a "systematic and holistic evaluation" encompassing all key aspects of personnel management: formal rules and regulations of the personnel management system as well as criteria for how party and government officials are recruited, trained, evaluated and promoted. The holistic approach is also reflected in their appreciation of the influence of the imperial past on the current meritocratic civil service system. References to the imperial examination (*keju*) as the main institutional pillar of meritocracy serve to contextualize the Chinese civil service reform. Imperial precedent underlines the contemporary goal of attaining an efficient and capable bureaucracy. At the same time, and as a result, meritocracy is conditioned by historical, cultural and political factors.

In Chapter 4, Jesper Schlæger examines the role of new management technologies in public sector reform in China. He especially looks at how information and communication technologies (ICT) have increased the capacity of government to monitor the work performance of both employees and government agencies. Schlæger introduces two theoretical concepts to guide his investigation. One is the concept of "virtual panopticon." The concept denotes the ability of superior government authority to comprehensively monitor the compliance of lower-level government employees and institutions. The monitoring is virtual since it applies ICT techniques and includes automated surveillance. The other key concept is "battering ram." This refers to government authority's attempt to use digital monitoring and ICT-based data to force institutional change. The battering-ram mechanism is deployed in cases of non-compliance with objective criteria such as performance indicators. In short, based on interview data from fieldwork in Chengdu, this paper not only contributes detailed empirical knowledge about Chinese public administrative reform, but also provides theoretical insights about mechanisms of institutional change by invoking new concepts keyed to new ICT-based management techniques.

Digital monitoring is also used to reduce inefficiency in communication. Reformers believe that real-time surveillance of screen-level bureaucrats will create a more performance-oriented and non-corrupt set of behaviors among employees. Digital techniques also make it easier to introduce quantitative measures of quality control. In short, digital monitoring introduces a new dynamic in administrative reform in the public sector. However, Schlæger cautions that the battering-ram mechanism appears to have failed repeatedly in solving problems of bureaucratic politics and administrative problems. The matrix-muddle of vertical and horizontal relations (*tiao-kuai*) in the Chinese administrative system often blunts both subtle and direct applications of ICT methods.

Reform of public service units

In Chapter 5 Kjeld Erik Brødsgaard and Chen Gang discuss the personnel management system in both civil service and the public service units (PSU). Although these two pillars of the public sector in China have been managed by two different personnel systems, there have been many similarities in terms of remuneration, pensions and other benefits. A great number of employees in public service units have in fact been managed according to civil service regulations (*canzhao gongwuyuan*). The government now wants to separate the civil service system and the public service units. As a result salaries, pensions and social security benefits for PSU employees will be less generous. Those affected are naturally critical of the reform, which consequently has been slow in getting off the ground. Another aspect of this reform is to reclassify PSUs into three categories: (1) government-like organs with administrative functions and civil service status; (2) not-for-profit organizations or public benefit units which will continue to have PSU status and will receive government funding; and (3) self-financed or purely for profit organizations which will be turned into enterprises.

The authors show that the status of the employees in the public sector is closely associated with the concept of *bianzhi* (authorized staffing). This is a key concept in Chinese public management. It refers to the authorized number of established posts in the public sector. There are three main categories of *bianzhi*: administrative *bianzhi* (*xingzheng bianzhi*), enterprise *bianzhi* (*qiye bianzhi*) and the *bianzhi* which applies to PSUs (*shiye danwei bianzhi*). The *bianzhi* lays down the number of agencies, organizations, and units and the number of personnel (*renyuan*) allocated to these institutions. The *bianzhi* also involves budget outlays in the form of salary and allowances.

For the individual employee the *bianzhi* is of utmost importance because it gives job security and stipulated state-financed salary and benefits. The current reform implies that some PSU employees in the future will not have a fixed *bianzhi* as their unit will rely on private funding. This again has implications for social security and pension as new schemes have to be designed to replace the old schemes based on civil service comparisons. The chapter shows that employees in the public sector units face a loss of social status and position as well as pension and welfare benefits, whereas the Party-state by contrast will retain welfare privileges for its own officials. This may be politically and economically efficient, but is also perceived as morally incorrect and unfair by the people adversely affected. The new policy has provoked huge resistance and boycotts among employees in public sector units. Only in April 2012, after several years of debate, was it possible to pass the regulatory guidelines for reform in this sector.

In Chapter 6 Daniele Brombal focuses on the health care system, which is a key part of the PSU sector. In the past health care was in the hands of the state in the cities and the collectives in the countryside. Now there are strong pressures for privatization. In fact, Brombal shows that public funding in the hospital sector has been cut so much that hospitals increasingly are left to generate their own income. They do this by prescribing excessive amounts of medicine and by overcharging for the drugs provided. This in turn gives rise to economically driven private interests on the part of doctors who prescribe the drugs and companies that produce them. He estimates that hospitals account for four-fifths of all pharmaceutical sales and that on average 40–50 percent of hospital revenues come from drug prescriptions. Drawing on data collected through fieldwork between 2008 and 2011, Brombal investigates this state of affairs and the effect of this unleashing of private interests on the health care sector.

In his contribution Brombal highlights an area where the retrenchment of the state from social services work left an important part of the public sector ill-regulated and underfunded. He argues that although the government has retained ownership of the majority of health care providers, reliance on user fees has resulted in a de facto privatization of health care.

While there is no doubt that important parts of health care in China are being outsourced to non-public providers as part of public sector reform, hospitals may not be totally commercialized. The current reform of PSU units would make it possible for hospitals to retain their PSU status as public benefit units. However, this would require an increase in public funding, so that they would have less motivation to overcharge patients for medical treatment and overprescribe drugs. It would also require an attempt to break up the significant vested interests that have emerged within this sector, threatening the efficiency and fairness of the system.

Public sector reform and state-owned enterprises (SOEs)

Chapters 7 through 9 shift the focus to public sector reform and state-owned enterprises (SOEs). These enterprises are still an important part of the public sector. Until the early 1980s enterprises were not independent production units, but were part of the centralized economic planning system. As a result of administrative reforms during the 1980s, many heavy-industrial ministries were abolished and turned into companies. The state continued to hold the formal ownership of these companies, but in practice they developed considerable autonomy.

In Chapter 7, Huang Yanjie and Zheng Yongnian discuss China's centrally managed SOEs during the reform era. They show how, through enterprise reform, China's large SOEs evolved from loss-making giants with feet of clay to powerful and autonomous corporate and political actors. Although China has seen considerable private sector development since the 1980s, the strategic sectors of the economy—such as oil and gas, power, electricity, aerospace, aviation, shipbuilding, telecom, etc.—are still dominated by state-owned companies, in particular around 115 large companies managed by the State Assets Management and Supervisory Commission (SASAC). They command enormous resources and generate huge profits, retained by the companies instead of handed over to the state, the nominal owner.

Acting in their own interests, these SOEs have become a source of strong vested interests which prevent further economic reform and liberalization. They enjoy monopoly status in important sectors of the economy and prevent foreign and private companies from entering their markets. Huang and Zheng point out that new studies show that if hidden subsidies from the state are factored in, the SASAC companies are not as profitable as commonly thought. In fact, serious economic problems exist ranging from inefficiency to income inequality. Moreover, their political might in the Party-state bureaucracy and their fiscal contributions to state coffers have made it difficult for the central government to control and regulate them effectively either through regulatory agencies like SASACs or other alternative channels. Based on a discussion of the power and autonomy of centrally managed SOEs vis-à-vis the state and the economy, the chapter seeks to illustrate some of the most vexing problems faced by China's central government when it comes to further reform of the state sector. The authors note that the large SOEs no longer carry the extensive social security burdens they used to in the old system, when the livelihood and the welfare of the workers were the responsibility of the workplace. The corporatization process of the 1980s allowed them to shed many of their welfare obligations, leaving these to the state. The authors sympathize with Chinese observers who argue that the central enterprises should bear more social responsibility by handing over more of their profits to the state to pay for needed welfare and pension benefits.

In Chapter 8 Jean C. Oi and Zhang Xiaowen also show how corporate restructuring in China has made SOEs more, not less, dominant in key industrial sectors. The number of SOEs may have gone down, but those companies that remain have become more dominant and have grown in size. With the hope that the strong would help turn the fortunes of the weak and the need to minimize or at least delay worker layoffs, the state merged weak firms with strong ones, leading eventually to the creation of corporate groups (*jituan*), into which most central SOEs are organized today.

Of particular interest are the large central state-owned companies under SASAC that are nurtured by the Chinese state in order to create global giants. However, while the state wants to create national champions that are competitive internationally, the question remains as to whether the government's earlier strategy of merging the weak with the strong has left some SOEs with a set of historical burdens and costs that will prove to be obstacles to further reform. The subsidiaries of the *jituan* may do well on the stock exchange, but the parent companies are still struggling with problems of inefficiency, backward technology and lack of innovative capabilities. The parent companies will eventually also have to reform, but so far have been given much longer timelines entailing less visible but very real costs to the economic system.

The authors emphasize that a distinction should be made between privatization and corporatization. When large firms were restructured they were corporatized, not privatized, which meant that the state no longer was the sole owner. It sold shares to others, such as workers or managers of the firm, but in most instances the state held a controlling number of shares. The large *jituan* are completely owned by the state. The subsidiaries that are spun off as listed companies may have other types of shares, but the mother company will still hold the controlling number of shares.

The authors also emphasize that China's goal in restructuring never was to fully privatize or marketize its industrial sector. In terms of public sector reform this is an important point to make. It indicates that China may learn from the West and may be eager to adapt to forces of globalization. However, wholesale privatization is not on the agenda. On the contrary, within important sectors of the economy, the state is advancing rather than retreating.

In Chapter 9 Andrew Walder's analysis of the corporate steel sector in China reinforces the view that the state sector of the economy is still strong. In fact he argues that the notion of a shift "from plan to market" no longer accurately describes the transformation taking place in Chinese industrial sectors. He uses the steel sector to show how large bureaucratic corporations or business groups have been assembled through mergers of existing state companies pushing back private firms. The same process has taken place in other strategic sectors of the economy. As part of the corporatization process, also analyzed by Oi and Zhang, the labor forces in these SOEs have been cut drastically. In the past SOEs not only employed tens of thousands of employees, they also provided extensive welfare in the form of child care, schools, housing, clinics, medical insurance and pensions. The restructured firms are increasingly trying to transfer these welfare obligations to local governments.

Walder also argues that even though the restructured state firms have been listed on domestic and international stock exchanges, they have not been privatized in any meaningful sense. They are as tightly integrated into national political structures as older socialist enterprises. The process analyzed by Walder is completely different to developments in the former Soviet where state enterprises were either spontaneously privatized or privatized in a more systematic manner. In China, larger firms continued under state ownership and still form an important part of the public sector and the national political structure.

The chapter also discusses a unique feature of integration of the large SOEs into the Party-state. This is the appointment system for top executives in the 115 SASAC companies. They are part of the nomenklatura system and the leaders of the 53 largest companies are in fact appointed by the Party's Central Organization Department. They are regarded as leading cadres and are often rotated to government positions as governor or vice-governor or even minister. There are also numerous examples of government bureaucrats moving into top positions in big business. This shows that top executives of the large state-owned corporations are an integral part of the Party-state's bureaucratic leadership system. In fact business executives from these companies are informally ranked similar to civil servants.

Public sector reform in India and China: a comparative perspective

Chapters 10 and 11 bring in a comparative perspective by comparing public sector reform in China and India. These are both huge developing countries that initiated their post-World War Two growth trajectories by introducing economic development strategies that focused on high investment and heavy-industrial growth. India has broken with this pattern of growth whereas China essentially is still locked into it. Thus disinvestment of public enterprises has gone further in India than in China. Jayan Jose Thomas and Manoranjan Mohanty agree that state-owned public sector enterprises and publicly funded welfare and social security provisions are needed in large countries such as China and India and that disinvestment and privatization of the public sector are not the answers to the problems and challenges they face.

In Chapter 10 Jayan Jose Thomas argues that public sector units in India and China are frequently portrayed as "inefficient" producers, causing a drain on the national economies. His chapter, reviewing the relation between public sector and economic growth in India and China since the 1950s, contests this view. In India, the public sector contributed significantly to raising the savings and investment rates and to reviving the overall economic growth of the country, especially between 1950 and the mid-1960s. However, the success of India's state-led development in reducing societal inequalities and in generating non-agricultural jobs has been rather limited. The Chinese record has been far superior in this respect. Another difference, according to Thomas, is that although the disinvestment process in India has slowed down after 2004, policy-makers in India do not envisage a significant role for the public sector in the country's future. He indicates that the greater focus on state-led development and a limit on disinvestment or privatization of the public sector in China may account for that country's superior economic performance. Here Brombal, on the other hand, would argue that an important part of the public sector in China is being hollowed out by lack of funding, which in the case of the hospital sector gives rise to de facto privatization as doctors and hospital managers seek to make up for lack of funding by overprescribing drugs, often in collusion with large pharmaceutical companies.

According to Thomas, given the dominance of Western multinational companies in the global innovation economy, public sector units will have to emerge as generators of crucial knowledge assets in countries like India and China. For instance, the public sector can help generate innovations in agriculture and labor-absorbing industries that can transform the lives of millions of poor in these and other developing nations. SOEs also have an important role to play and here Thomas is critical of the fact that disinvestment deals in India during the early 2000s often resulted in handing over profitable public sector companies in strategic areas of the economy to private monopolies. He applauds the fact that in China the government has retained direct control over the large SOEs, while the smaller SOEs in sectors of non-strategic significance have been privatized.

In Chapter 11, Manoranjan Mohanty, contextualizes the public sector reform in China by investigating the building blocks of the political discourse on this topic in both India and China. In both countries the state has played an important role in initiating economic growth and establishing basic welfare provisions for the population. In fact, according to Mohanty the experience of public sector reforms, and the discourses accompanying reform in India and China, challenge basic categories and beliefs that have dominated development thinking in the contemporary world. In his mind, experiences in China do not substantiate the neo-liberal view that the way ahead for developing countries is to reduce the size and role of the state and basically dismantle the public sector. In the West critics of "big government" even advocate the privatization of health, education and other social services. Mohanty shows that periodic attempts to reduce public investment in basic welfare and social services in China and India have "created havoc."

His paper takes up some comparable as well as distinct examples from both countries to argue that the future course of reforms in general and public sector reforms in particular is likely to be along novel lines rather than following the New Public Management practices and the neo-liberal script that have been advocated by the sponsors of globalization. However, there is contestation on these issues as there are decision makers and planners in both India and China who subscribe to Western management ideas and are eager to reduce the scope and reach of the state. In short, according to Mohanty, Indian and Chinese experiences, encompassing both state policies as well as social dynamics, contribute to continued critical reflection on basic issues in development theory, thereby overcoming many dichotomies created by the neo-liberal discourse. The state and the public sector are necessary in public welfare and social security provisions as well as in managing and developing key sectors of the economy.

It is noteworthy that both Thomas and Mohanty stress the achievements of the state sector and warn against far-reaching privatization and disinvestment of the public sector. They believe that a strong state sector is the best solution to the problems and challenges large countries such as India and China will face in their efforts to modernize and develop. Here they are in disagreement with other contributors, including Huang and Zheng, Oi and Zhang, and Walder who see problems of inequality, vested interests, inefficiency and the monopolization of profitable economic sectors. Currently, the debate on these issues is also growing in China. How the debate plays out and what further policy measures will be taken remains to be seen.

Notes

1 Margaret Thatcher's Conservative government of 1979 was elected on an explicit commitment to control public expenditure and reduce the size of the public sector. See Bach and Winchester (1994).
2 Core personnel in Party and state organs are civil servants. On civil service reform, see Lam and Chang (1995); Brødsgaard (2001); Burns (2004); OECD (2005a); Chou (2009); Wang (2012).
3 For this method of calculating the number of civil servants, see Zhu (1998).
4 On public service units, see Lam and Perry (2001); OECD (2005b); World Bank (2005).
5 On Chinese SOEs, see Steinfeld (1998); Keister (2000); Hsueh (2011); Walter and Howie (2011); Oi (2011).
6 This point is most forcefully made by Peter Nolan. See Nolan (2001, 2012).

References

Bach, S. and Winchester, D. (1994) "Opting Out of Pay Devolution? The Prospects for Local Pay Bargaining in United Kingdom Public Services," *Journal of Industrial Relations*, 32(2): 263–282.
Bender, K. A and Elliott, R. F. (2003) *Decentralised Pay Setting: A Study of the Outcomes of Collective Bargaining Reform in the Civil Service in Australia, Sweden, and the UK*, Aldershot: Ashgate.
Bertucci, Guido and Jemiai, Yolande (2013) "Public Sector Reform Revisited in the Context of Globalisaton," available online: http://unpan1.un.org/intradoc/groups/public/documents/caricad/unpan000477.pdf (accessed July 2, 2013).
Brødsgaard, Kjeld Erik (2001) "China's Civil Service Reform: Changing the Bianzhi," *EAI Background Brief* (81).
Brødsgaard, Kjeld Erik (2002) "Institutional Reform and the Bianzhi System in China," *The China Quarterly*, 170(June): 361–386.
Brødsgaard, Kjeld Erik (2011) "Western Transitology and Chinese Reality: Some Preliminary Thoughts," *Copenhagen Discussion Papers* (38).
Brødsgaard, Kjeld Erik (2012a) "Cadre and Personnel Management in the CPC," *China: An International Journal*, 10(2): 69–83.
Brødsgaard, Kjeld Erik (2012b) "Politics and Business Group Formation in China: The Party in Control?" *The China Quarterly*, 211 (September): 624–648.
Brødsgaard, Kjeld Erik and Grünberg, Nis (2013) "Leadership Changes and Structural Reform after the 18th Party Congress in China," *The Copenhagen Journal of Asian Studies*, 31(1): 81–94.
Brødsgaard, Kjeld Erik and Young, Susan (eds.) (2000) *State Capacity in East Asia: Japan, Taiwan, China, and Vietnam*, Oxford: Oxford University Press.
Burns, John P. (2004) "Governance and Civil Service Reform," in Jude Howell (ed.) *Governance in China*, Lanham, MD: Rowman & Littlefield, pp. 37–57.

Chan Hon (2009) "Politics Over Markets: Integrating State-Owned Enterprises into Chinese Socialist Market," *Public Administration and Development*, 29(1): 43–54.

Chan Hon and Suizhou, Edward Li (2007) "Civil Service Law in the People's Republic of China: A Return to Cadre Personnel Management," *Public Administration Review*, 67(3): 383–398.

Cheung, Anthony B. L. (1997) "Understanding Public-Sector Reforms: Global Trends and Diverse Agendas," *International Review of Administrative Sciences*, 63(4): 435–457.

Chou, Bill K. P. (2009) *Government and Policy-Making Reform in China*, Abingdon: Routledge.

Christensen, Tom, Dong Lisheng and Painter, Martin (2008) "Administrative Reform in China's Central Government—How Much Learning from the West?" *International Review of Administrative Sciences*, 74(3): 351–371.

Fukuyama, Francis (2004) *State-Building: Governance and World Order in the Twenty-First Century*, London: Profile Books.

Gore, Lance L. P. (2013) "China's New State Council and the 'Super-Ministry' Reform," *EAI Background Brief* (810).

"Guowuyuan jigou gaige fang'an (caoan)" (2009) (Draft Plan for Institutional Reform of the State Council), available online: www.mykh.net/bbs/ viewthread.php?tid=170593 (accessed April 7, 2013).

Haley, Usha C. V. and Haley, George T. (2013) *Subsidies to Chinese Industry: State Capitalism, Business Strategy, and Trade Policy*, New York: Oxford University Press.

Hsueh, Rosalyn (2011) *China's Regulatory State*, Ithaca, NY: Cornell University Press.

Keister, Lisa (2000) *Chinese Business Groups*, New York: Oxford University Press.

Lam, Tao-Chiu and Chang Hon S. (1995) "The Civil Service System: Policy Formulation and Implementation," in Lo Chin Kin, Suzanne Pepper and Tsui Kai Yuenn (eds.) *China Review*, Hong Kong: The Chinese University Press, pp. 2.3–2.43.

Lam Tao-Chiu and Perry, James L. (2001) "Service Organizations in China: Reform and Its Limits," in Peter Nan-Shong Lee and Carlos Wing-Hung Lo (eds.) *Remaking China's Public Management*, Westport, CN: Quorum Books, pp. 19–40.

Lan Zhiyong (2001) "Understanding China's Administrative Reform," *Public Administration Quarterly*, 24(4): 437–468.

Ngok, K. and Chan, H. (2003) "Introduction," *Chinese Law and Government* 36(1): 5–13.

Ngok, Kinglun and Zhu Guobin (2007) "Marketization, Globalization and Administrative Reform in China: A Zigzag Road to a Promising Future," *International Review of Administrative Sciences*, 73(2): 217–233.

Nolan, Peter (2001) *China and the Global Business Revolution*, New York: Palgrave.

Nolan, Peter (2012) *Is China Buying the World?* Cambridge: Polity Press.

OECD (2005a) "Civil Service Reform in China," in OECD (ed.) *Governance in China*, Paris: OECD, pp. 49–74.

OECD (2005b) "The Reform of Public Service Units: Challenges and Perspectives," in OECD (ed.) *Governance in China*, Paris: OECD, pp. 75–100.

Oi, Jean (ed.) (2011) *Going Private in China: The Politics of Corporate Restructuring and System Reform*, Stanford, CA: Stanford University/Walter H. Shorenstein Asia-Pacific Research Center Books.

Steinfeld, Edward (1998) *Forging Reform in China: The Fate of State Industry*, Cambridge: Cambridge University.

Walter, Carl and Howie, Frazier, J. T. (2011) *Red Capitalism: The Fragile Financial Foundation of China's Extraordinary Rise*, Singapore: John Wiley & Sons.

World Bank (2005) *China: Deepening Public Service Unit Reform to Improve Service Delivery*, Beijing: CITIC Publishing House.

Worthley, J. and Tsao, K. (1999) "Reinventing Government in China: A Comparative Analysis," *Administration and Society*, 31(5): 571–587.

Wang Xiaoqi (2012) *China's Civil Service Reform*, Abingdon: Routledge.

Zhang Mengzhong and Straussman, Jeffrey D. (2003) "Chinese Administrative Reforms with British, American and Japanese Characteristics?" *Public Administration and Policy*, 12(2): 143–179.

Zhu Guanglei (1998) *Dangdai Zhongguo shehui gejieceng fenxi* (Analysis of Social Strata in Contemporary China), Tianjin: Tianjin renmin chubanshe.

2 Looking West

The impact of Western ideas on public sector reform policies in China

John P. Burns

Introduction

During the Cultural Revolution in China (1966–76) the radicals in power criticized and denounced everything foreign and persecuted Chinese citizens who they suspected of looking West in virtually all areas of human activity, from science to the arts, including public policy and public administrative. Xenophobia writ large characterized public discourse during these years and for anyone to suggest that China could learn from the West was strictly forbidden. In a major change of course, however, in December 1978 newly anointed paramount leader Deng Xiaoping announced an opening to the West that welcomed foreign investment and sought to develop the economy through trade with the West. The opening allowed leaders and intellectuals in China to examine what was going on in the West. They came to understand that public sector reform ideas then current in the West might, suitably adapted, either help solve problems in China or provide the symbols of modernity that the leadership sought.[1]

The post-Cultural Revolution receptivity to Western ideas undoubtedly started at the center, in Beijing. In 1980 provincial and local leaders were too traumatized to experiment with what had been denounced as the evils of Western capitalism on their own. I argue that although the central government led the (at first very tentative and cautious) policy of looking West, the incentive system put in place by the central government soon encouraged local officials to look West (and anywhere else, for that matter) that might improve their chances of promotion. Indeed, from the perspective of 2012, when 420 million-plus Chinese are connected to the internet, it may seem puzzling to consider whether Western ideas have an impact on public sector reform. Of course they do now, but how did this come about?

In this chapter I examine three examples of Western ideas that officials in China considered, starting from the mid-1980s. In the first case, I examine Chinese officials' attempt to introduce what they perceived to be a modern (that is, competitive) civil service system. In the process they considered and discarded other features of Western civil service systems, such as separate roles for politicians and bureaucrats. In the second case, I discuss officials' consideration of certain "new public management"-like techniques. Local Chinese leaders, especially, adapted and then popularized these techniques in pursuit of improved performance and accelerated promotion. In the third case I discuss the impact of a "good" governance paradigm, associated to a large extent with Western multilateral aid agencies, on public sector reform in China. Leaders, motivated by a mixture of altruism and self-interest, reacted cautiously at first but after considerable hesitation adapted the principle (symbols are important), and then endorsed and popularized a limited version (that is, "good" governance with Chinese characteristics). I examine China's experiments with "open" government, initially designed to increase central leaders' control of local subordinates.

Theoretical considerations

Following Pollitt and Bouckaert (2000), I understand that ideas play some role in the process of public management reform. Adapting their model, which seeks to explain reform outcomes in Western capitalist democracies, I understand that "new management ideas," filtered through the political system, reach political leaders as they consider what reforms are needed and what reforms are feasible. Leaders lay down the content of public sector reforms in particular environments and subject to chance events.

The literature on the impact of Western ideas on public sector reform policies in China focuses on two key issues: the nature of diffusion of innovation from the West and the mode of transfer.[2] These issues are examined in the paragraphs below.

Convergence versus national trajectories

Some scholars argue that organizations facing similar environmental pressures tend to evolve towards similar solutions (isomorphism). The convergence hypothesis suggests that due to cultural and goal similarity (Morgan 1981), comparable environmental constraints and opportunities (Osborne and Gaebler 1992), and attempts at imitation (Oh 1976), China's administrative reforms are broadly analogous to those found in other countries (Worthley and Tsao 1999). For example, Worthley (1984) notes that Chinese and American administrations share a common "value structure" that promotes both "administrative expertise and political control," and seeks to reconcile these basic values (Worthley 1984: 519). Although there may be some deviations in technical details between the two countries, they do not undermine the fundamental commonalities in the direction of reform and the nature of the political and administration challenge the reformers in both countries face. The proponents of an emerging global paradigm in public administration (Aucoin 1990; Lan and Rosenbloom 1992; Osborne and Gaebler 1992) share this view. In this view, administrative reforms in China should develop administrative and organizational solutions similar to those already in use in countries with common meta-policy orientations (Chan and Chow 2007; Liou 1997). Both the rise of a global market and China's rapid transition to a capitalist economy create challenges that are universal to governments across the globe (Cheung 1997; Ngok and Zhu 2007). They argue that the force of economic globalization, rather than domestic forces, has determined China's administrative reforms since the 1990s (Christensen *et al.* 2008). In commenting on China and Hong Kong, Huque and Yep (2003) point out that China's ultimate task is to adapt its socialist institutions to a global economic order operating under capitalist principles, and therefore convergence is "possible despite markedly different points of departure" since "the forces of globalization will overwhelm the strong pulls from within the system" (Huque and Yep 2003: 151). Macro-level convergence is facilitated by micro-level dialogue between Chinese officials and Western administrators (Foster 2005; Tong *et al.* 1999). Those involved in the exchange are influenced by their experience and exposure (Lan 1999).

Critics of the convergence hypothesis consider China's reform conditions and objectives to be sufficiently unique that attempts to compare them with foreign experience—even for the purpose of illustration—is inherently misguided (Lam and Chan 1996a). First, China's formulation of administrative reforms ascribes to a unique political philosophy that combines political authoritarianism with economic liberalism (Chan 2004; Chan and Li 2007). In China, public administration reforms are an attempt to replace general centralized economic planning with a targeted consolidation of state control over strategically critical industries and corporations. Most state-owned enterprises are reformed to only the extent that the pragmatic goals of raising the global competitiveness of domestic companies and expanding access to natural resources overseas can be achieved without compromising state control (Chan 2009). As for the public sector in China, it is "actually being re-politicized" despite "the outward appearance of de-politicization" (Chan and Li 2007: 382). The result is the continued inhibition of citizen participation and the strengthening of the traditional superior/subordinate relationship between the Party and the state in spite of growing economic freedom (Burns 1989), a development not mirrored in any of the Western democracies. Moreover, Confucian traditions, the legacy of Communist rule, and developmentalism jointly determine the outlook of China's reform initiatives (Aufrecht and Li 1995; see also Bing 1992; Lam and Chan 1996a). At the more technical level, "imported" administrative practices are often adjusted to local needs and conditions, even when the officials initiating the reform programs engage in active learning and imitation (Foster 2005). Indeed, the Chinese localization of administrative practices closely associated with the post-progressive governance paradigms has led to "a partial return to progressivism rather than a move away from it" (Hood 1995: 109).

An important aspect of the convergence debate is that common reform objectives and outcomes are not necessarily the result of diffusion and transfer: It is possible that reformers of different administrative systems are spurred by a common set of problems and environmental conditions alone in reaching independent yet similar conclusions as to how their respective system should be changed. To a certain extent, researchers comparing foreign administrative reforms with China's own experience do not necessarily suggest diffusion: Tsao and Worthley (1995) compare civil service reforms in contemporary China with the Pendleton Civil Service Reform Act of the United States in 1883. They argue that because of the unique problems leaders in China have faced and the particular reform objectives they have pursued, the process has produced a system that is markedly different from a Western model of public administration both in principle and practice (Lam and Chan 1996a).

Nonetheless, the absence of convergence has not led to a rejection of diffusion as a characteristic of China's reforms. Chinese public sector reformers continue to draw inspiration and even legitimacy from Western ideas (Ngok and Zhu 2003), even though reform programs are often infused with technical changes to limit perceived "negative" impacts on existing government practices (e.g., Horsley 2004; Lam and Chan 1996b). In general, the literature abounds with examples of diffusion that are similarly subject to local variations in context and agenda (Cheung 1997). Writing in the late 1990s Lan (1999: 50) contends that "while attempts at learning from the west have never entirely had their way in China," Western ideas will continue to influence "the pivotal forces that lead China into a modern age." A decade later Christensen *et al.* (2008: 363) observed that, absent the identical mix of problems and political context prevalent in the West, Western models still impact "more generally on the way problems were defined and the solutions selected" in China. The case studies presented here provide additional evidence of this view.

Mode of innovation transfer: top-down and bottom-up

As we shall see in the case studies that follow, some reforms have come from the bottom, through local officials (see Foster 2005). In the cases of many performance management reforms, local governments more or less on their own adopted ideas from the West; the central government was only involved when they became convinced of the idea's utility. In other cases, such as civil service reform discussed below, the central government itself first "looked West" for ideas, initiated the reform, and then required local governments to adopt them (Bing 1992; Burns and Wang 2010). While there is a high level of local spontaneity in the first scenario, direct involvement by national-level actors in the second scenario means that local governments are much less important in importing and initiating reform programs. In both scenarios the involvement of the central government is crucial; reform programs cannot be nationally implemented without the support and commitment of the central government. But the act of importing and experimenting with Western reform programs may actually involve local governments directly.

Various models of innovation diffusion appear to agree on the fundamentals, including the range of actors, the key importance of a leadership committed to the reform programs, the general path of diffusion, and the importance of historical and institutional forces. A key area of unresolved contention concerns the role of the local actors. While some scholars see local leaders as a drag on reform (Christensen *et al.* 2008), others see a degree of local autonomy as important for adapting imported reform programs to local conditions (Ngok and Chan 2003). The resistance of local governments is a manifestation of how the special socio-political setting of China can channel administrative reforms into unique developmental trajectories (Burns 2001). Local actors may undermine reforms initiated by the central authorities, but they also face pressures to innovate and initiate changes given appropriate incentives and conditions (Foster 2005). Any model of diffusion focusing on the long-term tension between the central government and local authorities must also consider local spontaneity in importing and promoting reform programs by specifying the incentive structure of local bureaucrats. Both top-down and bottom-up strategies are illustrated in the case studies below.

Officials' motives

Because I am interested in the incentives for officials to adopt Western ideas we need to have some understanding of the motives of officials generally. Following Downs I assume that officials seek to maximize their utility where utility is defined broadly to include power, both within the bureaucracy and/or outside it, money, prestige, convenience, security, personal loyalty, pride in a job well done, a desire to serve the public interest, and a commitment to a specific program or policy (Downs 1967: 84). Among Chinese officials I am most interested in those Downs calls "climbers," who are motivated almost exclusively by power, income, and status, and for whom promotion is everything. I argue that among the various leadership types in China,[3] climbers are the most likely to adopt Western ideas that will improve the performance of their unit and thus their chances of promotion. I argue that promotion is a strong incentive for most Chinese officials and, therefore, climbers especially have had the incentive to adopt new management ideas, sometimes from the West. They are, however, constrained by promotion rules.

Given reformist China's efficiency and economic development orientation, I expect that official promotion rules would stress performance. Officially, promotion is mostly based on performance (merit). According to the Civil Servants Law officials should be promoted based on the principles of "both moral integrity and ability, and appointment of those on merits, paying special attention to work accomplishments" (National People's Congress 2005). In the Chinese system superiors assess subordinates in annual appraisals and through tests and interviews. In the 1990s officials established elaborate lists of performance targets that local leaders were assessed against, the most important of which at the time was growth of gross national product. Other indicators were added such as the extent to which officials achieved the one-child-per-couple target and the extent to which all children received nine years of education. The party further has expanded these criteria since 2000 to include measures of social stability, including the incidence of social protest and petitioning (Gao 2007; Burns and Zhou 2010).

Studies have shown that local leaders whose counties, districts, or provinces do well on the economic indicators, especially economic growth and remittances of taxes, tend to have a greater chance of promotion (Li and White 1990; Bo 2002; Lin 2008). I understand that promotion rules in practice also include seniority, bribery (purchase of offices) and other forms of corruption (Burns and Wang 2010). However, in this chapter I assume that promotion is mostly performance based and I argue that this provides the key incentive for local leaders to scan for methods and styles that can boost their performance credentials.

The case studies

I turn now to a discussion of three cases in which Chinese leaders considered Western ideas for China's administrative reforms. In the first case (top-down and internal), the political elite at the center, having determined that their current system for managing officials was inefficient, introduced a competitive selection mechanism, which they perceived to be Western.[4] In the process they also considered a Western "new public management"-like reform—separate roles for politicians and bureaucrats, but ultimately rejected this idea. In the second case (bottom-up and internal), climbers in local governments picked up Western notions of performance management (such as performance pledges) to enhance their credentials. Climbers in the central government then pushed the reforms there as well. In the third case (bottom up and external) multilateral aid organizations such as the World Bank and the UNDP introduced the notion of "good" governance to Chinese leaders who were initially skeptical. The central leadership, encouraged by China's establishment intellectuals, then picked it up, adapted it, and popularized it. Climbers scrambled on board.

Civil service reform

In the mid-1980s the inefficiencies of China's centralized "cadre" personnel system had become increasingly obvious (for example, skill and interest mismatches; egalitarian pay systems; rigid transfer systems [Barnett 1967]) and reformers in China began looking for new ideas, including to the West, searches that were legitimized by Deng's new open door policies. Reformers did not look to China's imperial past which they perceived as having kept the country poor and undeveloped (Dai 1990–91: 68).[5] Reformers observed approvingly that the civil service system in the West had "created an environment in which people feel that they are able to compete on the basis of equality and this has helped to draw talented people into government, thereby facilitating the stability of capitalist society" (Dai 1990–91: 68). How did Chinese officials come to see that the competitive element of the Western civil service system might be appropriately adapted for China?

While acknowledging that China in 1980 and Western capitalist democracies had fundamentally different political and economic systems, a high-level party policy making small group acknowledged that leaders in various counties could learn from each other (Dai 1990–91: 68). The small group studied the civil service systems of various foreign countries (Cao 1985) and concluded that

China could benefit from so-called Western practice including recruitment of personnel through open competition; rigorous evaluations, reviews, and promotion on the basis of merit; acknowledgement and protection of civil servants' rights; and using the legal system to manage the civil service (Dai 1990–91: 68–69). Leaving aside the question of the extent to which these characteristics are Western (clearly strengthened training is not peculiar to Western civil service systems), Chinese officials apparently endorsed certain techniques they perceived to be Western. Not surprisingly given the CCP's monopoly position in China, Chinese officials excluded from consideration the broader political environment of Western civil service systems, which was characterized by multi-party competition and political neutrality (Dai 1990–91: 69).[6] That is, adopting some Western technique was acceptable if it would improve the performance of the Chinese system. Clearly, however, China's leaders perceived that they had borrowed from the West.

Early versions of the reforms called for separate roles for the party and the government (*dangzheng fenkai*). Officials anticipated that such a separation would result in a "relatively major shift" in the functions of party organization departments, the CCP's key personnel agency, which previously had directly managed the selection, training, and discipline of all white-collar employees in public institutions of all sorts in China. In their public statements reformers apparently considered that party organization departments would focus on research, policy making, and manpower forecasting ("comprehensive researching of the cadre and personnel system, on cadre and personnel policy, and on the forecasting of personnel conditions and needs for cadres") and not on the day-to-day management of the cadre corps (Dai 1990–91: 66). That is, party organization departments would select and manage directly only the most senior officials and most other civil servants would be managed by government agencies, staffed of course mostly by party members. In keeping with this policy direction, early versions of the civil service reforms distinguished between two types of civil servants: "political affairs" civil servants, those senior officials, elected by people's congresses and directly managed by party organization departments; and "professional" civil servants, selected through the new Western-inspired competition and managed by government agencies.[7] Arguably introducing separate roles for politicians and bureaucrats, a radical departure from both Confucian (Dao 1996) and Soviet traditions, would have been more significant borrowing from the West than introducing the civil service management techniques, discussed above.

After several false starts officials introduced China's "new" civil service system in 1993. The new system contained many elements that reformers had previously identified as Western, mostly techniques such as open competition, rigorous evaluations, promotion based on merit (Provisional Regulations on Civil Servants 1993 [Ministry of Personnel 1993]; Civil Servants Law 2005 [National People's Congress 2005]). The new system, however, omitted any reference to separate roles for politicians and bureaucrats. This policy was a casualty of elite-level in-fighting within the CCP that followed the June 4, 1989 incident (Burns 1994: 464). Still, the reforms have had a major impact and since

1993 hundreds of thousands of new civil servants have been selected based on competition (Burns and Wang 2010).

The incentives for China's political leaders to formally adopt civil service reform varied with their position. Although the reforms were introduced top-down, once they became official policy, local political leaders supported them for various reasons. Because the reforms were introduced with salary increases, they appealed to some income-maximizing officials. Officials seeking promotion (climbers) may have been motivated by the need to improve their performance, which hiring competent public servants might accomplish. More importantly they were motivated by the need to be seen to be implementing official policy. There seems to have been very little resistance to the policy, probably because in many places, after completing some formalities including sitting exams, most cadres were transferred into the new civil service. The real impact of the reforms if any was on the newcomers (Burns and Wang 2010).

Public management techniques

Many public management ideas currently adopted by Chinese officials have come from the West ("Everything modern is a Western idea" [Zhang 2007]). Local government authorities, charged with implementing public policy and increasingly evaluated based on their performance (Burns and Zhou 2010), adopted new public management techniques such as contracting out, vouchers, and balanced score cards (Zhang 2007; *People's Daily* 2006). At least initially, the writing of local academics, aid agency training, and overseas study tours introduced Chinese officials to these public management ideas.

Unlike the top-down civil service reforms, many public management reforms were initiated by local political leaders undoubtedly to improve their chances of promotion. The 1994 and 1995 experiment with performance (or service) pledges in Yantai, Shandong, clearly inspired by practice in the United Kingdom and Hong Kong, is a case in point (see Foster 2005). In this case the Mayor of Yantai City learned about performance pledges which had been introduced in Hong Kong in 1993. The system requires government agencies to publicly pledge to handle business with the public (for example, granting licenses, handling particular cases) within a particular time period. The agency then monitors its own performance and publishes the extent to which it met its pledges. Generally, government agencies set the pledges at levels that allow them to achieve them relatively easily. That is, their impact on performance has been mostly symbolic. But they do indicate to agencies that political leaders are watching (Burns 2010). In 1996, the central government picked up the practice and adopted performance pledges there on an experimental basis (Hu 1998: 1092–1093). Since then they have been widely adopted throughout the country. Local leaders took the initiative to introduce the performance pledge system to burnish their credentials. Our discussion indicates, then, that officials in China have borrowed Western public management techniques quite liberally. As with the civil service system, they have adapted them to China's circumstances.

"Good" governance

Although the notion of good governance is not well defined (Doornbos 2003; Nanda 2006), the concept does have a common core of characteristics that include accountability, participation, transparency, and integrity (Asian Development Bank 1995). These ideas imply a strong civil society and the rule of law (World Bank 1994). At the same time local academics in China have popularized the concept among the intelligentsia (Yu 2000). Initially government officials resisted the idea which did not even have an agreed translation into Chinese but they came to see that it could be adapted to suit their purposes. Indeed, elements of various "good" governance paradigms coincided with central government policy to impose greater bureaucratic accountability on local government and on state-owned enterprises. After some hesitation and reflection the central government accepted a version of "good" governance that has emphasized bureaucratic accountability, more stakeholder participation, and increased transparency, especially at the grassroots. In the paragraphs that follow I focus on one of these characteristics, increased transparency, offering an explanation of the incentive structure for officials to move in this direction.

Although public administration in China has been among the most secretive in the world, from the 1990s central leaders began to encourage local governments to become more open about the process of governance. For example, in 2000 the central government required that town and township authorities make public information on a long list of government budgetary, social policy, and personnel matters (New China News Agency 2000), largely to reduce corruption and increase compliance with official policies. I argue, then, that central leaders sought to improve transparency to consolidate their power. From 2002 in response to the central government's policy of "opening up government affairs" (*zhengwu gongkai*) many provinces and municipalities in China adopted their own "open government" legislation (Horsley 2007). Among the first was Guangzhou in southern China whose "Provisions on Open Government Information"[8] became effective on January 1, 2003. Unusually for China (the Chinese Constitution includes no right to information among citizen's rights), these regulations established a presumption that government-held information should be made public (Horsley 2003). They were drafted with the assistance of academics from Guangzhou's Zhongshan University and took into account "international experience" (Horsley 2003). The Guangzhou government's resolve to implement the new provisions was sorely tested a few months later, however, with the spread of severe acute respiratory syndrome (SARS). The government initially suppressed all information about the disease, denying its existence and declaring any information about a virulent infection in Guangdong a "state secret." The government's ability to make such declarations easily indicated a major loophole in the regulations. Other local governments followed with their own provisions. In May 2008 the national-level "Regulations on Open Government Information"[9] (*zhengfu xinyi gongkai tiaoli*), came into force. The central-level regulations were drafted based on local experience and on foreign examples and expertise, including "Western" freedom of information laws (Horsley 2007).

China's open government regulations followed the basic structure and many of the mechanisms found in information access systems in the West (Horsley 2007). For example they acknowledged the types of information that government agencies should voluntarily provide to citizens on their websites, in press releases, and other open communications. They also provided a mechanism for citizens to request information, institutions to oversee compliance (the State Council's General Office and local government General Offices), laid down a requirement that governments at all levels produce annual reports on how they have complied with the regulations, and for a system of adjudicating disputes between citizens and the government over information requests (through the courts).

In significant respects, however, the central government's regulations depart from international (Western) practice. First, unlike Western freedom of information laws, the central government regulations provided no clear statement favoring disclosure over non-disclosure. Rather they hedged the open information regime with all sorts of restrictions (see Articles 5, 6, 7, and 8) ending with the statement that any disclosure may not harm "state security, public security, economic security, or social stability" (Horsley 2007). Specific exemptions from disclosure involve state security, commercial secrets, and privacy, and referred specifically to the vaguely drafted State Secrets Law (1988) which defines state secrets broadly. In general, the regulations do not weaken the presumption of secrecy that exists in contemporary Chinese public administration. Although the regulations exempt disclosure of commercial secrets and private information, as do Western regulations, these areas are also vaguely defined in China. There is, for example, no law in China establishing and defining the right to privacy. Thus, the central government's regulations favor non-disclosure as the default. Second, they narrowly describe the scope of information that may be requested from government. Third, they provide for no independent decision-making body to resolve disputes between citizens and government agencies. (The Shanghai government's regulations, do, however, provide for such an independent body.) Fourth, the regulations leave adjudicating disputes between citizens and government agencies over what may be disclosed to China's highly politically dependent courts. That is, the regulations, while following the structure and mechanisms of Western freedom of information laws, lay down a regime that leaves citizens with little room to challenge state authority.

By 2007, 11 provinces and more than 40 city-level jurisdictions had issued their own open government regulations. Many central government ministries also implemented transparency regimes, spurred on by China's drive for e-government. Among the most successful has been Shanghai. From 2004–06, according to Shanghai's annual compliance reports,[10] government agencies made public more than 200,000 documents, accepted in part or in full 80 percent of the some 30,000 information requests, and 95 percent of the public were aware of the open government rules (Horsley 2007; Chang 2007). However, in Shanghai, by 2007 in none of the lawsuits filed by citizens to gain access to government information were citizens successful. The government simply classified the information as secret and the courts did not question the classification (Chang 2007).

Civil society has begun to challenge the state using the open government regime. In 2004 Peking University Law School established the Center for Public Participation Studies and Supports to monitor central and local government compliance with the new laws. According to the Center's ranking, based on an internationally developed compliance index, local governments did better than the central government, and among central government agencies the Bank Regulatory Commission, Ministry of Commerce, and Customs more often complied than those agencies with less external contacts (Beijing University Center for Public Participation Studies and Supports 2008). The project gave provincial governments a 40 percent "pass rate" (with Beijing, Tianjin, Guangdong, and Shanghai leading the pack) compared to only 5 percent for central government agencies. For the project, participating units in seven universities scattered around the country (the "open government information watch alliance") submitted requests for information to various government agencies to test their responsiveness. The summary report concludes that provincial and local governments were better at disclosing information on their own initiative and on supervision and remedy than agencies in the central government. Increasing demands from citizens and civil society monitoring has put pressure on authorities and has led to more information being revealed about, for example, the national budget (Horsley 2010).

Increased transparency has some benefits, widely cited by Chinese officials themselves, such as reducing state–society tensions, improving efficiency, and supporting economic development. Most important, however, is that through the judicious use of open government regimes, officials can maintain tighter control over subordinates.

Conclusion

In this chapter I examine three cases in which Chinese officials considered and then adapted some notionally Western ideas of public sector reform. In the first case, central leaders, determined to reform the political and administrative leadership system, examined foreign, primarily Western, experience of personnel competition. The top-down exercise resulted in the CCP adopting some civil service management techniques it perceived to be Western (such as competition), but rejecting potentially more radical structural changes such as separate roles for politicians and bureaucrats. The reforms, grafted on to China's cadre system, produced a "new" civil service that continued to be highly centralized, operating a nationwide uniform rank and grade structure, and that pays pensions. Once the reforms became official policy, local leaders, eager for promotion, implemented it to please their superiors. In contrast to the top-down civil service reforms, local leaders initiated the search for public management techniques, the subject of our second case. They saw contracting out, vouchers, and performance pledges as evidence of their commitment to improving public sector performance. Local leaders, eager for fame and to improve their career prospects, adopted techniques from the West. China's experience of "good" governance and improved transparency came from both the top and the bottom. On the one hand, the central government could see the benefits of increased transparency for controlling local agents. Local leaders, too, benefited because they also could better control their subordinates. The transparency regime as adopted, we have seen, relatively narrowly circumscribes what information citizens may be given, and leaves the state in a relatively strong, although not unchallenged, position to protect its secrets.

The incentive to adopt Western ideas (or new ideas from any quarter) has varied. The strongest incentives, I have argued, are associated with the promotion system. Where local officials can see their careers furthered by the adoption of a Western technique, and that technique is allowed within the system, they have pursued it.

Notes

1 This a revised version of a paper that appeared in a festschrift for B. Guy Peters: Burns, John P. (2010) "Western Models and Administrative Reform in China: Pragmatism and the Search for Modernity," in Jon Pierre and Patricia W. Ingraham (eds.) *Comparative Administrative Change and Reform: Lessons Learned*, Montreal: McGill-Queens University Press, pp. 182–206.
2 I gratefully acknowledge the assistance of Norbert Chan Kwan-Nok, PhD candidate at Indiana University, who wrote the literature review contained in this paper.
3 Downs (1967) also identifies conservers (single-motive officials who seek to maintain their positions as all costs) and various mixed-motive officials such as zealots, advocates, and statesmen.
4 Competition had been a key feature of the traditional civil service system in China since the Song Dynasty.
5 Dai Guangqian was a senior official of the Ministry of Personnel and directly involved in policy discussions leading to the introduction of the civil service reforms. Dai (1990–91) is the English language translation of a speech he gave on 25 July 1988 in which he outlined the process of drafting the reform plan and the principal considerations of the CCP leadership.
6 In one-party China, civil servants may join the CCP (most are party members), vote, stand for election, and participate in party activities.
7 See the 1988 draft "Provisional Regulations on State Civil Servants" Articles 3, 4, and 9 available in English translation in Burns and Cabestan (1990–91).
8 For an English-language translation see: www.freedominfo.org/documents/ provisions.pdf (accessed January 12, 2014).
9 For an English-language translation of the "Central Government's Regulations on Open Government Information," see www.law.yale.edu/documents/pdf/ Intellectual_Life/CL-OGI-Regs-English.pdf (accessed January 12, 2014).
10 By 2007 only two governments (Shanghai and Wuhan) had issued annual reports on their compliance (Chang 2007).

References

Asian Development Bank (1995) *Governance: Sound Development Management*, available online: www.adb.org/documents/governance-sound-development-management (accessed December 19, 2013).
Aucoin, P. (1990) "Administrative Reform in Public Management," *Governance* 3: 115–137.

Aufrecht, S. and Li, S. (1995) "Reform with Chinese Characteristics: the Context of Chinese Civil Service Reform," *Public Administrative Review* 55(2): 175–182.

Barnett, A. D. (1967) *Cadres, Bureaucracy, and Political Power*, New York: Columbia University Press.

Beijing University Center for Public Participation Studies and Supports (2010) Summary of the 2009 Annual Report on China's Administrative Transparency, September 28, available online: www.law.yale.edu/documents/pdf/ Intellectual_Life/ch_OGIWA_2009_Report_Exec_Summary_English_FINAL__1-28-11_.pdf (accessed September 13, 2011).

Bing, S. (1992) "The Reform of Mainland China's Cadre System—Establishing a Civil Service," *Issues and Studies* 28(10): 23–43.

Bo Z. Y. (2002) *Chinese Provincial Leaders: Economic Performance and Political Mobility since 1949*, Armonk: M. E. Sharpe.

Burns, J. P. (1989) "Chinese Civil Service Reform: The 13th Party Congress Proposal," *The China Quarterly* 120: 739–770.

Burns, J. P. (1994) Strengthening Central CCP Control of Leadership Selection: The 1990 *Nomenklatura*," *The China Quarterly* 138: 458–491.

Burns, J. P. (2001) "Public Sector Reform and the State: the Case of China," *Public Administration Quarterly* 24(4): 419–436.

Burns, J. P. (2010) "Western Models and Administrative Reform in China: Pragmatism and the Search for Modernity," in J. Pierre and P. W. Ingraham (eds.) *Comparative Administrative Change and Reform: Lessons Learned*, Montreal: McGill-Queen's University Press 2010, pp. 182–206.

Burns, J. P. and Cabestan. J. P. (eds.) (1990–91) "Provisional Chinese Civil Service Regulations," *Chinese Law and Government* 23(4): 10–23.

Burns, J. P. and Wang X. (2010) "Civil service Reform in China: Impacts on Civil Servants' Behaviour," *The China Quarterly* 201: 58–78.

Burns, J. P. and Zhou, Z. (2010) "Performance Management in the Government of the People's Republic of China: Accountability and Control in the Implementation of Public Policy," *OECD Journal on Budgeting* 2: 1–28.

Cao, Z. (1985) *Guowai renshi zhidu gaiyao* (Outline of Foreign Civil Service Systems), Beijing: Beijing daxue chubanshe.

Chan, H. (2004) "Cadre Personnel Management in China: The *Nomenklatura* System, 1990–1998," *The China Quarterly* 179: 703–734.

Chan, H. (2009) "Politics over Markets: Integrating State-owned Enterprises Into Chinese Socialist Market," *Public Administration and Development* 29(1): 43–54.

Chan, H. and Chow, K. (2007) "Public Management Policy and Practice in Western China: Meta-policy, Tacit Knowledge, and Implications for Management Innovation Transfer," *The American Review of Public Administration* 37(4): 479–498.

Chan, H. and Li, S. E. (2007) "Civil Service Law in the People's Republic of China: A Return to Cadre Personnel Management," *Public Administrative Review* 67(3): 383–398.

Chang, T. (2007) "Open Government: A Step Forward, But With Sideways Shuffles Too," *China Development Brief*, May 24, available online: www.chinadevelopmentbrief.com/node/1111 (accessed August 18, 2008).

Cheung, A. (1997) "Understanding Public-Sector Reforms: Global Trends and Diverse Agendas," *International Review of Administrative Science* 63(4): 435–457.

Christensen, T., Dong L., and Painter, M. (2008) "Administrative Reform in China's Central Government—How Much 'Learning from the West'?" *International Review of Administrative Science* 74(3): 351–371.

Dai G. (1990–91) "Proposing a Reform of the Cadre and Personnel System and the State," in J. P. Burns and J. P. Cabestan (eds.) *Chinese Law and Government* 23(4): 61–73.

Dao M. C. (1996) "Administrative Concepts in Confucianism and Their Influence on Development in Confucian Countries," *The Asian Journal of Public Administration* 18(1): 45–69.

Doornbos, M. R. (2003) "'Good Governance': The Metamorphosis of a Policy Metaphor," *Journal of International Affairs* 57(1): 3–17.

Downs, A. (1967) *Inside Bureaucracy*, Boston, MA: Little, Brown.

Foster, K. (2005) "Chinese Public Policy Innovation and the Diffusion of Innovations: An Initial Exploration," *Chinese Public Administration Review* 3(1): 1–13.

Gao J. (2007) "Performance Management in the People's Republic of China During the Market Reform Era: A Case Study of Two Counties in Shaanxi Province," PhD dissertation, City University of Hong Kong.

Hood, C. (1995) "Contemporary Public Management: A New Global Paradigm?" *Public Policy and Administration* 10(2): 104–117.

Horsley, J. P. (2003) "China's Pioneering Foray into Open Government: A Tale of Two Cities," *Freedominfo.org*, July 14, available online: www.freedominfo.org/ 2003/07/ chinas-pioneering-foray-into-open-government-a-tale-of-two-cities/ (accessed December 19, 2013).

Horsley, J. P. (2004) "Shanghai Advances the Cause of Open Government Information in China," available online: www.law.yale.edu/documents/pdf/ Shanghai_Advances.pdf (accessed June 28, 2011).

Horsley, J. P. (2007) "China Adopts First Nationwide Open Government Information Regulations," *Freedominfo.org*, May 9, available online: www.freedominfo. org/2007/05/china-adopts-first-nationwide-open-government-information-regulations/ (accessed December 19, 2013).

Horsley, J. P. (2010) "Update on China's Open Government Information Regulations: Surprising Public Demand Yielding Some Positive Results," available online: www. freedominfo.org/2010/04/update-on-china-open-government-information-regulations (accessed September 13, 2011).

Huque, A. S. and Yep, R. (2003) "Globalization and Reunification: Administrative Reforms and the China-Hong Kong Convergence Challenge," *Public Administration Review* 63(2): 141–152.

Hu, N. S. (1998) *Zhongguo zhengfu xingxiang zhanlue* (Strategic Images of China's Government), Beijing: Central Party School Press.

Lam, T. C. and Chan, H. (1996a) "China's New Civil Service: What the Emperor is Wearing and Why," *Public Administration Review* 56(5): 479–484.

Lam, T. C. and Chan, H. (1996b) "Reforming China's Cadre Management System: Two Views of a Civil Service," *Asian Survey* 36(8): 772–786.

Lan, Z. Y. (1999) "The 1998 Administrative Reform in China: Issues, Challenges, and Prospects," *Asian Journal of Public Administration* 21(1): 29–54.

Lan, Z. Y. and Rosenbloom, D. H. (1992) "Public Administration in Transition?" *Public Administration Review* 52(6): 535–537.

Li, Cheng and White, Lynn (1990) "Elite Transformation and Modern Change in Mainland China and Taiwan: Empirical Data and the Theory of Technocracy," *The China Quarterly* 121: 1–35.

Liou, K. T. (1997) "Issues and Lessons of Chinese Civil Service Reform," *Public Personnel Management* 26(4): 505–514.

Lin T. (2008) "Explaining Intra-Provincial Inequality in Education in China: The Roles of Institutions and Provincial Leaders," PhD thesis, University of Hong Kong, Hong Kong.

Ministry of Personnel (1993) *Provisional Regulations on Civil Servants*, Beijing: mimeo.

Morgan, M. C. (1981) "Controlling the Bureaucracy in Post-Mao China," *Asian Survey* 21(12): 1223–1236.

Nanda, V. P. (2006) "The 'Good Governance' Concept Revisited," *Annals of the American Academy of Political and Social Science* 603: 269–283.

National People's Congress (2005) "Civil Servants Law," available online: www.gov.cn/ziliao/flfg/2005-06/21/content_8249.htm (accessed July 27, 2008).

New China News Agency (2000) General Office of the CCP Central Committee and State Council General Office, "Implementing in an All-Around Manner the System of Opening Government Affairs to the Public by Organs of State Power in Towns and Townships throughout the Nation," Beijing: New China News Agency, in Chinese, translated in Foreign Broadcast Information Service (FBIS) Article ID: CPP2001010500097, December 25, 2000.

Ngok, K. and Chan, H. (2003) "Introduction," *Chinese Law and Government* 36(1): 5–13.

Ngok, K. and Zhu G. (2003) "Reinventing the Communist Government in a Transitional Economy—A Review of China's 1998 Central Government Restructuring," *Asian Profile* 41(1): 1–14.

Ngok, K. and Zhu G. (2007) "Marketization, Globalization and Administrative Reform in China—A Zigzag Road to a Promising Future," *International Review of Administrative Sciences* 73(2): 217–233.

Oh, T. K (1976) "Theory Y in the People's Republic of China," *California Management Review* 19(2): 77.

Osborne, D. and Gaebler, T. (1992) *Reinventing Government: How the Entrepreneurial Spirit is Transforming the Public Sector*, Reading, MA: Addison-Wesley.

People's Daily 17 August 2006.

Pollitt, C. and Bouckaert, G. (2000) *Public Management Reform: A Comparative Analysis*, Oxford: Oxford University Press.

Tsao, K. and Worthley, J. (1995) "Chinese Public Administration: Change with Continuity During Political and Economic Development," *Public Administration Review* 55(2): 169–174.

Tong, C. H., Straussman, J. D., and Broadnax, W. D. (1999) "Civil Service Reform in the People's Republic of China: Case Studies of Early Implementation," *Public Administration and Development* 19(2): 193–206.

World Bank (1994) *Governance: The World Bank's Experience*, Washington, DC: World Bank.

Worthley, J. (1984) "Public Administration in the People's Republic of China: An Overview of Values and Practices," *Public Administration Review* 44(6): 518–523.

Worthley, J. and Tsao, K. (1999) "Reinventing Government in China: A Comparative Analysis," *Administration and Society* 31(5): 571–587.

Yu K. (2000) *Zhili yu shanzhi* (Governance and Good Governance), Beijing: Shehui kexueyuan chubanshe.

Zhang C. (2007) World Bank, personal communication, October 23.

3 Transitional meritocracy?

Institutions and practices of personnel management in state-building in contemporary China

Zhengxu Wang and Dragan Pavlićević

Introduction

Since China's gradualist reform started in the early 1980s, its governance record has been relatively successful. Despite a large number of severe challenges, the government in Beijing has managed outstanding economic performance and large-scale social transformation (Naughton 2007). Overall, the regime seems to enjoy relatively high levels of public support (Gilley 2006; Wang 2009), and a reform and state-building process controlled by the ruling Chinese Communist Party looks set to continue for the next ten to 20 years.

One key element of the Chinese political or governing system is management of its Party and government officials, or "cadres" in its own terminology. We argue that the Party-state's personnel management features a meritocratic system that has so far largely evaded scholarly attention. This system retains strong influences from the Confucian scholar-official tradition of China's imperial past, as well as the Leninist "vanguard party" tradition that was established in the revolutionary and Maoist eras. In recent years, however, this system has paid increasing attention to nurturing managerial competence for the purpose of administering a modern economy and a modern society. How the Party attempts to strike a balance between political loyalty and professional competence is the focus of this study.

We will examine several aspects of the Chinese cadre management system. These include the formal rules, institutions, and actual practices regarding (1) recruitment, (2) development, and (3) promotion of officials. From this analysis we will understand how political loyalty and professional competence are defined and measured in the Party's personnel regime, and how a balance is sought between the two. We will also look at the changes that are taking place in the relative importance, or weights, of these two criteria as the Party-state tries to build a modern governance machine.

We find that while political reliability and commitment still feature prominently when the Party staffs the state and party bodies, rapid economic development and social changes have amplified the need for capable and competent managers and administrators, in order to deliver successful governance. Whereas in the past political loyalty played a crucial role for officials' success within the state ranks, today professional competence has become more central. Whether this trend will continue, to a future state in which political loyalty becomes almost irrelevant, will be discussed toward the end of the chapter.

Meritocracy and contemporary China's politics

Meritocracy as a concept in political science and public administration has been frequently referred to, but rarely clearly defined. When it was first invented, it referred to a hypothetical society of the future, organized according to talent and achievement (Young 1958). Further development of the concept has picked up different aspects, partially resulting in fragmentation and confusion. Most commonly, the importance of educational attainment for social mobility is taken as a strong indicator of the meritocratic nature of a society (Goux and Maurin 1997; Longoria 2007). Others have investigated the relationship between economic modernization, productivity and efficiency on one side and meritocratic education on the other (Ranson 1998). Another important line of research relates to the so-called "New Class" theories, which look at the likelihood of a scientific and intellectual elite governing industrial society (Szelenyi and Bill 1989). Indeed, it has been noted that meritocratic tendencies have been present since as early as the nineteenth century, in the works of Saint-Simon and his followers, who envisioned society ruled by technocrats and scientists (Andreas 2009: 1–2). Yet another line of research can be found in the sciences of organizational behavior and management, which interpret meritocracy as the just allocation of career opportunities according to one's talent and ability (e.g., Alveson and Karreman 2001). Furthermore, the idea is certainly not limited only to academia. For example, Tony Blair's New Labour political discourse gave it a central place; here meritocracy is understood as "a society in which the most able and committed people can succeed in attaining the most desirable, responsible and well rewarded positions" (Aldridge 2001: 6).

Hence, as Amartya Sen puts it, "The idea of meritocracy may have many virtues, but clarity is not one of them" (Sen 1999: 5). While there is obvious lack of consensus on how to define meritocracy, it is suitable, however, to conclude that meritocracy is best directly linked to competence. In a meritocracy, it is one's *competence*—be it educational attainment, ability to perform one's duties, or accomplished achievements—that is the main prerequisite for one's success. Social, economic, political, and professional opportunities within a society or any organizational framework should be allocated to the most competent people. We call this a "one-dimensional" meritocracy concept.

The Chinese understanding of meritocracy differs quite significantly. To begin with, meritocracy is an ancient practice in China. The imperial examination (*keju*) was the main institutional pillar of meritocracy in the Confucian Middle Kingdom. Established during the Sui Dynasty in AD 605 and maintained for 1,300 years, it served as the ultimate ladder for social mobility for the talented, irrespective of family pedigree. In general, attaining the position of civil servant in imperial China depended on a series of outstanding performance in the *keju* exam. By contrast, a person that could not excel at the exam would in turn have no chance of entering the higher level institution, or any government institution at all (Elman 2002). This concept retained its centrality for the governance system in China long after the collapse of imperial order. The roots of civil servant recruiting institutions in contemporary China and neighboring Asian countries can be clearly traced back to the meritocratic system founded on the imperial examination.[1]

Yet, taking talent as the only determinant of success within the Chinese imperial civil service would be an obvious mistake. Confucian ethics essentially equated ethics with good governance, and moral rightness with authority. In that sense, under the imperial system, "the ultimate yardstick for assessing the acceptability of bureaucratic behavior was ethical norms, and the criteria for evaluation were sincerity, loyalty, and reliability, all of them more important than administrative efficiency and effectiveness" (Zhang 1993: 7). The traditional Chinese concept of "merit" clearly had two dimensions: the talent (*cai*) was crucial, yet moral virtue (*de*), was also highly regarded and even decisive for one's success once within the ranks.

Since the Chinese Communist Party came to power in Mainland China in 1949, meritocracy has taken on a new life. The new ideological context has reinterpreted and reproduced the virtue vis-à-vis talent (*de/cai*) dichotomy into a redness vs. expertise one (*hong/zhuan*). During the Maoist period, redness (*hong*) referred to ideological purity and political loyalty and expertise (*zhuan*) referred to professional competence. For a long time, redness became far more important than expertise, especially in peak times of radicalism such as during the Cultural Revolution.[2] In post-Mao China, with progressive de-ideologization and increasing focus on economic development, expertise gradually assumed a more prominent role in personnel appointments and promotion.[3] Yet, the two dimensions of merit continued to coexist, and political or party loyalty still plays a significant role in determining an official's fate. In the 1990s, the country's Administrative Law still defined that "the public personnel are being employed by their merits and criteria of being revolutionary, professional, intellectual and young," with "being revolutionary" pointing to ideological purity and loyalty.[4] The Civil Servant Law that came into force on January 1, 2006, states that civil servants should have qualifications of "good moralities" as well as "having the educational level and working capacity as required by the post" (Civil Servant Law of the People's Republic of China 2006: Chapter 2, Article 11). Therefore, the concept of meritocracy within the Chinese Party-state differs significantly from that in the West, in that it consists of two inter-related dimensions: competence—as seen through notions of talent (*cai*) and expertise (*zhuan*), and ideopolitical reliability constituted by moral rightness and (*de*) and ideological commitment and loyalty (*hong*). We call this "two-dimensional meritocracy."

The Party and state building in contemporary China

In the Chinese Party-state, Party officials and government officials are both treated as civil servants. In other words, full-time Party workers are also state employees. Meanwhile, "government" agencies also include both government offices and Party institutions.[5]

It is clear that the ongoing modernization and development of the last 30 years have greatly altered the sociopolitical landscape of China, consequently bringing into question the legitimacy of the Chinese Communist Party (hereafter CCP) and putting pressure on the Party-state to deliver good governance.[6] In this context, the appointment, management, and cultivation of members of the Party-state apparatus becomes a critical component of China's state-building effort. This taps into a time-tested belief, succinctly expressed in Mao's quote: "When the political lines are set, it is the cadres that are the decisive factor" (*Zhengzhi luxian queli zhihou, ganbu jiushi juedingxing yinsu*) (*Selected Works of Mao Zedong* 1991: 526). The Party-state's perception of critical need can be seen in its major early twenty-first century policy document, "Decision on Strengthening the Party's Governing Ability," which focuses on "strengthening the Party's governing ability," which deems "upgrading the quality of cadre corps" and "producing outstanding leadership" at all levels of government as of paramount importance (Brødsgaard and Zheng 2006: 1; Shambaugh 2008a: 124–127).

As argued above, the Chinese understanding of meritocracy has traditionally encompassed a dimension consisting of virtue and morality, ideological purity, and political loyalty. Echoes of that tradition are perceptible in the CCP's concept of meritocracy: It is aware that developing competence is necessary for delivering good governance, but also holds ideopolitical monopoly to be of utmost importance in maintaining its grip on power (Shambaugh 2008a: 104–106). It can be argued that achieving good governance and successful management depends on government officials' knowledge, expertise, and competence in modern economic and social affairs, while government bureaucrats' ideopolitical convictions are of much less relevance. Ideopolitical convictions may even become barriers to innovation and changes in policies that are necessary when dealing with rapidly changing social, economic, and political issues.[7] Therefore, a conflict between the two dimensions of meritocracy, the overall goals of promoting competent government on the one hand, and ensuring the ideopolitical monopoly on the other, is set to emerge.

In other words, to achieve good governance by competent staff, the Party should build a meritocratic state at the opposite end of the spectrum to that of a government rigidly defined by ideological considerations (Figure 3.1). If the modern Chinese state began with a one-dimensional focus on ideology created by Maoist discourse, the twenty-first century should see it gradually move toward the left-end of the spectrum, giving much more emphasis to competence and expertise.

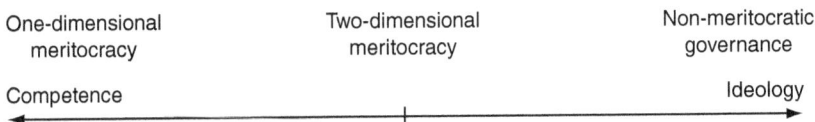

One-dimensional meritocracy	Two-dimensional meritocracy	Non-meritocratic governance
Competence		Ideology

Figure 3.1 Meritocracy and governance in contemporary China.

Conceptualization and research design

This study aims to find out how this conflict is resolved in the Chinese Party-state's personnel management regime. In its effort to learn about government management and other modern Western know-how, is China also adopting a Western one-dimensional notion of meritocracy and discarding its "old" two-dimensional concept?[8]

Figure 3.2 presents the research model for this study: We create an innovative platform for *systematic* and *holistic* evaluation of personnel management institutions and practices, an *approach that would encompass all key aspects of personnel management*. While previous literature cited throughout this chapter tended to focus mainly on individual aspects of personnel management, e.g., performance management, training, or promulgation of new rules and laws, we include and discuss all key aspects: the formal rules and regulations of the personnel management system, and how government and party officials are recruited, trained, evaluated, and promoted.

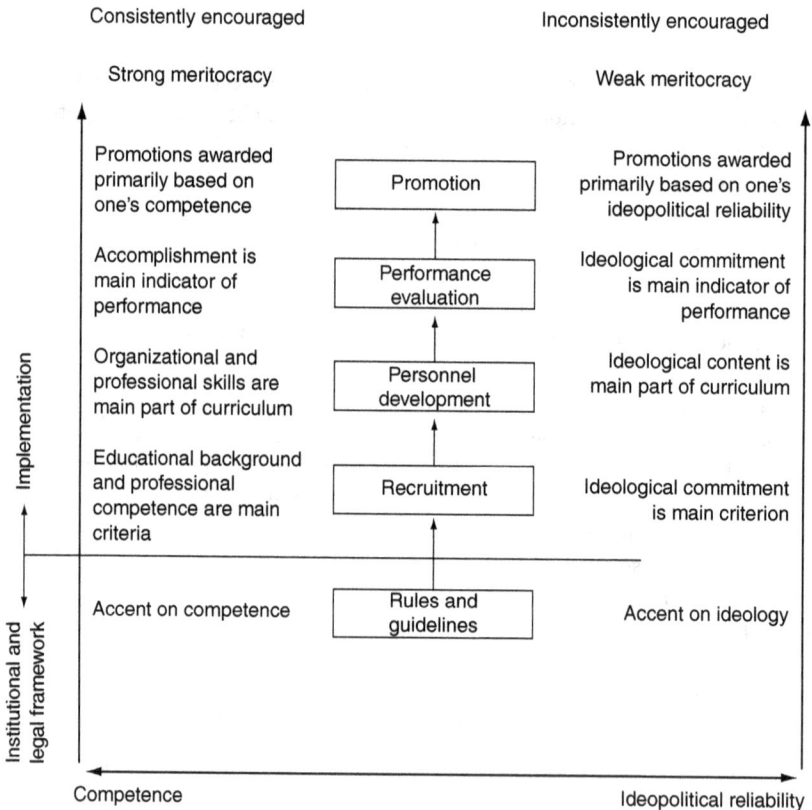

Figure 3.2 Research model.

We hypothesize that:

1   The Party's meritocracy system has established *education, professional expertise*, and *performance record* ahead of political reliability and loyalty as crucial human resource management principles; and
2   As a result, such a one-dimensional concept of meritocracy has been *strongly* promoted and encouraged within the Party-state system.

We aim to test our hypotheses by comparing the importance of competence-related elements to ideological-related elements within the given area of Party-state's personnel management and contrasting currently available evidence with the evaluation of bureaucratic reforms in 1990s, when, it has been argued, attempts to institutionalize the principles of merit, competition, fairness, and transparency have been partial and inconsistent (Chou 2004). Given the necessity of its ideological foundation for legitimizing the undisputed leadership role of the CCP, it is expected that Marxism–Leninism and its Chinese derivates such as Mao Zedong's Thought, Deng Xiaoping's Theory, and the important theories of Three Represents and Scientific Development would frequently appear in Party documents. Yet, the important question is, are they there only out of necessity to provide continuity and legitimacy to CCP rule and to provide general guidance, or is ideological content translated into practical measures? Our approach is that only if ideological content has *direct practical consequences*—when requiring full commitment and loyalty to Party and ideology has direct impact on institutional procedures, decision-making processes, or personnel working priorities and performance—should it be acknowledged that ideopolitical reliability remain one dimension of today's Party-state's meritocracy?

If our hypotheses is confirmed, we also need to ask whether the Party's ideopolitical monopoly has been brought into question? Some of the recent research has argued that this is not the case, as the reform has still failed to improve administrative efficiency, capacity, and integrity, while it primarily aimed to strengthen the command chain by emphasizing "inverse accountability" of local cadres to upper echelons.[9]

The rest of this chapter is organized according to the areas of personnel management presented in Figure 3.2. For "Rules and guidelines" we present an analysis of the Chinese Civil Servant Law valid since 2006. Second, for "Recruitment" we analyze the Party's membership structure and civil servant examinations. Third, for "Personnel development" we examine China's cadre training system. Fourth, for the "Performance Evaluation" we look at the cadre responsibility system that determines the performance of government officials at every level. Lastly, for "Promotion" we will look at the career patterns of the provincial leaders in China. After these analyses, we assess the state of meritocracy in contemporary Chinese state cadre management.

Rules and guidelines: the Civil Servant Law of 2006

Effective since January 1, 2006, the Civil Service Law applies to an estimated 70 million state servants in central and local governments, public service units and state-owned enterprises (Burns 2007: 60). It represents one of the most important efforts of the Party to build a more responsive, high-quality, effective, and competent government.[10] To build such a government, between the political and the competence dimensions of meritocracy, the Party's civil servant management law should clearly establish virtues of talent and expertise as the main qualities of government officials. The Law's success in doing so would indicate the Party-state's genuine shift away from the traditional two-dimensional concept of democracy, while adopting a competence-based, one-dimensional meritocracy.

Indeed, the Civil Service Law shows clear intentions in this direction. To be sure, in its General Provision it carries a highly ideopolitical passage, stipulating that "The civil servant system shall take Marxism, Leninism, Mao Zedong Thought and Deng Xiaoping Theory and the important thought of the 'Three Represents' as its guide" ("Zhonghua Renmin Gongheguo gongwuyuan fa" 2006: Chapter 1, Article 4). While this helps set the ideological tone of state administration (and any other state-building efforts), once the Law starts to stipulate the operating practices of the civil service, the ideopolitical requirements become completely absent.[11]

For example, in terms of recruitment, the General Provision explicitly states that superior applicants should be selected as civil servants through open competition (*zeyou luqu*).[12] Recruitment should rely on "measures of open examination, strict inspection, equal competition and employment on the basis of competitive selection" (ibid.: Chapter 4, Article 21). No references to political concerns were made. In terms of training, the Law clearly focuses on the development of technical and professional skills, with no ideological studies or political training being mentioned. In particular, those civil servants taking posts in technical positions shall be given special technical training (ibid.: Chapter 10, Article 61). To be sure, the assessment of a civil servant "shall examine the morality, capability, diligence, achievement, and uprightness" of him or her. But in this context "uprightness" and "morality" seem concerned with non-political moral conduct, such as avoidance of power abuse, rather than political integrity and loyalty. Furthermore, the same clause states that the assessment should "focus on the practical achievements of his or her work" (ibid: Chapter 5, Article 33).

Furthermore, the Law explicitly links pay levels to a civil servant's performance. Clearly one's capability to perform one's managerial or technical duty is the sole criterion here. Additional provisions of rewards also focus on "outstanding working performances" and "noticeable achievements" related to work in social, economic, and administrative areas (ibid: Chapter 8, Articles 48–49). Conversely, unacceptable performance will be penalized: "Where a civil servant is assessed as incompetent during the periodical assessment, he or she shall be demoted to a lower-level post" (ibid: Chapter 7, Article 47). In fact, if "having been assessed as 'incompetent' in the annual assessment for two consecutive years," dismissal will follow (ibid: Chapter 13, Article 83).

Hence, the Law aims at establishing professional competence as the main criterion by which civil servants are selected and rewarded. Professional competence of individual civil servants forms the basis for the ultimate quality of the regime's civil service. Political loyalty and ideological principles are clearly pushed to the background. The remaining ideopolitical requirements seem to be of limited practical value. What is required from a civil servant are operational and managerial knowledge and skills rather than ideological and political commitment.

Recruitment: civil service examination and Party membership

Conventional wisdom states that as a communist regime transits from a revolutionary to a post-revolutionary agenda, it will prioritize effective administration of a complex society. It is then that it starts to emphasize educational and professional credentials over political and ideological standards (Burns 2006: 53). When applied to the selection of bureaucratic elites in China, given the inseparable connection between Party and state organizations, it would imply that both civil servants *and* Party members are recruited based on their competence rather than political loyalty. We look at the selection of both civil servants and Party members below.

Civil servant examination

In China's effort to build a competent civil service, annual examinations are now held by central and local government departments, and increasing numbers of posts are being contended by applicants, including those for leadership positions (Pieke 2009a: 166–173). In 2011, for example, over 1.3 million candidates took part in examinations to compete for around 16,000 government posts ("China's Civil Servants Exam Attracts 1.3 Mln Applicants" 2010).

Available evidence shows that consideration of competence dominates the civil service examination process. The exam consists of written and oral sections. The written exams test the applicant's administrative and professional knowledge. The test on administrative knowledge consists of three parts, on general knowledge, administrative skills and capacity, and practical application, respectively. Depending on the post one applies for, examination of professional knowledge is divided into segments focusing on the technical requirements of the specific post. Most often, these would include legal knowledge, and computer and secretarial skills. Furthermore, foreign language skills are required for those applying for posts in central departments and diplomacy. Equally, finance and accounting abilities are examined for those applying for posts in the finance sector or finance regulatory bodies (State Administration of Civil Service 2010).

By applying this unified examination system, the civil service selection process seems capable of identifying a pool of recruits based on talent and competence. According to the State Administration of Civil Service, more than 70 percent of the civil servants recruited in 2010 had earned at least a bachelor degree ("China Recruits Civil Servants in a Fair Way, Via Examinations" 2011). Among those recruited by the central government departments, over 90 percent came from ordinary families, and their parents were workers, farmers, teachers, doctors, or engineers. Family background and connections, and whether one is a Party member or not, do not seem to matter in this process. The recruitment process of civil servants seems to present evidence of a move towards emphasizing competence over political consideration.

Awarding Party memberships

It has been argued that the Party, with more than 70 million members, represents the political community of China, from which government officials are drawn (Backer 2009). In fact, 95 percent of public officials above the *chu* (division) level are Party members (including a large number of officials working in the Party's various agencies and departments) (Brødsgaard and Chen 2009).[13] Hence how Party memberships are awarded can also reflect whether the system is putting professional competence over political loyalty, or vice versa.

Of late, the Party's Three Represents theory has, among other, called for active recruitment of Party members from among social groups believed to represent the advanced technologies and knowledge of modern society, such as private entrepreneurs and intellectuals. The need to improve the quality of Party members has continued to feature in the discourse of former President and Party Secretary Hu Jintao up to the present day (Shambaugh 2008a: Chapters 6 and 7). During one of his major speeches elaborating the concept of Three Represents the then Party Secretary Jiang Zemin stated that Party members' recruitment and promotion should be conducted "through open and fair competition on the basis of merits" (Jiang 2001). This tends to suggest a tendency toward emphasizing competence when awarding Party memberships.

Yet political loyalty and political trustworthiness still loom very large regarding admission to the CCP. According to the official line, the Party should "give equal importance to both professional competence and political integrity." The Party applicant should be judged "mainly by his or her political awareness, moral integrity and performance" as well as "his or her actual contribution to the cause of building socialism with Chinese characteristics" (Jiang 2001). By repeatedly bringing attention to political awareness and political integrity and in the same sentence citing professional competence and performance, the Party seems to be trying to strike a balance between the competences and political dimensions in evaluation of candidates.

The same duality of criteria is found regarding the importance of educational background for Party membership. Historically, education did not represent a major criterion for Party recruitment. During the revolutionary period, the Party recruited a large number of "proletariat" with low levels of education. Having a high level of education even had a negative impact on the probability of Party membership during the anti-intellectual Cultural Revolution (Bian *et al.* 2001). However, after economic reform started in the late 1970s, individuals with higher education began to be favored. Walder, for example, shows that the possibility of a college graduate becoming a Party member during the 1987–96 period is almost six times higher than that of the 1949–77 period. Other researchers have noticed the increasing ratio of college graduates among party members (Walder 2006; Sato and Eto 2008; Pieke 2009a). Indeed, recent Party reports show a steep increase in the percentage of CCP members with a college education (*People's Daily* 2009a, 2009b).

But, "educational credentials are neither replacing nor reducing political criteria ... the increasing significance of educational credentials coexists with the continued screening for political loyalty" (Bian *et al.* 2001: 833). A lengthy and rigorous screening process applies to the allocation of Chinese Communist Party memberships. After officially submitting an application for membership, the applicant must declare loyalty to the CCP and actively participate in political activities, including off-work sessions to study the CCP constitution and current policies. The candidate would need to regularly report his or her self-assessments to the Party cell at his or her workplace. After a period of time, the Party cell engages its full members to examine thoroughly the applicants' political performance.[14] Information is collected through applicants and through the formal channels of the party cell and is compared in order to test the applicants' political trustworthiness (Bian *et al.* 2001: 813–814). More information along these lines is unavailable, but what we have is sufficient to enable us to conclude that ideological and political reliability remain major criteria in the recruitment of new CCP members.

Personnel development: cadre training

We will now turn our attention to cadre training and, especially, the regime's main platform for personnel development—the Central Party School (CPS). Ever since its inception, the CPS has adjusted its orientation and curriculum in line with prevailing political circumstances and the Party's ideological evolution (Wibowo and Fook 2006: 142). Therefore, it would be reasonable to expect that the Party's priorities would be clearly reflected in the CPS' curriculum. As CPS classes are open only for high-level and future leaders,[15] it seems inevitable that the central leadership would use CPS education programs to communicate its political position and priorities to these backbones of the state. The CPS curriculum would also serve to shape top officials' understanding of current affairs and how governance-related issues should be tackled. Consequently, the CPS curriculum would expectedly reflect the Party's commitment to improving officials' competence through the inclusion of non-ideological practical and administrative–technical contents.

Recent research has detected a decline in the coverage of Marxian theories and Party history compared to studies of economics, international relations, and public administration, among others. In fact, the latter contents have gained in prominence in recent years (Liu 2009; Shambaugh 2008b). Broadly speaking, the CPS offers two types of teaching programs. Non-degree short-term training programs typically lasting three months to one year constitute the CPS' "Principle Classes."[16] The other type includes MA and PhD programs under the School's "Graduate College."[17] The second type is less relevant to our discussion here, but focusing on the Principle Classes, we can see our two dimensions of meritocracy at play clearly: The curriculum is divided between practical and operational courses and theoretical and ideological ones. Practical and operational courses are represented by a Strategic Thinking and Major Practical Issues cluster, while theoretical and ideological courses are grouped under the so-called Three Basics.

The Strategic Thinking classes aim at sharpening the trainees' grasp on complex social and economic issues, with classes titled The Current Situation, State of the Nation, and Policy; System Theory; and Theories of Technological Innovation and Application, among others. However, the Three Basics classes aim at enhancing the political and ideological strengths of the officials, and consist of intensive studies of selected works of Marx, Lenin, Mao, Deng, and Jiang. The Party is apparently concerned with ideological unity among its rank and file. But nevertheless, the Three Basics curriculum shows a clear tendency towards practical knowledge, i.e., linking the Party classics to current development and policy priorities. In fact, most of the curriculum in this group, roughly 50 percent, is devoted to studies of Deng's theories. This emphasis on studying Deng's theories instead of dwelling on the old Marx–Lenin–Mao material is a change that has taken place in recent years, and it likely represents an attempt by the recent leadership (Jiang Zemin and Hu Jintao) to give more weight to practical and empirical knowledge at the expense of ideology. Very significantly, this segment is occasionally supplemented with lessons on Modern Theories of Management, Scientific Theories of Management, and Party-building and Party Spirit and Ethics, which are focused on corruption and organizational discipline. Further additions include Administrative Rules, Regulations, and Implementations and a substantial selection of specialized lessons on agricultural development, finance, taxation, policy-making, the art of leadership and personnel management among others (Liu 2009: 114–115). To further highlight the importance of practical knowledge, in-field investigation and tours have been made integral parts of the curriculum.

The CPS curriculum seems to display a great deal of effort towards balancing ideological and practical content.[18] At first sight, the curriculum seems to be divided equally between the two, yet, even the ideo-theoretical content is presented in a contemporary and practical context and approached critically.[19] For example, within the Three Basics module Principle Courses, a noticeable weight is put on the practical and specialized knowledge relevant for day-to-day management duties.[20]

It is important to note that the CPS sits at the top of the pyramid, composed of a nationwide network of over 2,600 party schools that stretch across all administrative levels.[21] The content of studies at lower-tier institutions (Tran

2003; Pieke 2009a) similarly reflects a dual purpose and in many ways reproduces the CPS formula described above: These schools retain the function of informing local cadres on party ideology and policies, but also "provide real training in concrete practical skills that local cadres can use on the job" (Shambaugh 2008a: 145–148). Furthermore, establishing the National School of Administration (recently renamed The Chinese Academy of Governance) in 1994 illustrates the prioritization of cadres' expertise. The Chinese Academy of Governance trains provincial and ministerial level cadres, as well as SOE leaders, outstanding young and middle-aged cadres, and even high- and mid-level civil servants of foreign governments who have come to China for training (such as African and Southeast Asian government officials). In general, it has a strong focus on specialized managerial and administrative skills (Wibowo and Fook 2006: 141).

In conclusion, training for leading cadres retains political and ideological components, but we observe a clear trend toward establishing capacity building as the main function of the regime's mid-career training system.[22]

Performance evaluation: the Cadre Responsibility System

In line with the drive to enhance the Party's governing ability and related campaigns, we should expect to see a clear reliance of Party-state apparatus on measurable performance indicators for assessing cadres' work. One major vehicle in this regard is the working performance contracts, enforced from the top down to township levels. This contract, together with measures of intra-party democracy which put officials' performance to evaluation by fellow Party members, and sometimes even citizen evaluation of officials' performance (Wu 2009), constitutes a "Cadre Responsibility System."[23] This system serves as an ultimate tool for evaluating an official's performance, and is applied to leaders both in Party and state organizations.[24]

While a critical institution for the Party and state's functioning, the Cadre Responsibility System has not been widely researched by scholars. Each year, an official signs a working performance contract, which stipulates objectives and targets, negotiated with the leadership one level up. Each contract contains a number of, in ascending order of importance, soft targets, hard targets and veto targets.[25] The veto targets are of utmost importance: Failing to achieve any of these targets, an official will be judged as having failed to accomplish his or her annual obligations, however successfully he or she performed regarding the targets in the other two categories.[26] The targets in these three categories, against which the performance of an individual official is measured annually, include economic and social indicators[27] as well as administrative effectiveness, and, as of recently, levels of service-orientation (Burns 2007: 71). Assessing an official through such a responsibility system suggests "emphasis being on the evaluation of the work performance" (Zhai 2008; Edin 2003a).

While it seems to be the case that performance appraisals focus mostly on competence-related criteria,[28] the current arrangement still carries ideopolitical considerations. The evaluation criteria also include "moral integrity," which has been interpreted as the extent to which the official implemented CCP policy during the reporting period ("Provisional Regulations on Civil Servants" 1993). Furthermore, apart from these targets (from higher levels of government), "spiritual civilization"—arguably referring to not only ethical and moral, but also the Party's theoretical standards—is also part of the assessment. It is also worth noticing that the CCP organizational departments participate directly in and approve personnel movements of all those holding leadership positions, no matter how low within the vast regime apparatus they might be (for example, section chief and deputy chiefs) (Burns 2007: 73). Furthermore, all personnel officials in government departments and agencies are Party members (ibid.: 75). Therefore, although ideopolitical considerations may not be explicitly stated, the whole Party-state is at the same time immersed in Party ideologies that have spread through the whole system.

The practices of resorting to intra-party democracy in performance evaluation are even less understood. Available evidence suggests that, "democracy" in this sense means the representatives of one's own working unit and subordinate units provide inputs when an official is being evaluated for his or her performance.[29] Such information is provided via questionnaire surveys and opinion polls, normally administered by the Party's organizational department (Edin 2003a: 8; Heimer 2006: 125). The demotions are prescribed for officials that are evaluated negatively by a third of those polled ("Regulations on the Work of Selecting and Appointing Leading Party and Government Cadres" 2002: Chapter 11, Article 55). Where employed, citizens' evaluations seem to attach significantly greater weight to competence than cadre evaluation, as the public is largely unconcerned with officials' ideological convictions and commitment to uphold party lines but rather with their effectiveness in doing their jobs.

In general, while provisions are made to judge cadres' work according to their political reliability, the emphasis in the cadre evaluations system is being placed on their ability to perform their duties in a competent and efficient manner.

Promotion: provincial leaders

During Maoist times ideological commitment played the most important role in affecting one's promotion. But the general tendency to curb ideological and personality factors in promoting high-level leaders has been notable ever since the kick-off of reforms. Critics of the current Chinese political system often argue that corrupt and incompetent cadres enjoy stable and progressing careers due to strong networks and the indolence of the legal system.[30] The Party, however, has made significant steps toward making cadre appointment and promotion processes competitive, predictable, and institutionalized.[31] While the Party's actual processes of deciding who gets a promotion are a matter of extreme secrecy, we can look at whether the system has successfully put the most competent leaders in the top positions of national governance. For that we look at provincial leaders. These include all the provincial Party secretaries and provincial governors. They provide a relatively large group of top leaders with relatively accessible data for analysis.

Available Party documents promulgate six basic requirements for evaluating whether an official can be promoted to a leadership position. At their face value, at least three of these have no reference to a candidate's competence, while at least four refer clearly to the ideological standings of the appointee. For example, "cherish a lofty aspiration for communism and unswerving confidence in socialism with Chinese characteristics," "be highly dedicated to the revolutionary cause," and "attain the level of Marxism–Leninism, Mao Zedong Thought and Deng Xiaoping Theory as required for performance of duties and responsibilities" all stress the ideopolitical strengths of the candidate. The other provisions include "have the organizational ability, educational level and professional knowledge commensurate with the work of leadership" or "effectively carry out the work" ("Regulations on the Work of Selecting and Appointing Leading Party and Government Cadres" 2002: Chapter 2, Article 6). Among seven necessary "qualifications," three prescribe desirable experience, one physical health, one education level, one received training, and the final one "length of Party standing as required by the Constitution of the Communist Party of China" (ibid.: Chapter 2, Article 7). By looking at these guidelines one can easily gain the impression that in the promotion of officials at this level (provincial governor-level), ideopolitical purity dominates over competence and expertise.

Yet how these vague ideological requirements are enforced is the real issue. Indeed, who gets to be promoted, those who show stronger ideological purity or those who perform better? We could look at economic performance at a provincial level to support the latter: the most recent systematic study found that leaders whose provinces contributed most to the central budget had the best chances.[32] With limited data, a few other general findings can be constructed. First, the average educational profile of provincial leaders has been improving steadily and significantly. As of early 2010 over 60 percent of provincial leaders hold advanced degrees (Master degrees and PhDs) (Li 2010). This suggests a strong focus on educational attainment, even beyond what related regulations prescribe: a college degree is normally required for high level positions ("Regulations on the Work of Selecting and Appointing Leading Party and Government Cadres" 2002: Chapter 2, Article 7). Another potential sign of prioritizing competence in promotion can be found in the dominance of economics, management, business, politics and law over other academic backgrounds among the provincial leaders. For example, at the peak of the technocrats' grip over elite politics in China in 2001, 62.9 percent of provincial leaders had engineering degrees, and less than 10 percent had a background in economics and management, with none in law and politics (Li 2004b). By 2010, those with a background in economics, management, or politics and law accounted for over 60 percent of provincial leaders (Li 2010). Hence we note a clear trend in putting people with higher-ranking academic degrees with more practical relevance for contemporary state management and administration in leadership position. In addition, the central authorities have recently made concerted efforts to recruit non-CCP elites into high-ranking offices (Li 2005). In 2007, a non-CCP member top hematologist became the country's Minister of Health, and another non-CCP scientist became the country's Minister of Science and Technology. Similarly, in provincial governments, a large number of non-CCP scholars or experts have taken up positions such as deputy governors.

In conclusion, we can see that the current provincial leadership has the highest educational profile along with the most diverse and relevant professional background since the foundation of the People's Republic of China. Yet, as we can see from the regulations relating to promotion, the ideopolitical dimension is still very important. Additionally, while not the focus of our examination here, factional and client relations also appear to be important factors in the career mobility of current provincial governors (Li 2005, 2010).

Discussion: transitional meritocracy in China

For this study, we hypothesized that the imperatives in governing a modern society and economy have forced the Chinese regime to embrace the Western, one-dimensional, competence-focused meritocracy. This would take place at the expense of the Party-state's two-dimensional model that also emphasizes ideopolitical reliability. After analyzing the various components of the Chinese meritocracy, we can now summarize whether competence and ideopolitical reliability are emphasized in each of these areas. This is presented in Table 3.1.

Our hypotheses proved to be only partially true. Generally, we could agree that "attempts to improve governance in China have been accompanied by civil service reforms to make the bureaucracy more meritocratic"—with being meritocratic here meaning focusing more on talent instead of political considerations (Burns 2007: 58). Yet the tendency to encourage professional competence has coexisted with a dimension, albeit a weakened one, that includes loyalty to the Party's ideology, policy lines, and leadership. This status quo, however, represents marked differences from the orthodox "red and expert" meritocracy regime in the Maoist era, as well as the imperial period when "virtue" and talent were woven together in the single being of each scholar-official. As presented in Figure 3.3, there has been a clear shift toward "expertise" in identifying, grooming, promoting, and evaluating a civil servant and political leader. We call such trend a *transitional meritocracy* (Figure 3.3).

Table 3.1 Summary

Area	Competence	Ideopolitical reliability
Legal framework	Strong	Weak
Recruitment	Strong	Medium
Personnel development	Strong	Medium
Performance evaluation	Strong	Medium
Promotion	Strong	Medium

One-dimensional meritocracy	Two-dimensional meritocracy	Non-meritocratic governance

Competence   **China's traditional meritocracy**   Ideology

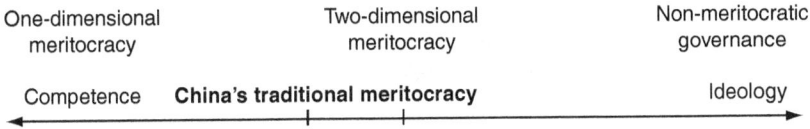

Figure 3.3 Meritocratic tendency in contemporary China.

Given current priorities in the provision of good governance, identifying, developing, and promoting officials with strong capacity has become a major objective of the Party's state-building enterprise. The regime's Civil Servants Law, Cadre Responsibility System, strong emphasis on diverse and practical training focused on the art of administration, and improving educational profiles and achievement records among top members of the leadership, indicate that meritocracy is increasingly understood as focusing on relevant knowledge, skills, and expertise. While political loyalty maintains a presence, it is increasingly balanced, and quite often overshadowed by factors associated with competence.

The difficulty lies in the maintenance of the political and ideological foundations of the state. We predict that the ideopolitical dimension in China's meritocracy will be increasingly marginalized as the modern and complex society increasingly requires efficient and competent governance. As such, the ability to perform in practical terms will gradually outstrip ideopolitical commitments in importance. For that reason, we conclude that China's Party-state meritocracy is in a state of transition. Its traditional conception consisted of two distinct components, morality and political loyalty on one side and competence on the other, but competence will become increasingly important at the expense of the former.

However, it would be too hasty to conclude that this two-dimensional concept of meritocracy will be completely discarded, and the Chinese state will change to a one-dimensional meritocracy that solely focuses on competence. The traditional idea of virtue or morality (*de*) is still important in cadre practices, and efforts are still being continuously injected into a morality discourse. The political and ideological requirements for the officials will also remain, given the one-party regime's determined goal of staying in power.

The challenges lie on two fronts. First, the Party needs to ensure its ideological package remains coherent and relevant. An obsolete ideology will lose its appeal to Party members, leading to a collapse of belief systems and reference frameworks among the rank and file. Second, the Party needs to ensure it can effectively channel its ideological lines to its members. Here its institutions regarding recruiting, training and developing, evaluating, and promoting state and party employees will be put to the test.

Predicting how well the Party will live up to these challenges is difficult. Suffice to say that the Party so far has demonstrated an ability to adapt to ever changing governing priorities (Shambaugh 2008a). Since the early 1980s, the Party has already escaped the rigidity of traditional Marxist–Leninist ideology and embraced innovations that followed the invention of "Socialism with Chinese characteristics." New ideological frameworks such as Deng Xiaoping Theory, Three Represents, and Scientific Development have been developed, not by individual leaders but mostly as collective products of the Party. However, whether the future cohorts of the Party leadership can continue to do so remains to be seen.[33] As to the second challenge, what is presented in this chapter indicates a serious effort by the Party to ensure political loyalty remains at the heart of recruiting, training, and promoting state and party employees. But clearly, the ideological component is declining in importance. Additionally, an increasing number of Party members now focuses on political and economic benefits brought about by membership, being unable or unwilling to internalize the Party's ideological beliefs and objectives (Shambaugh 2008a: 113–114; Walder 2006: 23; Guo 2005).[34]

Implications for state-building and democratization

State-building refers to the effort of developing or constructing institutions that enable effective governance (Tilly 1975). According to Huntington, political parties are important institutions in this effort (Huntington 1968). More importantly, Leninist parties take a much more proactive approach in building state institutions. Such a party sees itself as the vanguard of society, and serves as the political organization that carries out the country's revolutionary and governing functions. In our case, the Party takes responsibility for the staffing system of the Chinese state, a system composed of identifying, recruiting, training and developing, assessing, and promoting government employees. In this process the Party builds two elements into the system: ideopolitical reliability that aims at ideological unity and loyalty to party, and competence that aims at the quality of the individual officials.

Given the increasing recognition of the importance of state-building and government capacity in recent years (Fukuyama 2004; World Bank 1997), the Chinese Party's effort in building a strong meritocracy in personnel management, will serve future democratization well. Strong institutions in government personnel, taxation, fiscal management, regulation of commerce (food safety, for example) (Yang 2004), and welfare provision (Schwartz and Shieh 2009), among others, will prepare an effective state that can provide good governance when and after formal democratization takes place in the future.

Bureaucratic reform of the kind described in this chapter indeed may not necessarily immediately lead to democratization, and it may well be strengthening the party's grip on power by increasing organizational efficiency and cohesion. But what is being neglected in such a view is that in the reform process new forces are brought into play and new possibilities emerge. Reform erodes the status quo by creating a new context in which openness, rule of law and accountability gain normative strength and operational importance, as discussed in this chapter, which may eventually confuse and eclipse the ruling Party's instincts for self-preservation. As we hinted above, the Party's effort to maintain ideological coherence and unity will prove increasingly challenging. With the Party's ideological monopoly continuing to erode, in due course, a one-party system may prove incapable of supplying an encompassing ideological framework for a hugely pluralized society. It is then that different political articulations will have to fight each other out, and the one-party system might have to give way. Clearly, for democratization to take place in China, it is better that the collapse of CCP ideological unity arrives sooner rather than later. But, as argued elsewhere, democratization preceding complete state-building could prove to be not a way forward but backwards (Rose and Shin 2001). Hence, it is also important to allow sufficient time for the main state-building tasks to be completed, before radical political transitions come in to derail them. How things will actually play out will, however, remain out of the control of scholars.

Notes

1 The imperial examination was terminated in 1905, yet in the early Republican period of the 1920s, Sun Zhongshan (Sun Yat-sen) proposed that one of the five separate powers of the Republic would be responsible for managing and administering a civil service examination, mandatory for all civil servants. This idea is practiced in Taiwan today, as Examination Yuan is one among its five government branches. In Mainland China, the civil servant exam is a major selection and screening tool for the recruitment of government employees, and promotion within government hierarchy is often at least partially determined by various kinds of exams.

2 However, even Mao reportedly regarded non-competent cadres as "pseudo-red, empty headed potatoes" (Shirk 1984: 64).

3 In the words of Deng Xiaoping: "Being expert does not necessarily mean one is red, but being red means that one must strive for expertise." Quoted in Li (2001).

4 The original terms in Chinese were: *geminhua, zhuanyehua, zhishihua, nianqing hua.* See Li (1993).

5 In this study, unless specifically noted, "government" refers to the Party-state and its agencies, which may include both government and Party bodies.

6 As a vast amount of scholarship on contemporary China suggests, this is the result of the convergence of many factors including rising social inequalities, rampant corruption and occasional governmental incompetence, greater openness to foreign ideas and concepts, overall improvements in quality of life and the consequent turn toward post-modern values among Chinese citizens, to name just a few. See for example Pei (2006).

7 The conclusion that there is a necessity to de-politicize decision making in order to effectively govern modern society is echoed by Samuel Huntington (1970) as discussed in Burns (2006: 53).

8 The questions about why and how China "learns" and implements administrative concepts and mechanisms from the West has been raised in recent scholarship. In this chapter we will primarily discuss the suggestions that this process is characterized by the filtering of imported ideas through China's cultural and institutional context and the leadership's aim to claim symbolic rather than instrumental aspects of administrative reforms that help to boost its reform credentials. See: Christensen *et al.* (2008); Dong *et al.* (2010).

9 For different but complementing accounts, see: Chan and Gao (2009); and Chou (2004).

10 For the broader context, for example, see Schubert (2008).

11 The only other instance where the ideopolitical element is given high importance is when it is prescribed that "The appointment of civil servants shall adhere to the principle of making appointment on abilities and having both political integrity and professional competence, and attach importance to practical achievements of work" ("Zhonghua Renmin Gongheguo fa" 2006: Chapter 1, Article 7).

12 Moreover it is further stipulated that "The administration of civil servants shall persist in the principle of openness, equality, competition and selecting of the superior ones" (ibid.: Chapter 1, Article 5).

13 This does not include a large number of civil servants who are not categorized as "officials," or officials below the *chu* level.

14 Personal and parental histories and sometimes even kinship and marriage connections are also examined. Out of these obvious political criteria, there are only indications that a family background no longer increases chances of one's admission to CCP ranks. While having a father who is a CCP member would increase one's chances of Party membership two times in pre-reform era, since the 1980s it does not play any important role anymore. See Bian *et al.* (2001: 814); Walder (2006: 22).

15 These include ministerial and provincial leaders, selected mayors and county party secretaries, cadres involved in ethnic work and young cadres at central level before their promotion to vice-ministerial or equivalent level positions. Shambaugh (2008a: 149).

16 These are primarily aimed at provincial, prefecture and county cadres as well as cadres from Xinjiang and Tibet. See: Liu (2009: 111).

17 These are primarily aimed at future political instructors in Party, state and educational institutions (ibid.: 118).

18 Regarding MA and PhD programs under the Graduate College, the division is similar. For example, out of four compulsory segments for MA students, two are ideological, while the other two are geared toward specialization and broader academic knowledge. This balancing is mirrored by the choice of two compulsory courses for PhD students: Marxism and Contemporary Social Trends of Thought; and Social Survey. Designed research fields at the CPS are much diversified and while the majority relates to Marxist and the CCP's historical experience and philosophy, Western philosophical and theoretical achievements are also strongly emphasized. See Liu (2009: 118–119); Wibowo and Fook (2006: 153).

19 A recent study of Yunnan Party School confirms this finding on the provincial level, although it argues that "cadre training is thus the party's chief instrument to avoid that cadres become apolitical technocrats who simply put their education and skills to the solution of administrative problems." See Pieke (2009c).

20 This trend of rebalancing the content of training toward contemporary and technical components will likely continue as further practical courses dealing with very up-to-date subjects such as information theory and cybernetics theory as well as postmodern values is reportedly under consideration for inclusion in the curriculum, and even into Marxian courses. Additionally, during the training program at party schools, even those classes addressing the ideological foundations of CCP, there are lively discussions among the professors and students, marked by critical and practical perspectives. See, for example, Liu (2009: 122); Pieke (2009a: 68, 110–111).

21 Additionally, large government departments, SOEs, and large service organizations have their own party schools and training centers. See Pieke (2009a: 61–62).

22 Pieke argues that training in the Party school at and below the province level works at both directions: For the more technically educated cadres, the Party school trainings enhance their ideological commitment, while for the cadres with stronger ideological backgrounds, such trainings improve their technical and administrative knowledge and skills. Another major argument of his points to such trainings as a very important socialization experience for the trainees. See Pieke (2009a).

23 For an overview and examples of both central- and local-level documents on Cadre Responsibility System see Chan and Gao (2008).

24 The performance contracts are likely modeled after the household responsibility con-tracts that kicked-off the reform era in modern China. See Heimer (2006: 124–125).
25 These are further refined to indicators to measure their achievement—even as many as over 1,000 in total. See Gao (2009).
26 The veto targets are usually family planning and social order, though it is known that environmental protection has also been included for certain areas. See Heimer (2006: 129).
27 Targets related to social management and economic growth amount to roughly 75–80 percent of total evaluation. See Chan and Gao (2009).
28 Even in the 1990s, according to an official handbook, work achievement should account for 60 to 70 percent and political integrity, competence and diligence should together account for 30 to 40 percent of the evaluation. See Edin (2003b: 37).
29 See, for example, Office of the Chinese Communist Party (2005).
30 For a more detailed account see Pei (2006: 186–187).
31 See for example, Pieke (2009a: 166–173); Brødsgaard (2004).
32 This study, however, was based on data from the second half of last century. See Bo (2002).
33 Walder seems to suggest that with Party membership closely mirroring the social structure, it is able to design policy directions that meet the needs of society. See Walder (2006).
34 According to Huntington, when members join the Party for professional and eco-nomic benefits, instead of for its ideological appeals, the Party is close to its demise. See Huntington (1968).

Bibliography

Aldridge, Stephen (2001) *Social Mobility, A Discussion Paper*, Performance and Innovation Unit, Cabinet Office, London, available online: http://scholar.google.co.uk/scholar_url?hl=en&q=http://kumlai.free.fr/RESEARCH/THESE/TEXTE/MOBILITY/mobility%2520salariale/SOCIAL%2520MOBILITY.pdf (accessed December 20, 2013).

Alveson, Mats and Karreman, Dan (2001) 'Perfection of Meritocracy or Ritual of Bureaucracy?—HRM in a Management Consultancy Firm', Paper presented at the 2nd International Conference on Critical Management Studies, Manchester, July 11–13.

Andreas, Joel (2009) *The Rise of the Red Technocrats*, Stanford, CA: Stanford University Press.

Backer, Larry Cata (2009) "The Party as Polity, The Communist Party, and the Chinese Constitutional State: A Theory of State Party Constitutionalism," *Journal of Chinese and Comparative Law* 16(1): 101–168.

Bakken, Borge (2002) "Norms, Values and Cynical Games with Party Ideology," *The Copenhagen Journal of Asian Studies* 16: 106–137.

Bell, Daniel A. (2006) *Beyond Liberal Democracy*, Princeton, NJ: Princeton University Press.

Bian, Yanjie, Shu, Xiaoling, and Logan, John R. (2001) "Communist Party Membership and Regime Dynamics in China," *Social Forces* 79(3): 805–841.

Bo, Zhiyue (2002) *Chinese Provincial Leaders: Economic Performance and Political Mobility Since 1949*, Armonk, NY: M. E. Sharpe.

Brødsgaard, Kjeld Erik (2004) *Management of Party Cadres in China*, in Kjeld Erik Brødsgaard and Yongnian Zheng (eds.) *Bringing The Party Back In*, Singapore: Eastern University Press, pp. 57–91.

Brødsgaard, Kjeld Erik and Chen, Gang (2009) "China Civil Service Report: An Update,"

EAI Background Brief No. 493, available online: www.eai.nus.edu.sg/BB493.pdf (accessed April 13, 2010).

Brødsgaard, Kjeld Erik and Zheng, Yongnian (2006) 'Introduction: Whither the Chinese Communist Party?' in Kjeld Erik Brødsgaard and Yongnian Zheng (eds.) *The Chinese Communist Party in Reform*, London: Routledge, pp. 1–15.

Burns, John P. (2006) "The CCP's Nomenklatura System," in Kjeld Erik Brødsgaard, and Yongnian Zheng (eds.) *The Chinese Communist Party in Reform*, London: Routledge, pp. 33–58.

Burns, John P. (2007) "Civil Service Reform in China," *OECD Journal on Budgeting*, 7(1): 57–81.

Chan, Hon S. (2004) "Cadre Personnel Management in China: The Nomenklatura System, 1990–1998," *The China Quarterly* 179: 703–734.

Chan, Hon S. and Chow, King W. (2007) "Public Management Policy and Practice in Western China: Metapolicy, Tacit Knowledge, and Implications for Management Innovation Transfer," *The American Review of Public Administration* 37: 479–498.

Chan, Hon S. and Gao, Jie (eds.) (2008) "Performance Measurement in Chinese Local Governments," *Chinese Law and Government* (special edition) 41(2/3): 4–9.

Chan, Hon S. and Gao, Jie (2009) "Putting the Cart Before the Horse: Accountability or Performance?" *The Australian Journal of Public Administration* 68(1): 51–61.

"China's Civil Servants Exam Attracts 1.3 Mln Applicants" (2010) Available online: http://english.gov.cn/2010-10/25/content_1729958.htm (accessed October 25, 2010).

"China Recruits Civil Servants in a Fair Way, Via Examinations" (2011) Available online: http://english.gov.cn/2011-01/19/content_1788328.htm (accessed January 19, 2011).

Chou, Bill K. P. (2004) "Civil Service Reform in China, 1993–2001: A Case of Implementation Failure," *China: An International Journal* 2(2): 210–234.

Christensen, T., Dong, Lisheng, and Painter, Martin (2008) "Administrative Reform in China's Central Government: How Much 'Learning From the West'?" *International Review of Administrative Sciences* 74(3): 351–371.

Civil Servant Law of the People's Republic of China (2006) Chapter 2, Article 11, English-language translation available online: www.asianlii.org/cn/legis/cen/laws/ tcs-lotproc462 (accessed on December 31, 2013).

Dong, Lisheng, Christensen, Tom, and Painter, Martin (2010) "A Case Study of China's Administrative Reform: The Importation of the Super-Department," *The American Review of Public Administration* 40(2): 170–188.

Edin, Maria (2003a) "Remaking The Communist Party State: The Cadre Responsibility System at the Local Level in China," *China: An International Journal* 1(1): 1–15.

Edin, Maria (2003b) "State Capacity and Local Agent Control in China: CCP Cadre Management From a Township Perspective," *The China Quarterly* 173: 35–52.

Elman, Benjamin (2002) *A Cultural History of Civil Examinations in Late Imperial China*, London: University of California Press.

Fewsmith, Joseph (2004) "Promoting the Scientific Development Concept," *China Leadership Monitor* No. 11, available online: http://media.hoover.org/documents/ clm11_jf.pdf (accessed April 1, 2010).

Fukuyama, Francis (2004) *State Building: Governance and World Order in the Twenty-First Century*, New York: Cornell University Press.

Gao, Jie (2009) "Governing by Goals and Numbers: A Case Study in the Use of Performance Measurement to Build State Capacity in China," *Public Administration and Development* 29(1): 21–31.

Gilley, Bruce (2006) "The Meaning and Measure of State Legitimacy: Results for 72 Countries," *European Journal of Political Research* 45(3): 499–525.

Goux, Dominique and Maurin. Eric (1997) "Meritocracy and Social Heredity in France: Some Aspects and Trends," *European Sociological Review* 13(2): 159–157.

Guo, Gang (2005) "Party Recruitment of College Students in China," *Journal of Contemporary China* 14(43): 371–393.

Heimer, Maria (2006) "The Cadre Responsibility System and the Changing Needs of the Party," in Kjeld Erik Brødsgaard and Yongnian Zheng (eds.) *The Chinese Communist Party in Reform*, London: Routledge.

Huntington, Samuel P. (1968) *Political Order in Changing Societies*, New Haven, CT: Yale University Press.

Huntington, Samuel P. (1970) "Social and Institutional Dynamics of One-Party Systems," in Samuel P. Huntington and Clement H. Moore (eds.) *Authoritarian Politics in Modern Society*, New York: Basic Books, pp. 3–47.

Jiang, Zemin (2001) "Speech at the Meeting Celebrating the 80th Anniversary of the Founding of the Communist Party of China," available online: www.china-un.ch/eng/zgbd/smwx/t85789.htm (accessed April 3, 2010).

Landry, Pierre F. (2004) "The Political Management of Mayors in Post-Deng China', in Kjeld Erik Brødsgaard and Yongnian Zheng (eds.) *Bringing The Party Back In*, Singapore: Eastern University Press.

Lee, Hong Yung (1991) *From Revolutionary Cadres to Party Technocrats in Socialist China*, Berkeley, CA: University of California Press.

Li, Bobai (2001) "Manufacturing Meritocracy: Adult Education, Career, Mobility, and Elite Transformation in Socialist China," PhD dissertation, Stanford University.

Li Cheng (2004a) "Analyses of Current Provincial Leaders," *China Leadership Monitor* 7.

Li Cheng (2004b) "Educational and Professional Backgrounds of Current Provincial Leaders," *China Leadership Monitor* 8.

Li Cheng (2005) "Hu's New Deal and the New Provincial Chiefs," *China Leadership Monitor* 10.

Li Cheng (2008) "From Selection to Election: Experiments in the Recruitment of Chinese Political Elites," *China Leadership Monitor* 26.

Li Cheng (2010) "China's Midterm Jockeying: Gearing Up for 2012 (Part 1: Provincial Chiefs)," *China Leadership Monitor* 31.

Li, Kang Tai (1993) "Administrative Law in China," in Miriam K. Mills and Stuart S. Nagel (eds.) *Public Administration in China*, Westport, CT: Greenwood Press.

Liu, Alan P. L. (2009) "Rebirth and Secularization of the Central Party School in China," *The China Journal* 62: 105–125.

Longoria, Richard T. (2007) *Meritocracy and Americans' Views on Distributive Justice*, Lanham, MD: Lexington Books.

Naughton, Barry (2007) *The Chinese Economy: Transitions and Growth*, Cambridge, MA: MIT Press.

Office of the Chinese Communist Party (2005) "Evaluation Methods on the Objective Responsibility System in Zhouzhi County," *Chinese Law and Government* 41(2/3): 35–44.

Pei, Minxin (2006) *China's Trapped Transition: The Limits of Developmental Autocracy*, Cambridge, MA: Harvard University Press.

People's Daily (2009a) "2008 CCP Statistics Notice," July 3, available online: http://english.peopledaily.com.cn/90001/90776/90785/6692814.html (accessed April 9, 2010).

People's Daily (2009b) "Ranks of CCP Members Full of Life and Vigor," available from: http://english.people.com.cn/200209/02/eng20020902_102501.shtml (accessed December 31, 2013).

Pieke, Frank N. (2009a) *The Good Communist*, New York: Cambridge University Press.

Pieke, Frank N. (2009b) "Marketization, Centralization and Globalization of Cadre Training in Contemporary China," *The China Quarterly* 200: 953–971.

Pieke, Frank N.(2009c) "The Production of Rulers: Communist Party Schools and the Transition to Neo-Socialism in Contemporary China," *Social Anthropology* 17(1): 25–39.

"Provisional Regulations on Civil Servants" (1993) available online: www.china.com.cn/chinese/MATERIAL/385908.htm (accessed July 22, 2013).

Ranson, Baldwin (1998) "Education for Modernization: Meritocratic Myths in China, Mexico, The United States and Japan," *Journal of Economic Issues* 22(3): 747–762.

"Regulations on the Work of Selecting and Appointing Leading Party and Government Cadres" (2002) Available online: www.china.org.cn/english/features/45399.htm (accessed April 12, 2010).

Rose, Richard and Shin, Doh Chull (2001) "Democratization Backwards: The Problem of Third-Wave Democracies," *British Journal of Political Science* 31(2): 331–354.

Sato, Hiroshi and Eto, Kaiya (2008) "The Changing Structure of Communist Party Membership in Urban China, 1988–2002," *Journal of Contemporary China* 17(57): 653–672.

Schubert, Gunter (2008) "One-Party Rule and the Question of Legitimacy in Contemporary China: Preliminary Thoughts on Setting up a new Research Agenda," *Journal of Contemporary China* 17(54): 191–204.

Schwartz, Jason and Shieh, Shawn (eds.) (2009) *State and Society Responses to Social Welfare Needs in China: Serving the People*, New York: Routledge.

Selected Works of Mao Zedong (1991) Beijing: People Publishing House.

Sen, Amartya (1999) "Merit and Justice," in Kenneth Arrow, Samuel Bowles and Steven Durlauf (eds.) *Meritocracy and Economic Inequality*, Princeton, NJ: Princeton University Press, available online: http://press.princeton.edu/chapters/s6818.pdf (accessed March 20, 2010).

Shambaugh, David (2008a) *China's Communist Party: Atrophy and Adaptation*, Washington, DC: Woodrow Wilson Center Press.

Shambaugh, David (2008b) "Training China's Political Elite: The Party School System," *The China Quarterly* 196: 827–844.

Shirk, Susan (1984) "The Decline of Virtuocracy in China," in William Watson (ed.) *Class and Social Stratification in in Post-Revolution China*, Cambridge: Cambridge University Press.

State Administration of Civil Service (2010) "2011 niandu kaoshi luyong zhongguo zhengjianhui canzhao gongwuyuan faguanlishiye danwei gongzuo renyuan gonggao" (Public Notice on 2011 Annual Examination on Recruitment of Civil Servants in Management Institutions of China State Regulatory Commission According to Civil Servant Law) available from: www.scs.gov.cn/Desktop.aspx?PATH=/gjgwyjsy/ksly/lnksly (accessed February 1, 2011).

Sun Yat-sen (1945) *Fundamentals of National Reconstruction*, Taipei: China Cultural Service.

Szelenyi, Ivan and Bill, Martin (1989) "The Three Waves of New Class Theories," *Theory and Society* 17(5): 645–667.

Tilly, Charles (1975) "Western-State Making and Theories of Political Transformation," in Charles Tilly and Gabriel Ardant (eds.) *The Formation of National States in Western Europe*, Princeton, NJ: Princeton University Press.

Tran, Émilie (2003) "From Senior Official to Top Civil Servant," *China Perspectives* 46, available online: http://chinaperspectives.revues.org/document257.html (accessed June 23, 2010).

Walder, Andrew G. (2006) "The Party's Elite and China's Trajectory of Change," in Kjeld Erik Brødsgaard and Yongnian Zheng (eds.) *The Chinese Communist Party in Reform*, New York: Routledge, pp. 15–32.

Wang, Mengkui (ed.) (2008) *Good Governance in China—A Way Towards Social Harmony*, New York: Routledge.

Wang, Zhengxu (2006) "Hu Jintao's Power Consolidation: Institutions and Power Balance in China's Elite Politics," *Issues and Studies* 42(4): 97–136.

Wang, Zhengxu (2008) *Democratization in Confucian East Asia: Citizen Politics in China, Japan, Singapore, South Korea, Taiwan and Vietnam*, New York: Cambria Press.

Wang, Zhengxu (2009) "Citizens' Satisfaction with Government Performance in Six Asian-Pacific Giants," *Japanese Journal of Political Science* 11(1): 51–75.

Wibowo, Ignatius and Fook, Lye Liang (2006) "China's Central Party School: A Unique Institution Adapting to Changes," in Kjeld Erik Brødsgaard and Yongnian Zheng (eds.) *The Chinese Communist Party in Reform*, New York: Routledge, pp. 139–156.

Wu, Jiannan (2009) "Difang zhengfu pinggu de chuangxin yu wanshan" (The Reform and Improvement of the Local Governments' Performance Evaluation Activities), in Yu Keping (ed.) *Scientific Concept of Development and Government Innovations*, Beijing: Blue Book of Chinese Government Innovations 2009, Social Science Academic Press.

Whaites, Alan (2008) "States in Development: Understanding State-building," London: Department for International Development, available online: www.gsdrc.org/go/display&type=Document&id=3264.

World Bank (1997) *World Development Report 1997: The State in a Changing World*, Oxford: Oxford University Press.

Yang, Dali (2004) *Remaking the Chinese Leviathan: Market Transition and the Politics of Governance in China*, Stanford, CA: Stanford University Press.

Young, Michael (1958) *The Rise of the Meritocracy*, London: Thames and Hudson.

Young, Michael (2001) "Down with Meritocracy," *Guardian*, June 29, available online: www.guardian.co.uk/politics/2001/jun/29/comment (accessed March 20, 2010).

Zhang, Cheng F. (1993) "Public Administration in China," in Miriam K. Mills and Stuart S. Nagel (eds.) *Public Administration in China*, Westport, CT: Greenwood Press.

Zhai, Tianshan (2008) "A Study of How to Improve the System of Civil Servant Performance Evaluation," in Menkui Wang (ed.) *Good Governance in China—A Way Towards Social Harmony*, New York: Routledge.

"Zhonghua Renmin Gongheguo gongwuyuan fa" (Civil Servant Law of the People's Republic of China) (2006) In *Renshi gongzuo wenjian xuanbian* (Selected Documents of Personnel Work), Beijing: Renshibu zhengce faguisi, 28: 56–57.

4 Digital monitoring and public administrative reform in China

Jesper Schlæger

Introduction[1]

Information and communication technology (ICT) has increased the monitoring capacity of the Chinese state thereby facilitating performance management in public administration. Even so, the consequences of ICT adoption in terms of power redistribution and control within the politico-administrative system are unclear. The existing literature has contradictory theories of the dynamics that are a consequence of the implementation of new information systems. A number of interpretations argue that citizen empowerment and pluralization of society are taking place, which may be precursors of a process of democratization or steps towards good governance (Damm and Thomas 2006; Zheng 2007). Nevertheless, others point out that the regime has been successful in using the new media to its own benefit to increase control and monitoring capacity (Kalathil and Boas 2003; Seifert and Chung 2009). Studies with a particular focus on ICT in the public administration converge on arguments that ICT leads to reinforcement of the existing power structures (Kluver 2005; Seifert and Chung 2009). It raises the question of whether the central government can use ICT to support organizational reforms to attain better control of local governments and thereby promote good governance (Lagerkvist 2005; Zhang 2005).

A technological determinist position would argue that the inherent character of technology will decide the new organizational form (Song and Cornford 2006) whereas a constructivist position, on the contrary, would focus on how powerful actors are able to shape technology to suit their interests (Bijker 1995). Whereas these positions exist, the majority of studies of the use of ICT in public administration (e-government) argue for a middle way (Agre 2002; Danziger and Andersen 2002; Yildiz 2007). It depends upon the 'affordances' of the particular technology in a particular context of ideas and institutions (Agre 2002; Hansen and Hoff 2006; Schlæger 2010). This chapter takes as its point of departure this last position. Consequently, it will focus on exploring through which mechanisms the new technologies affect processes of administrative reforms.

The problem addressed in this paper is: how does digital monitoring affect government capacity to implement public administrative reforms? Digital monitoring can be understood as a means to address the information asymmetry that exists in principal–agent relations within the state. The purpose of this paper is to trace the mechanisms that drive processes of technology-mediated organizational reform. This is done in order to explore regularities in the way digital monitoring influences organizational behaviour through changes in principal–agent relations. Underlying this is the question whether the party-state is able to increase transparency, efficiency and effectiveness and reduce corruption within the bureaucracy. Such improvements could lead to better governance and over the longer term could legitimize the regime as the government shows its ability to deliver what people need from the state (see, e.g. Shue 2010).

The question is answered through an exploratory case study which traces the processes of two instances of ICT adoption in Chengdu. The study is based on 21 qualitative interviews, participant observation, and documentary sources collected during a half-year of fieldwork. The logic behind choosing Chengdu instead of more developed cities such as Shenzhen, Shanghai or Beijing is that the impact of ICT will most likely be more visible. The level of informatization is lower in Chengdu and hence changes are easier to observe. The first case of government affairs service centres is the most likely place to see an effect of digital monitoring as administrative approval takes places in a stationary office setting. Furthermore, the development of service centres is the result of an explicit government goal of organizational reform. Hence, it presents a most likely case of organizational changes enabled by digital monitoring in an area of China where changes would be easy to spot. The second case of urban management probes further into the individual level to find the limits of digital monitoring. It is a particularly useful heuristic case, because government has explicit focus on organizational reform. So, the purpose of the second case is to explore the limits to attaining total digital monitoring. The cases are intended to empirically develop the medium-range concepts of 'virtual panopticon' and 'battering ram' that can help explain the role of digital monitoring in processes of public administrative reforms.

New digital ICT such as networked computing and mobile telephony afford new ways of monitoring and can therefore potentially lead to changes in organized practices and new rules of the game. In the case study such institutional changes will be traced on two levels; first, the individual level concerning how and why employees change behaviour when carrying out their work; and second, at the organizational level regarding how and why relations between organizations in terms of tasks and authority change.

To guide the analysis a key concept is linked to each level. On the individual level, the analysis identifies the presence of a virtual panopticon. A virtual panopticon is when a superior government authority applies a range of ICT including automated surveillance to comprehensively monitor the level of compliance of lower-level government employees. The virtual panopticon takes to the extreme what Bentham did with his panoptic prison where centrally placed guards could monitor all the inmates yet remain unseen (Bentham 1995). The difference between the original idea and the one characterizing the virtual panopticon is that of automated surveillance. It makes the panopticon even more pervasive. In the classic panopticon, the point is to create a prison where inmates self-regulate because there is a risk that they will be caught they if transgress (Foucault 1977). Additionally, in the virtual panopticon the surveillance is automated and hence constant, so any unsanctioned behaviour will definitely be revealed.

The virtual panopticon is in many ways similar to the 'electronic panopticon' of call-centres (Bain and Taylor 2000). In the debate about implications of electronic panopticon, the focus has been on strategies of autonomy: how employees avoid being constrained. Such strategies can be individual or collective. It has been argued that the monitoring can lead to worker organization, e.g. in the form of labour unions. In a Chinese public-administration context this is not feasible under the present conditions where the state opposes all non-state political organizations. Consequently, this leaves individual-level shirking as the main focus for analytical attention in the following. In particular, analysis must address if the virtual panopticon turns street-level bureaucrats with considerable discretionary power into screen-level bureaucrats with no or very limited power to make independent decisions (Bovens and Zouridis 2002). This could be expected to happen as a consequence of digitally mediated regulation and standardization of the work process.

On the organizational level, the battering ram is used as the key concept. This is when a government authority uses ICT-based data to induce institutional change in other agencies by problematizing non-compliance with 'objective' criteria, e.g. performance indicators. This mechanism has been hypothesized to potentially lead to organizational changes in the Chinese administration (see, e.g. Lagerkvist 2005). If this is the case it would be a very important tool in the Chinese government's attempts to implement administrative reforms.

The following sections first provide a short background on informatization in Chengdu and introduce a shared ICT system. Then, government affairs service centres and digital urban management reform processes are analysed to assess to what extent the virtual panopticon and the battering ram mechanisms are present in the cases and with what outcomes. Finally, the processes are compared and the implications of the findings are discussed.

Background: informatization of the public administration in Chengdu

In Chengdu, government agencies called informatization offices play a central role in standardization of shared Internet platforms. The offices are government internal functions on city and district levels, and their task is to implement digital solutions in all government operations. Decisions on ICT procurement are centralized here to counter a tendency of locally developed systems to become detached information islands (*dudao*). Formally, the offices are responsible for policy making concerning informatization, but in practice they work as consultants to the overall planning which is undertaken by the government. In effect, the key task of the offices is the co-ordination and standardization of information systems.

The other district-level organizations presented in the case study (service centres and urban management) are both influenced by the work of the informatization offices through the latter's involvement in development and procurement of information systems for their use. The offices have played an important part in drafting the plans for implementation of networks to support the new institutional structures built up later.

Determining the code of a system implies making political choices and this leads to an 'automation of bias' in the sense that it reinforces the interests of those who shape the technology (Dutton and Kraemer 1980; Lessig 1999). In order to use the platform, agencies have to comply with standards set by the informatization office. The main affordance of the integrated government network is that it allows access-control, so if an agency does not heed the standard, they cannot use the resources of the network. A part of this is the shared database which requires collection of particular process data such as time of case entry, type of case, and name of employee responsible for the case. By setting standards the informatization offices determine what will be possible with the technologies, and they shape the technologies in terms of the software. The decisions about which parameters are measured as part of the work flow analysis are highly political decisions, as they define the measurable criteria for the evaluation of government agencies. The local government, through the informatization offices, ensures that government priorities are reflected in the standards and evaluation criteria embedded in the software which all agencies have to use. The government applies this 'automation of bias' to enhance control over administrative processes on the organizational and individual level as shown in more detail in the sections below.

Government affairs service centres

Corruption and inefficiency characterized the application for business licences in Chengdu in the 1990s. A business man showed his license with 100 different stamps to the mayor who reacted to a perception that so much 'running around' was a bad thing for local GDP growth. As this is the main performance indicator for leaders, it would diminish his chances of promotion. Reform was put in motion to increase the efficiency of administrative approval procedures thereby improving the soft environment for business investment by creating a service-oriented government. The ideas behind the concept of 'service-oriented government' were similar to the ideas behind New Public Management, the well-known ideological basis of reinventing government in the OECD countries (Hood 1991; Osborne and Gaebler 1992). Consequently, there was a drive to make government lean, effective and responsive to customer citizens. The problem of administrative process corruption, the abuse of public power for illegal gain performed in relation to administrative approval, is facilitated by the veto-power of the single employee. The entire application process can be stopped because the applicant needs to have a particular seal before any further work can be done, which makes it possible to press for grease or an outright bribe. Furthermore, opaque rules make it even easier to find an excuse to stall the process. In practice, rules of administrative application were considered a state secret until the reforms of government affairs began in 2001. Up until then, there was thus no way of knowing exactly which rules would apply to a particular type of application. This created problems of unfettered administrative power. Hence there is a good reason for autonomy-seeking employees to prefer this situation since the information asymmetry is clearly in their favour, both in relation to superiors and to the clients. As a countermeasure, the political leaders gave high priority to tackling the issues related to administrative corruption. They perceived ICT as an important part of the anti-corruption efforts (see Li *et al.* 2009).

A number of key events characterize the reform process. In 2001, the government implemented a service centre at the provincial level, and this was accompanied by a significant reduction in the number of items for approval. This was the first of a number of reductions in the administrative burden of businesses. The provincial-level centre proved successful, and it was followed by centres at city and district levels in 2004. Due to the distribution of authority, the district-level centres have more contact with local clients than the provincial-level centre, which primarily addresses national or international clients. In varying numbers between districts, the centres collect about 25–30 agencies in co-production. In 2007 a new system of parallel processing allowed these to process complex cases more fluently. It is also relevant to point out that the reforms entailed the addition of government agencies and an increase in budget and personnel allocations. The scope of rules was reduced and, combined with the organizational expansion and new work processes, the administrative quality in terms of efficiency and effectiveness improved considerably. The process so far culminated in 2009 when one district tried to move decision authority from co-producing agencies into the service centre, a reform that gave rise to fierce bureaucratic turf-wars, and the reforms were rolled back. In the following, key elements of the reform are described and analysed to explore how ICT shaped the reform outcomes.

Whereas research has been looking for innovation online on government websites (Hartford 2005; Lagerkvist 2005; Zhang 2005), the physical centres are still the main scene of encounters between clients and the state. Indeed, the service centres established an 'online government affairs office' to complement the off-line office. Even so, the online channel does not in itself solve the problems of running around. Most original documents still have to be handed in to the centre, and therefore the usefulness of the system is mainly as a platform for pre-application to assess if the materials are complete before going to the centre. The centres address the issues of inefficiency in two ways. First, all of the participating agencies have a window or counter so the centre serves as a 'one-stop-shop' even if an application concerns several of them. Second, supported by the affordance of information exchange on the digital system, it is possible to process cases in parallel in multiple agencies as opposed to the previous serial processing.

The key to understanding the role of ICT lies in the back-office processes. The service centres rely on an Internet-based case processing system which demands that all applications are entered into the system as soon as they are received. All procedures, ranging from the basic form of journalizing file-numbers to complete online processing, require interaction with a computer system. The information is then transferred to the relevant authority, and a countdown commences according to strict time commitments. Case loads and time consumption can be followed on an individual basis through the statistics of the system. One of the effects of applying a computer system to the administrative working procedures is that it becomes easier to monitor the work of government employees. On the level of the individual 'screen-level bureaucrat' (see Bovens and Zouridis 2002) a system of pervasive monitoring was established in 2004. Their superior, the office manager (*ke zhang*), and the Bureau of Supervision (*Jiandu Ju*) can trace all work routines in real time and retrospectively through the statistics. Furthermore, among the rules which confer rights on the clients, there is a time commitment for any type of case. The system registers whenever an employee opens a new case, which results in a countdown. When the timer reaches the limit, an automated 'red alert' warning (*liang hongdeng*) will be issued to the office manager and to the Bureau of Supervision. The screen-level bureaucrats can lose their job over this and, naturally, it creates pressure on them to finish in time. A potential tool to reduce arbitrary government discretion thus exists, because if any irregularities occur the higher levels can intervene in the process.

Additionally, the interconnection between systems combined with automated procedures creates more constraints on the employees. An example is the connection of the real estate tax payment system and the system to confer real-estate documentation. Previously, a citizen could evade tax and be registered as such, yet still get an official document stating ownership of an apartment or a house because two different agencies were concerned with the matter. Now, a case of tax evasion is registered in the tax database. This database is connected to the database from where real estate documentation is printed. When the tax has not been paid, the print function is automatically disabled. As a result, a client who attempts to cheat the tax system will be unable to get documentation for his or her real estate. It is not possible to bribe employees responsible for printing, because they cannot manually override the system.

As a supplement, managers can also monitor their employees visually through CCTV (closed-circuit television). The surveillance cameras serve to protect employees against dissatisfied clients as well as to monitor the behaviour of the employees themselves. If this had been a simple adoption of CCTV, the feed from the surveillance cameras would have been visible only from the manager's office or from a special internal unit responsible for monitoring. In the service centres in Chengdu this is more sophisticated. The CCTV signal is transmitted over an Internet connection, which enables several access points to the data. Both the centre manager and personnel from the Bureau of Supervision can follow the feed.

The opportunities for the screen-level bureaucrats to commit administrative process corruption are significantly changed in the environment of pervasive surveillance which is supported by rewards and sanctions. The number of applications has been reduced; the ones left are more transparent. In other words, there is no way of making up rules, the case processing leaves a digital trail that can be followed, and hence it is difficult for the employee to hide any irregularities. There is surveillance in real time and even automated monitoring so that time limits must be met. Furthermore, no single office is in a veto-position anymore, as cases can be processed in a parallel manner. To support the control over employees, the management uses a range of rewards and sanctions. Performance pay amounts to 20–30 per cent of the salary, and the performance indicators include items related to work efficiency as well as positive evaluations by clients. In these respects, the reality for the employees working in the interface between citizens and state differs substantially from previous times.

On the organizational level the changes are more modest as core bureaucracies and authority relations have not been altered. To process an application in a parallel fashion more communication is needed between the agencies involved. Furthermore, there is a new role for the service centre as a central node co-ordinating the efforts. As it is often the case in government reform and in particular those involving complex ICT systems, there are apparently still unresolved problems, in particular when seen from the point of view of clients. The point of one-stop-shopping is that the needs of the client should be met at the centre. Nevertheless, some complex cases cannot be handled there, e.g. environmental licensing of industrial production facilities. Therefore, a client who needs this kind of license will be sent to the Bureau of Environmental Protection (*Huanbao Ju*) where the authority and expertise for this kind of government affairs are vested, even though they have a representative at the service centre.

There are several unfortunate consequences seen from the client's side. First, it is inconvenient to have to go to another office because of distance and because the relevant person may not be present. However, the issue of 'running around' (*pao lu*) and the resulting waste of time and energy is the least of the potential problems. More serious problems include that the process requirements are not necessarily known to the public, and that the process cannot be monitored from other agencies. This is a potential site of corruption. Such problems are foreseeable and there are no signs of systematic failure on the part of the service centres. Nevertheless, under such circumstances effectiveness is low, and the government has attempted to change this through delegation and restructuring of authority.

In sum, the one-stop-shopping reform has increased government capacity to monitor the screen-level bureaucrats and at the same time reduced how much clients need to run around between government offices to acquire business licences or pay tax. The monitoring system applied in relation to the service centre employees fits closely the definition of the virtual panopticon of total monitoring: it allows real time monitoring of government employees and produces a 'red alert' if a time commitment for case processing is exceeded. The reform has reduced administrative discretion and direct administrative process corruption. At the same time, new problems arise on the organizational level because the authority relations and incentive structures are not attuned. Consequently, even though the district party committee had intentions to use ICT as a battering ram for organizational reform, it did not succeed in breaking down the barriers between different government agencies.

Urban management

As the virtual panopticon seems to be successfully applied within the service centres, it is relevant to examine other cases to find the limits of this mechanism. To this end, the following pages analyse the use of digital monitoring in urban management. The government has used ICT to challenge existing organizational structures in urban management. The problems facing urban management boil down to co-ordination and co-production between bureaucracies to attain higher efficiency in maintaining public infrastructure and the general appearance of the city. A new Internet-based digital urban management system was adopted in Chengdu first in the central districts between 2007 and 2009 and then in the periphery. The system is built upon 'network management' which at its core is a management system that literally splits the city up into digits. It is done so that routine inspections of infrastructure can be performed using the *chengguan-tong*—a smart phone—and this is complemented by surveillance through access to Skynet, the police CCTV network. Employees at urban management control centres watch monitors displaying live-feeds from surveillance cameras in the streets and virtual maps with moving red dots. These dots show the position of city inspectors who, equipped with a smart phone, hunt for infrastructure problems. Chinese news media widely circulate images of these city managers performing their work routines of identifying potholes in the street, broken manhole covers etc. When it comes to controlling the employees, the system by and large achieves the goals set by policy based on a virtual panopticon. In contrast, the government decision makers do not achieve co-ordination between the large number of co-producing agencies by the battering ram of the ICT system alone, but resorts to the integrative mechanism of a leadership group (*lingdao xiaozu*).

Similar to the service centres, the most significant role of ICT is in back-office functions. The Urban Management Bureau has a website which mainly serves as a platform for the bureau to disperse information—primarily news—and not for any larger amount of interaction. Nonetheless, the Internet plays an important role for the operation of the system. Whereas the particular website application is not necessary for the operation of the system, the Internet nonetheless plays an important role because it facilitates communication across agencies and it enables the network management system. The term 'network' refers to the city district being divided into small administrative cells. Within these areas, all fixed infrastructure components such as, e.g. manhole covers, lamp posts, waste bins etc. are assigned unique identifying numbers in a digital system. Consequently, reports of a problem can be dealt with without misunderstandings about the precise location. The system's provision of real time work-flow statistics provides new, important data which is used in two main ways. First, it is used for efficiency improvements and discussions of further reform. Second, the data can be accessed by the Bureau of Supervision and allow the surveillance both manually and automatically through the same 'red alert' system as issued by the service centres.

Moreover, it is important to notice that other technologies than the Internet play a role. The technological infrastructure for the new system hinges on the so-called *chengguantong*. The word *chengguan* means city manager and *tong* refers to the first part of the word *tongxin* which means communication or to communicate. It alludes to a very popular device called the *xiaolingtong*, a wireless phone system, which in many places substituted mobile phones, because they were initially cheaper. Expectedly, at further examination the technology is well-known under names such as smart phone or PDA (personal digital assistant), and it also resembles a better quality version of the *xiaolingtong*. It is not without an innovative element, though: an important difference from the units more often used is that the *chengguantong* operates on its own dedicated network and not on the public mobile phone networks. So, even though the technology was well-known, the appropriation of it and the diffusion and development of the system in several Chinese cities warrants further attention. The thing itself can be used as a 3G (third generation) mobile phone with communication in sound and image. Furthermore, it has GPS (global positioning system), which combined with virtual maps (using a geographic information system, GIS) enables position tracking of the *chengguantong* unit on a virtual map.

The dual functions of the system (to increase efficiency and improve monitoring) are visible through the way the system works. The following sections describe the daily routine work process as it unfolds at city and district levels in Chengdu. As in the case of service centres, the issue confronting the government can be seen from two levels. On the individual level, the problems are to control that tasks are carried out and that workers do not collude in shirking. Table 4.1 summarizes the key actors, tasks and the role of ICT. Initially, the inspector identifies a problem, takes a photo with his mobile phone and sends it back to the control centre (*jiandu zhongxin*) along with information about the geographical

Table 4.1 Urban management work process

Actor	Task	ICT
Inspector	Problem identification	*Chengguantong*
Control centre	Open file	Internet
Command centre	Task dispatch	Internet
Responsible agency	Accept task	n.a.
Multiple actors	Handle problem	n.a.
Inspector	Verify handling	*Chengguantong*
Control centre	Close file and evaluate	Internet

Source: Folder from the Chengdu City Urban Management Bureau.

position. Then, the control centre opens a file in the Internet-based system. This file is subsequently passed on to a command centre (*zhihui zhongxin*) where employees examine the photo and description and determine how to fix the problem. They send a message to the agency responsible for the task, which dispatches a team to mend the pothole or change the light bulb in question. After the problem is solved, the inspector visits the place and confirms task completion with another photo which is sent to the control centre for verification, whereafter they close the file.

The ICT system also plays a role in evaluations at the individual level in the same fashion as in the service centres. Due to the computerized system, performance indicators can be closely linked to the production output of every single employee. For the screen-level bureaucrats the number of cases processed or problems resolved will count towards their salary bonuses, as well as count towards being awarded 'Star of the Month' which comes with a cash prize. The process of gathering statistical information about the work efforts of the employees has been facilitated by the Internet-based system, but of course it would be possible (yet much more costly in terms of time spent) to gather the data without such platform. For the office managers, evaluations are more complex but aggregate performance indicators also affect their salary and, more importantly, their chances of promotion. As illustrated next, what the system measures shapes the behaviour of the employees.

The movements of the inspector are traceable by GPS but the photos do not have a GPS stamp, so it is impossible to tell where it was taken, and this is used by the inspectors to gain autonomy. The inspector can cheat the system to avoid moving around. This point is not mentioned in the account provided by earlier studies of the system as it was applied in Beijing (Song and Cornford 2006). The motivation for shirking could be that it increases their apparent productivity and thereby their salary. Another motivation could be the more abstract to increase autonomy of decisions. To counter shirking, inspectors are now told to send photos which include identifiable surroundings. In the lack of a high-technological solution, this is a way of using process regulation instead to make the inspectors comply, and reduce risk that such cases recur.

A comprehensive control system based on several levels of supervision has been built up and with it the opportunity to manage by performance indicators. An incentive structure to solve the problems of urban management can be put in place by making the supervisors guard the inspectors who guard the work team, and all are awarded for getting the job done. The supervisors themselves are also guarded by the Bureau of Supervision, who can enter the system at any point through the Internet channel, and check on the work. Furthermore, failure to comply with time limits triggers the automated 'red alert' function similar to what happens in the government affairs service centres described above. The monitoring takes place not only in real time but can also take place retrospectively by looking at the production statistics. An autonomy-maximizing actor who attempts to preserve and exploit information asymmetries explains well the observed behaviour at street level. However, both financial incentives and threats of punishment if the shirking is revealed will draw him or her in the opposite direction. In the case of the cheating inspector there is no doubt that the person responsible for the final approval of the case will not be able to hide, because the employee's log-in details appear on the case file. The main motivation is interest-based self-regulation with its roots in fear of the sticks of punishment or salary deductions, and in hope of carrots of a monthly bonus and credit in shape of the 'Star of the Month' award. On the individual level the digital system combined with performance management has thus allowed increased control and better efficiency of the work process.

Urban management is a hard case with respect to the adoption of a virtual panopticon. In contrast, it is a most likely case for the adoption of a battering ram mechanism, because the entire reform of the agency revolves around the need to increase collaboration between different government bureaucracies. Seen from the city government level, control of employees alone does not solve the organizational challenges of co-ordination of urban management, which involves a number of different agencies with different interests. To this end, the output from the system in the form of statistics can create a new basis for discussing administrative reform. On the one hand, creating the new network management system brings simplification of the process of problem identification, because the identification is handled by one agency instead of a handful. On the other hand, increased complexity in terms of a whole new set of problem categories has been necessary along with the complexity it brings to assign unique numbers to all fixed infrastructure. In particular the definition of which problems are registered in the system and the deadlines for solving them are important for the function of the system as a battering ram, as it is non-compliance with these measures which is used to put pressure on the agencies that are supposed to handle the issues. It is fair to consider the system an expression of a battering ram mechanism because performance measures are created to induce a behavioural change among the co-producing agencies. A number of these receive very poor results in the internal evaluations, and for those agencies the performance indicators are in all cases set higher than the current level of co-ordination allows.

The organizational performance measures reflected in the computer system are sometimes counter-productive to other agencies, and the fact that a leadership group is adopted in the end reflects the need for hierarchical authority. A concrete example was provided by an office director during an interview (Author's interview 12, 6 January 2010): along the streets of Chengdu there is a large number of road trees planted and maintained by the Bureau of Forestry. Sometimes, trees die or break, and this has been coded as a problem in the digital urban management system. If an Urban Management Bureau inspector finds a dead tree, he will register it and there will be a call to the Bureau of Forestry asking them to remove it immediately. Surprisingly, this is not guaranteed to happen, as the Bureau of Forestry might wish to wait for a while until they can collect a couple of dead trees on the way for economies of scale; it is inefficient to send a lorry to pick up just one tree. In this situation there is a draw because the administrative authority of the agencies is on the same level. Consequently, who gets their way with things will ultimately be a question of negotiation, which takes time and energy. Such problems of co-ordination are often found within the context of Chinese public administration (Lieberthal and Oksenberg 1988).

The solution is also a well-known integrative mechanism with little relation to ICT: a leadership group. In 2009 the Office of the Urban-Rural Environmental Governance Leading Group (*chengxiang huanjing zhili lingdao xiaozu bangong-shi*) was assigned to the Urban Management Bureau. Thus, the bureau chief became the leader of the office, and consequently superior in rank to the heads of the other related bureaus. In cases like the one mentioned he—because of his higher rank—can issue an order to the relevant bureau to make them comply. According to a respondent, the lack of co-ordination was the main reason for the adoption of the leading group. Nevertheless, to the actors involved, this is not considered a permanent and stable solution. Instead, they argue, an organizational arrangement should be made so that such higher level interference becomes unnecessary (Author's interview 12, 6 January 2010).

In sum, network management affords monitoring of the employees involved in urban management as well as more efficient problem identification. The Internet-based system combined with the *chengguantong* works through total digitization of the fixed infrastructure of the city. It does not, however, reach the level of a complete virtual panopticon as the lack of a GPS-stamp on photos enables inspector to shirk. With respect to the battering ram mechanism, co-ordination between agencies continues to be an issue, and this is a question of authority more than technology. Hence, in this case, as in the previous one, the battering ram is ineffective as a tool for reform.

The role of digital monitoring in public administrative reforms

Comparing the findings from the two cases reveals different dynamics on the individual and organizational levels respectively. Reducing the monitoring costs through applying digital surveillance systems enables managers in the service centres and urban management control and command centres to monitor their employees in real time and in a pervasive manner. However, the implementation in urban management is incomplete in the sense that a loop-hole (*chengguantong* does not GPS-stamp pictures) allows for cheating. The employees have to follow the rules encoded in the system concerning when, how and what they report and register. In the context of a clear authority relation between them and their employer, backed up by incentive systems that reward and punish behaviour as measured by the system criteria, the mechanism 'fires'.

In contrast, at the organizational level the context for ICT as a battering ram is non-conducive. The findings in this chapter indicate that an important contextual factor for the mechanism to 'fire' is the existence of credible sanctions and clear authority relations. They are absent in both of the processes above. In the service centre case it results in rolling the reform back on district level. In urban management the solution was to adopt a leadership group, which was deemed only a temporary solution seen from the people who perform the everyday management in the agency. Certain institutional contexts are non-conducive to a particular mechanism, and for practical use this implies that ICT is not a solution in itself but has to fit with the context of institutions and ideas.

Based on the findings in Chengdu, it can be hypothesised that authority relations are an important contextual factor determining whether the mechanism of battering ram and virtual panopticon 'fire' or 'gel'. On the individual level, simple and clear performance indicators supported by a clear principal–agent relation are conducive for the virtual panopticon. On the organizational level, in contrast, the context is characterized by complex performance indicator clusters that are in play between organizations with two 'principals' following from the 'matrix-muddle' of horizontal and vertical relations in the Chinese administrative system.

The battering ram 'gels' in both situations. This would be an affirmation of the reinforcement hypothesis, which could be further specified on organizational and individual levels. Hypotheses can thus be proposed that when authority relations are challenged, the battering ram mechanism does not fire, which leads to a status quo. Under other circumstances, an existing power asymmetry can be further exacerbated as demonstrated by the virtual panopticon. In this sense ICT is conservative by reinforcing the existing power relations. As they are from the outset different at the individual and the organizational level the outcomes of ICT adoption on the two levels will also differ.

Conclusion

Through analysis of an exploratory case study this chapter suggests that the role of digital monitoring in administrative reform can be explained by the mechanisms of the virtual panopticon and the battering ram. On the individual level, ICT enables creation of a virtual panopticon, a total monitoring of employees, which allows a high degree of control of their behaviour in combination with a detailed system for performance management. The mechanism 'fired' and the reforms increased efficiency and reduced corruption. Organizationally, digital monitoring can be applied as a battering ram by creating statistics that assign 'objective' numbers to the level of co-ordination between agencies. Coupling this to performance indicators of the office directors then allow their superiors in district government to press for reform. However, this mechanism did not 'fire'. The organizational level reforms were unsuccessful both in the service centres where they were rolled back, and in urban management, where co-ordination was contingent on establishing a leadership small group. In both instances, lack of a clear hierarchical authority relation appears to be the reason.

The role of digital monitoring is mainly to reduce inefficiency through communication, and reduce administrative process corruption by increasing oversight capacity through real-time surveillance of screen-level bureaucrats. In the case study, the governance capacity of the party-state was strengthened, which illustrates a reinforcement of existing power structures. By creating a liveable city environment and making life easier for business entrepreneurs the government is creating an output which in a longer perspective might increase regime legitimacy. This paper demonstrates the existence of new dynamics in the way government uses ICT and goes about administrative reform. Even so, the findings are discomforting for anyone who hoped that the deeply ingrained problems of corruption and bureaucratic politics could be solved by technology as illustrated by the repeated failures of the battering ram mechanism. On the other hand, ICT can be put to work as a virtual panopticon to increase efficiency and reduce the administrative process corruption in relation to the clients in situations where an unambiguous authority relation exists. These findings require further inquiry into the necessary context for a successful application of the mechanism as a tool for administrative reform.

Note

1 Parts of this chapter have previously been published in: Schlæger, J. (2013) *E-Government in China: Technology, Power and Local Government Reform*, London: Routledge. The author wishes to thank Routledge (Taylor and Francis Group, Ltd.) for permission to use this material. The completion of this chapter was supported by the Sichuan University Fundamental Research Funds for the Central Universities (skyb201201).

References

Agre, P.E. (2002) 'Real-Time Politics: The Internet and the Political Process', *The Information Society* 18(5): 311–331.
Bain, P. and Taylor, P. (2000) 'Entrapped by the "Electronic Panopticon"? Worker Resistance in the Call Centre', *New Technology, Work and Employment* 15(1): 2–18.
Bentham, J. (1995) 'Panopticon', in M. Bozovic (ed.) *The Panopticon Writings*, London: Verso, pp. 29–95.
Bijker, W.E. (1995) *Of Bicycles, Bakelites, and Bulbs: Toward a Theory of Sociotechnical Change*, Cambridge, MA: MIT Press.
Bovens, M. and Zouridis, S. (2002) 'From Street-Level to System-Level Bureaucracies: How Information and Communication Technology Is Transforming Administrative Discretion and Constitutional Control', *Public Administration Review* 62(2): 174–184.
Damm, J. and Thomas, S. (eds) (2006) *Chinese Cyberspaces: Technological Change and Political Effects*, London: Routledge.
Danziger, J.N. and Andersen, K.V. (2002) 'The Impacts of Information Technology on Public Administration: An Analysis of Empirical Research from the "Golden Age" of Transformation', *International Journal of Public Administration* 25(2): 591–627.
Dutton, W. and Kraemer, K. (1980) 'Automating Bias', *Society* 17(2): 36–41.
Foucault, M. (1977) *Discipline and Punishment*, Harmondsworth: Penguin.
Hansen, H.K. and Hoff, J. (eds) (2006) *Digital Governance:://Networked Societies: Creating Authority, Community and Identity in a Globalized World*, Copenhagen: Samfundslitteratur NORDICOM.
Hartford, K. (2005) 'Dear Mayor: Online Communications with Local Governments in Hangzhou and Nanjing', *China Information* 19(2): 217–260.
Hood, C. (1991) 'A Public Management for All Seasons?' *Public Administration* 69(1): 3–19.

Kalathil, S. and Boas, T.C. (2003) *Open Networks, Closed Regimes: The Impact of the Internet on Authoritarian Rule*, Singapore: The Eastern Universities Press.

Kluver, R. (2005) 'The Architecture of Control: A Chinese Strategy for e-Governance', *Journal of Public Policy* 25(1): 75–79.

Lagerkvist, J. (2005) 'The Techno-Cadre's Dream: Administrative Reform by Electronic Governance in China Today?' *China Information* 19(2): 189–216.

Lessig, L. (1999) *Code: And Other Laws of Cyberspace*, New York: Basic Books.

Li J., Dong L. and Xu J. (2009) 'Jiyu zhengfu menhu wangzhan tuidong zhengwu liucheng zaizao' (Promoting Government Affairs Process Reengineering on the Basis of Government Portal Websites), *Zhongguo xinxijie* (*China Information Times*) 2009(3): 48–50.

Lieberthal, K. and Oksenberg, M. (1988) *Policy Making in China: Leaders, Structures, and Processes*, Princeton, NJ: Princeton University Press.

Osborne, D. and Gaebler, T. (1992) *Reinventing Government: How the Entrepreneurial Spirit is Transforming the Public Sector*, Reading, MA: Addison-Wesley.

Schlæger, J. (2010) 'Digital Governance and Institutional Change: Examining the Role of E-Government in China's Coal Sector', *Policy and Internet* 2(1): 37–61.

Seifert, J.W. and Chung, J. (2009) 'Using E-Government to Reinforce Government Citizen Relationships: Comparing Government Reform in the United States and China', *Social Science Computer Review* 27(3): 3–23.

Shue, V. (2010) 'Legitimacy Crisis in China?' in P.H. Gries and S. Rosen (eds) *Chinese Politics: State, Society and the Market*, Abingdon: Routledge, pp. 41–68.

Song, G. and Cornford, T. (2006) 'Mobile Government: Towards a Service Paradigm', in *Proceedings of the 2nd International Conference on e-Government*, Pittsburgh, PA: University of Pittsburgh, pp. 208–218.

Yildiz, M. (2007) 'E-Government Research: Reviewing the Literature, Limitations, and Ways Forward', *Government Information Quarterly* 24(3): 646–665.

Zhang, J. (2005) 'Good Governance Through E-Governance? Assessing China's E-Government Strategy', *Journal of E-Government* 2(4): 39–71.

Zheng, Y. (2007) *Technological Empowerment: The Internet, State, and Society in China*, Stanford, CA: Stanford University Press.

5 Public sector reform in China

Who is losing out?

Kjeld Erik Brødsgaard and Chen Gang

Introduction

Reform of the public sector has become an issue of great concern to the Chinese leaders as they realize that efficient public administration is a key to securing the regime's governing capacity and ultimately long-term survival. The public sector in China is enormous, comprising 64.2 million people, and efforts to reform the system as well as to change the work habits and routines of the personnel staffing the administrative organs are of a herculean nature. The Chinese government, starting from the abolishment of "iron rice bowls" or lifelong employment in state corporations, has taken very different approaches to reform the personnel management systems pertaining to the state-owned enterprises (SOEs), public service units (PSUs) and the civil service. Our investigation of the implementation of these disparate reforms applied to various categories of public sectors reveals that, while tens of millions of iron rice bowls have been broken in state business to invigorate the economy, the party-state still retains many of those privileges for its own officials in an effort to bolster its own rule. Despite being politically and even at times economically efficient, such discriminatory policies are morally incorrect and perceived as unfair. As a result the policies have caused enormous implementation problems, especially in the reform of more vaguely defined PSUs. In these enterprises the misery experience by SOE employees, having already suffered from previous reforms, has led to a boycott of changes to the pension and medical schemes they enjoyed previously under the the iron rice bowl. Case studies have shown that unfairness and discrimination in the initial reform design are major obstacles to the implementation of policies aimed at transforming PSUs. Privileged treatment reserved for all civil servants obstructs further reforms of other public sectors, promising erosion of the popularity of the ruling party in the long run.

A number of works on the Chinese civil service system have been published (Cabestan 1991; Lam and Chang 1995; Burns 2004; OECD 2005). However, there is a scarcity of studies on the reforms and changes that have taken place in the Hu Jintao Era and especially since the passing of a new Civil Service Law in Jaunaury 2006. Similarly, reform of public service units has been severely under-researched in Western and Chinese-language literature on the topic.

China's public sectors and the concept of "iron rice bowl"

The Chinese public sector can be divided into three institutions: party and state organizations (*dangzheng jiguan*), public service units (PSUs or *shiye danwei*), and state-owned enterprises (SOEs or *qiye danwei*).[1] Each category has its own personnel management system and personnel and budget allocations. Party and state organs are staffed with civil servants (*gongwuyuan*). The staff in PSUs are also on the state's payroll, but they are not regarded as civil servants.

"Iron rice bowl" (*tie fan wan*), a Chinese term to refer to guaranteed lifetime employment, was once provided for almost everyone in the public work units or *danwei* under the command economy. After 30 years of reform and opening up, the market economy has done away with such preferential job arrangements in most SOEs and numerous PSUs. Only civil servants (*gongwuyuan*) in party and state organizations (*dangzheng jiguan*) and staff in some PSUs like universities, schools, hospitals and the official media continue to enjoy the security of the iron rice bowl arrangement. For a number of years the line between party and state organizations and PSUs have been blurred and the staff of many PSUs have enjoyed almost the same privileges as civil servants. Recently attempts have been made to clearly separate the two systems in terms of personnel management, remuneration and pension arrangements. Due to the lingering concerns about potential downgrade of income, job security and welfare, which actually fell on SOE workers that had lost their iron rice bowls in the completed SOE reform of the 1990s, this PSU reform, with the visible goal of depriving PSU employees of iron rice bowls has caused new widespread objections even in its nascent period.

With the booming of the private sector and the transformation (*gaizhi*) of state-run firms into private or state-owned shareholding companies, the iron rice bowl concepts have been replaced by contract-based employment and "socialized" welfare (*fuli shehuihua*). For the latter, medical care, pension and unemployment compensations are provided on the basis of insurance funded jointly by the individual, the employer and the state. Only civil servants and some PSU staff members still enjoy the benefits of iron rice bowl job security. Apart from cradle-to-grave job security, these people are also entitled to free lifelong medical care and access to special hospitals. Cadres at Deputy Bureau Director level or above have access to the well-equipped Senior Cadre Wards (*gaogan bingfang*) when receiving in-patient treatment. Without contributing part of their wages to a social security fund on a monthly basis, these government employees still get to enjoy the government-paid lifelong pension that is much higher than that of a retiree relying on social security funds.

What guarantees the iron rice bowl: the power of *bianzhi*

Employees in Chinese public sectors are managed under the system of *bianzhi*, which is literally translated as "authorized staffing" and refers to the number of authorized personnel in a party/government unit, office or organization

(Brødsgaard 2002). Only staff within the *bianzhi* system can enjoy the iron rice bowl privilege. Today a large proportion of the work force without *bianzhi* are working for the Chinese government and PSUs, but they are excluded from the enviable iron rice bowl system. According to the Civil Service Law the term "civil servant" refers to "personnel who perform public duties according to laws and have been included into the state administrative *bianzhi* with wages and welfare borne by the state public finance" (Zhonghua Remin Gongheguo gong-wuyuan fa 2006: Article 2).

This formulation highlights the key role of the concept of *bianzhi* in Chinese public management. Until recently all posts included in the *bianzhi* system were financed by the state through the Ministry of Finance. This will still be the case for civil service positions. However, for other sectors, a *bianzhi* post may no longer be fully financed by the state, although the overall number is still state-controlled. Although the *bianzhi* is formally controlled by the state, in practice the Party is heavily involved in setting *bianzhi* targets. The Party is especially interested in controlling and managing the leadership positions associated with *bianzhi* system at various levels.

There are three main categories of *bianzhi*: administrative *bianzhi* (*xingzheng bianzhi*), enterprise *bianzhi* (*qiye bianzhi*), and the *bianzhi* which applies to PSUs (*shiye danwei bianzhi*). The administrative *bianzhi* is at the core of the administrative system and applies to civil servants. It refers to the authorized number of established posts in Party and government administrative agencies and organizations (*jiguan*). The administrative *bianzhi* lays down the number of administrative agencies and the number of personnel (*renyuan*) allocated to these agencies. The *bianzhi* also involves budget outlays in the form of salary and allowances. Collective and private enterprises are not part of the *bianzhi* system.[2]

Occupying a position defined by the *bianzhi* system is normally associated with lifelong tenure and a number of benefits and is therefore associated with prestige and social status. Particularly prestigious is the administrative *bianzhi*, since it denotes membership of the core government bureaucracy. However, it is possible to be part of the PSU *bianzhi* and yet enjoy the same benefits as officials on the administrative *bianzhi* (civil servants). This is the case for a considerable portion of the officials working in PSUs, in particular those having clear administrative functions and responsibilities.

It should be noted that *bianzhi* is not identical with the concept of nomenklatura, as indicated by some scholars (Schurmann 1968; Shambaugh 2000). The *bianzhi* specifies the number of positions and agencies as well as the budgetary outlays, whereas the nomenklatura system focuses on Party management of the leading positions in these agencies and organizations. Thus the nomenklatura system can be defined as a list containing those leading officials directly appointed by the Party as well as those officials about whom recommendations for appointment, release or transfer may be made by other bodies, but which require the Party's approval (Brødsgaard 2009: 80; Harasymiw 1969: 494). It should also be noted that the nomenklatura include lists of personnel to be recommended for future appointment. The *bianzhi* system neither contains such reserve lists nor does it describe mechanisms for leadership appointments.

Originally the officials performing public duties in post-1949 China were called cadres (*ganbu*). As the cadres were managed by the Party this system denoted that the Party was in control of the public sector. From the beginning of 1979, with the introduction of reform policies, many reformers argued for a professionalization of public functions and a separation of Party and government (*dangzheng fenkai*) functions. Thus the notion of a modern civil service system in China was born and the concept of civil servant (*gongwuyuan*) began to be used. However, the political climate following the Tiananmen incident did not allow less Party control over the state apparatus and these plans were stalled for several years. Only in 1993 was it possible to publish the legal basis for a new civil service system in the form of "The Provisional Service Regulations." However, by then the Party no longer intended to give up its control over the state bureaucracy. In fact, a lack of fundamental clarity as to whether civil servants are primarily to be managed by the state's civil service regulations or the Party's cadre regulations still permeates the public sector in China.

Number of civil servants

Exact estimations of the number of civil servants are difficult to arrive at and the literature on the subject reports conflicting numbers. The public sector as such has shrunk significantly and now only counts 65.5 million staff and workers compared to almost 110 million in 1995, when public sector employment peaked in China (*China Statistical Yearbook* 1996: 96; *China Statistical Yearbook* 2008: 115). This reduction is primarily the result of the restructuring of the state-owned enterprise sector that Zhu Rongji initiated in the mid-1990s. State-owned enterprises now employ 22.5 million people compared to 75.4 million in 1995. By contrast, employment in PSUs has increased steadily but slowly and now amounts to 27.4 million staff and workers. The number of civil servants can be found in the statistics under the category of "public management and social organizations" (*gonggong guanli he shehui zuzhi*).[3] In 2007, 12.6 million were employed in this category, up from 10.42 million in 1995 and 4.67 million in 1978 (*China Statistical Yearbook* 2008: 114, 127).[4] However, not all who work in these agencies and organizations are engaged in administrative work. We estimate that about 20 percent are engaged in ancillary functions such as cooks, drivers, janitors, etc. and temporary secretaries, although Zhu Guanglei notes that 8–13 percent of the employees in Party and government agencies and organizations are logistic workers (Zhu 1998). Thus we arrive at a figure for 2007 of about 10.08 million civil servants in core government bodies (see Table 5.1). About 93 percent of all civil servants work in government agencies (*jiguan*), 4.5 percent work in organs of the Communist Party and 1.7 percent in non-governmental organizations and social organizations. The social organizations are also often called "mass organizations" (*qunzhong shetuan*) and they primarily include a number of state-sponsored organizations such as the All China

Trade Union and All China Federation of Women. The remaining less than 1 percent work in the Political Consultative Conference and in the eight so-called democratic parties (Table 5.2).

Civil servants are not necessarily members of the Party. In fact, most of the rank and file civil servants do not hold a Party membership. However, 95 percent of civil servants in leading positions from division (county) level and above are Party members. Civil servants who formally occupy the "real" leadership position (*zhengzhi*) in a given agency or ministry are almost without exception Party members, whereas the deputy positions can be filled with non-Party members. In recent years the Party has, as a part of its strategy of professionalizing government work, appointed two non-Party members of the State Council, namely Wan Gang, minister of Technology and Science, and Chen Zhu, minister of Health. However their power was limited by the fact that they could not occupy the important Party secretary post in their ministries.

It is important to note that civil servants in China denote not only career bureaucrats who enter the bureaucratic system at the bottom of hierarchy and work

Table 5.1 Estimated number of China's civil servants, 1978–2008 (millions)

Year	Employees in state, Party and mass organizations	No. of civil servants
1978	4.67	3.74
1980	5.27	4.22
1985	7.99	6.39
1990	10.79	8.63
1991	11.36	9.09
1992	11.48	9.18
1993	10.30	8.24
1994	10.33	8.26
1995	10.42	8.34
1996	10.93	8.74
1997	10.93	8.74
1998	10.97	8.78
1999	11.02	8.82
2000	11.04	8.83
2001	11.01	8.81
2002	10.75	8.60
2003	11.46	9.17
2004	11.70	9.36
2005	12.13	9.70
2006	12.35	9.88
2007	12.60	10.08

Source: *China Statistical Yearbook* (various years).

Note
Calculated on the basis of the total number of staff and workers in organs of the CCP, government agencies, democratic parties and social organizations minus an estimated 20% logistic workers and temporary personnel.

Table 5.2 Distribution of civil servants (2007)

Organization	Number[1]	% of total
Organs of Chinese Communist Party[2]	448,000	4.48
Government agencies	9,313,000	93.09
PPCC[3] and democratic parties	71,200	0.71
NGOs and social organizations	172,000	1.72
Total	10,004,200	

Source: *China Statistical Yearbook* (2008: 124).

Notes
1 Calculated on the basis of total number of employed staff and workers minus an estimated number of 20 per cent logistic workers and temporary personnel.
2 This category excludes Party secretaries, deputy Party secretaries and other full-time Party workers in the Party committees and branches inside government agencies, public service units (*shiye danwei*) and state-owned enterprises. So the actual figure of all full-time Party workers and officials is much larger than this.
3 People's Political Consultative Conference.

their way up the career ladder. State leaders and cabinet members, who normally would be considered politicians in political systems with competing political parties and elections, are also part of the civil service system in China. Thus President Hu Jintao and Prime Minister Wen Jiabao are civil servants and are remunerated and have benefits in accordance with civil service regulations. They have climbed to the top vertically rather than horizontally, as is the case in parliamentary democracies.

Similarly, whereas all civil servants are cadres, not all cadres are civil servants. There are around 42 million cadres in China compared to ten million civil servants, meaning that around one fourth of the cadre corps can be classified as civil servants. The fact that civil servants are also classified as cadres has the significant consequence that they are also managed according to the various cadre regulations circulated by the Party and the Ministry of Personnel. The new Civil Service Law in fact stipulates that in cases where there are other regulations concerning the appointment, dismissal and supervision of leading civil servants, then these regulations apply. By this formulation it is indicated that the Party's regulations for leading cadres take priority over the Civil Service Law (Zhonghua Renmin Gongheguo gongwuyuan fa 2006: Articles 3 and 4). The formulation was not included in the "temporary regulations." That it has been necessary to do so in the new Civil Service Law indicates that the Party will insist on not losing control over the leading civil servants who are also Party members. However, these modifications to the law create a gray zone where it at times is unclear which regulations apply and which do not, thereby undermining one of the primary objectives of civil service reform, i.e., establishing clear and transparent procedures and objectives. A recent trend among Party officials is to restrict the concept of cadres to cover only civil servants, i.e., the core bureaucracy.[5]

Content and aim of recent reform of the civil service system

The new Civil Service Law contains a number of changes. The most important is the addition of a new chapter on appointment. The addition specifies the possibility of using the appointment system (*pinren zhi*) in connection with positions with strong specialties. However, using this possibility requires the approval of the administrative department above the provincial level. For positions which involve state secrets, the appointment system cannot be applied. The term for the employment contract is one to five years, preceded by a probation period of six months. The contract includes clauses on wage, welfare provisions, insurance treatment and breach of liabilities. The appointment system based on contract gives various administrative departments considerable flexibility to hire special expertise within areas that require attention. The system has been in use since the early 1990s but it is now regulated in a legal document. However, acquiring staff through the appointment system has to take place within the allocated *bianzhi* and will therefore affect the hiring of regular staff. In general the Civil Service Law focuses more than the regulations on stressing that staffing has to be within the prescribed *bianzhi*.

Concerning the hiring of regular staff the new Civil Service Law introduces a distinction between selection (*xuanren*) and appointment (*weiren*) (Article 38). The concept of selection does not appear in the 1993 regulations. It covers a recruitment system based on selecting civil servants among a wider number of candidates that have applied for the position in question based on a public announcement. The appointment takes place according to the result of an examination (*kaohe*) and a process of "hearing the masses." The difference between the new selection system and the traditional appointment system can more loosely be described as the difference between appointment from the bottom up and appointment from the top down.

The new law is generally also more specific on the rights and duties of the civil servants. For example it is illegal for civil servants to engage in enterprises or in for-profit public institutions (Article 102). This also applies for a three-year period after retirement. Civil servants may also not draw any financial reward from a part-time job (Article 42).

Concerning employment, the new law has more detailed provisions which indicate a greater focus on qualifications in terms of examination as well as making the recruitment process more transparent. The 2006 law stipulates that examinations for civil service posts shall be published and the notice should include information concerning the nature of the posts in question as well as the qualifications needed and the material to be included in the application to take part in the examination (Chapter 4).

The chapter on positions and ranks has also been modified. The most important is that the ranking system with 15 different grades is no longer explicated. It is mentioned that the corresponding relationship between post and rank of civil servants shall be prescribed by the State Council, thereby indicating that a new grading system was underway.

Appointing and selecting civil servants

The objective of civil servant management in China is to make sure that professionally competent people are recruited and promoted and that they remain loyal to the Party's ideological and political line (Brødsgaard 2001). To ensure their loyalty to the Communist Party, the privilege of the iron rice bowl has been retained for all civil servants amidst all sorts of institutional changes to improve their efficiency. Their job security rests not in a civil service statute but rather through a unified personnel management system that the Civil Service Law has sought to revitalize (Chan and Li 2007: 384).

All civil servants are managed by the Party according to detailed regulations relating to recruitment, appointment, transfer, reward, training etc. which supplement the Civil Service Law. Concerning the management of civil servants above division (*chu*) level, the most important provisions are contained in "Regulations on Selection and Appointment of Party and Government Leading Cadres" (Dangzheng lingdao ganbu xuanba renyong gongzuo tiaoli 2003) initially issued in 2002 by the CCP Central Organizational Department.

All these regulations emphasize that when selecting and appointing leading cadres in civil service in China, it is important to follow a number of basic principles. These include openness, equality, competition and the selection of the best. Although their selection and appointment are based on meritocratic principles (*ren ren wei xian*), it is also stressed that cadres should have both political integrity and ability (*de cai jian bei*) and that the Party should manage the cadres (*dang guan ganbu*) (Dangzheng lingdao ganbu xuanba renyong gongzuo tiaoli: Article 2). It is stipulated that civil servants to be promoted to leading Party and government posts at section (township)-head level must have college diploma (*dazhuan*) or above degree and have worked at the deputy post for more than two years (Article 19). Candidates to be promoted to posts higher than the county (division) level must have held at least two posts at lower level organs and candidates who are promoted from deputy post to a head post (*zhengzhi*), generally must have worked at the deputy post for more than two years. Leading cadres at bureau-level (*ju, si, ting*) or above should normally have a bachelor degree (*daxue benke*) or above.

Changing the egalitarian mindset on remuneration

Wage policy in developing countries tends to be more politically sensitive because of prevailing conditions of scarcity (Cooke 2005: 281). In response to a long-time criticism of the wage system in China's civil service for being egalitarian and insensitive to variations of performance, the government has been making cautious but substantial efforts to enlarge wage differentials among civil servants on the basis of administrative ranking and yearly performances. The results of these efforts are embodied in a reform document on the civil service wage system, published by the State Council in June 2006, which substantially widened the salary gap among civil servants with different job positions (*zhiwu*) and rankings (*jibie*), and institutionalized the one-off bonuses at the end of the year. The new wage system also introduced a new ranking system with 27 different ranks and a grade (*dangci*) system within each rank (at most 14 grades for each rank) to reflect seniority and performances (see Table 5.3). The old wage table only contained 15 different ranks. In general, the 2006 reform increased the average salary level of China's civil servants by large margins. Taking the Chinese president (or the premier) as an example, he/she could earn at most 2890 yuan per month (excluding all the monetary subsidies and non-monetary benefits) according to the salary standard set by the government in 2001 (China's Ministry of Personnel 2002: 404). In 2006, however, the president's monthly salary was more than doubled to 7820 yuan (excluding monetary subsidies and non-monetary benefits).

According to the 2006 reform plan, the present salary system for civil servants in China consists of a "position and ranking system" with two parts: position salary (*zhiwu gongzi*) and ranking salary (*jibie gongzi*) (China's State Council 2006). Compared with previous salary systems before 2006, another two components, namely basic salary and seniority salary, have been abolished because these two parts were the same for any civil servant regardless of rank and therefore reflected the egalitarian mindset. The basic salary was a fixed monthly contribution of 180 yuan and the seniority contribution amounted to one yuan for each year of service.

The new salary system is based on a classification of 12 levels of job positions and a 27-level ranking system with regard to nature of work, level of responsibility and qualification, capability, and seniority. Unlike the 2001 salary table, the rankings do not explicitly mention top job positions such as president, vice-president, premier and vice-premier. Instead these positions are incorporated into the categories of state-leader and vice-state-leader. The category of state-leader covers rank 1–3 and presumably covers the following positions: president, chairman of the National People's Congress (NPC), premier, chairman of the Chinese People's Political Consultative Conference (CPPCC) and vice-president, with only the first two positions in the top rank. The vice-state-leader rank would include the vice-chairmen of the NPC and the CPPCC, the vice-premiers and the state councilors. Not explicitly mentioning the positions in these top ranks opens the possibility of flexibility in remunerating the top leaders.

In general, correspondences between position and ranking are given in Table 5.4.

The new salary system follows a strict hierarchical order with widening income gaps. The president (state leader level) earns 7820 yuan per month at the top of the salary scale. This is based on a ranking salary of 3820 and a position salary of 4000. At the bottom of the scale an office worker starts off with a beginning ranking salary of 290 yuan per month and a position salary of 340. This amounts to 630 yuan per month, less than one tenth of the president. According to the 2001 salary scheme, the office workers' beginning salary was about one sixth of the president's. The new salary system has introduced a

Table 5.3 Standard table of nominal salary system (excluding monetary subsidy and other benefits) (yuan/month) (2006)

Dangci (Grade) Position	Ranking	1	2	3	4	5	6	7	8	9	10	11	12	13	14	Position salary
State-Leader level	1	3020	3180	3340	3500	3660	3820	—	—	—	—	—	—	—	—	4000
	2	2770	2915	3060	3205	3350	3495	3640	—	—	—	—	—	—	—	
	3	2530	2670	2810	2950	3090	3230	3370	3510	—	—	—	—	—	—	
Vice-State-Leader level	4	2290	2426	2562	2698	2834	2970	3106	3242	3378	—	—	—	—	—	3200
	5	2070	2202	2334	2466	2598	2730	2862	2994	3126	3258	—	—	—	—	
	6	1870	1996	2122	2248	2374	2500	2626	2752	2878	3004	3130	—	—	—	
Ministerial level	7	1700	1818	1936	2054	2172	2290	2408	2526	2644	2762	2880	—	—	—	2510
	8	1560	1669	1778	1887	1996	2105	2214	2323	2432	2541	2650	—	—	—	
Vice-Ministerial level	9	1438	1538	1638	1738	1838	1938	2038	2138	2238	2338	2438	—	—	—	1900
	10	1324	1416	1508	1600	1692	1784	1876	1968	2060	2152	2244	—	—	—	
Bureau-Director-level	11	1217	1302	1387	1472	1557	1642	1727	1812	1897	1982	2067	2152	—	—	1410, 1290[1]
	12	1117	1196	1275	1354	1433	1512	1591	1670	1749	1828	1907	1986	2065	—	
Deputy-Bureau-Director level	13	1024	1098	1172	1246	1320	1394	1468	1542	1616	1690	1764	1838	1912	1986	1080, 990[1]
	14	938	1007	1076	1145	1214	1283	1352	1421	1490	1559	1628	1697	1766	1835	
Division-Head level	15	859	924	989	1054	1119	1184	1249	1314	1379	1444	1509	1574	1639	1704	830,760[1]
	16	786	847	908	969	1030	1091	1152	1213	1274	1335	1396	1457	1518	1579	
Deputy-Division-Head level	17	719	776	833	890	947	1004	1061	1118	1175	1232	1289	1346	1403	—	640,590[1]
	18	658	711	764	817	870	923	976	1029	1082	1135	1188	1241	1294	—	
Section-Head level	19	602	651	700	749	798	847	896	945	994	1043	1092	1141	—	—	510,480[1]
	20	551	596	641	686	731	776	821	866	911	956	1001	—	—	—	
Deputy-Section-Head level	21	504	545	586	627	668	709	750	791	832	873	—	—	—	—	430,410[1]
	22	461	498	535	572	609	646	683	720	757	—	—	—	—	—	
Section member	23	422	455	488	521	554	587	620	653	—	—	—	—	—	—	380
	24	386	416	446	476	506	536	566	596	—	—	—	—	—	—	
Office worker	25	352	380	408	436	464	492	520	—	—	—	—	—	—	—	340
	26	320	347	374	401	428	455	—	—	—	—	—	—	—	—	
	27	290	316	342	368	394	420	—	—	—	—	—	—	—	—	

Note
1 Non-leading positions.

Table 5.4 Correspondences between position and ranking

1	State-Leader level: rank 1–3
2	Vice-State-Leader level: rank 4–6
3	Ministerial (Provincial) level: rank 7–8
4	Vice-Ministerial (Provincial) level: rank 9–10
5	Bureau-Director level: rank 11–12
6	Deputy-Bureau-Director level: rank 13–14
7	Division-Head level: rank 15–16
8	Deputy-Division-Head level: rank 17–18
9	Section-Head level: rank 19–20
10	Deputy-Section-Head level: rank 21–22
11	Section member: rank 23–24
12	Office worker: rank 25–27

Source: China's State Council 2006.

differentiation between leading and non-leading positions (see Table 5.3). An in-power bureau director (*juzhang*) is expected to earn 1410 yuan per month as his/her position salary, while an inspector with the same ranking can only get 1290 yuan per month because he/she does not head a bureau and therefore has no leadership and personnel responsibilities. In principle this would mean that a *juzhang* who is not moved up the career ladder at the end of his ten-year tenure would see his salary reduced.

Besides the position and ranking salary, almost all civil servants now receive some monetary subsidies (*butie*) that usually range from 2000 yuan to 5000 yuan per month. Such subsidies are usually related to local GDP performances, fiscal revenues, price levels and geographic conditions. Civil servants in metropolises like Shanghai and Beijing and coastal provinces like Guangdong and Jiangsu get the higher-level subsidies due to the high living standards there. Officials working in Tibet and Xinjiang are also subsidized for the harsh natural circumstances and geographic remoteness. All civil servants are supposed to receive year-end bonuses worth one month's salary if they make no serious mistakes. Regular salary increases are given to officials every two or three years upon passing an evaluation or performance appraisal. Hence even without promotion, a civil servant will still witness steady salary increase in the long run. Moreover, the monetary incomes at the various levels of the salary scale are adjusted upwards at regularly intervals. In recent years this has happened almost every year.

Besides all the monetary remuneration on the payroll, most civil servants today are still able to purchase their apartments at subsidized prices in convenient locations. This is not an option open to urban workers. The kind of housing a civil servant is entitled to buy reflects his position and ranking. A cadre at county or division level is entitled to buy a three-bedroom apartment, whereas a section head would only be allocated a two-bedroom apartment. In Beijing leading cadres at vice-ministerial level and above are allocated an apartment measuring at least 240 square meters. Such privilege could mean fringe benefits worth hundreds of thousands of yuan in big cities like Beijing and Shanghai where housing prices have rocketed in recent years. In addition, higher level cadres have a special car with a driver at their disposal. A vice-minister, for example, can have a car worth 350,000 yuan. Lower-level officials without such a privilege often draw on these benefits by using the office car for their own personal purposes. In some places, the authorities have tried to solve the problem by giving officials a transportation allowance. This should also be considered part of their total income (Zhu 1998: 148). Civil servants are entitled to have almost-free medical care and access to special hospitals. Cadres with ranking at deputy-bureau-director level or above have the access to the well-equipped Senior Cadre Wards (*gaogan bingfang*) when receiving in-patient treatment. Unlike other urban workers in private sectors or state-owned enterprises, civil servants do not need to contribute part of their wages to social security funds on a monthly basis, but they can enjoy the government-paid lifelong pension that is much higher than that of a retiree relying on the social security fund.

Influenced by the idea of paying high salaries to foster a clean government, the authorities have increased civil servants' salaries, subsidies and pensions remarkably in recent years. If all the non-monetary benefit is counted, civil servants are definitely much better paid compared to many other groups in Chinese society. This explains the fierce competition during the national civil service entrance exam in 2008, when 775,000 people, mostly college-educated, were vying for 13,500 national civil service posts (*China Daily* 2008). In recent years the authorities have pushed a so-called "Sunshine Project" (*yangguang gongcheng*) which aims to make salaries and benefits of civil servants more transparent. Associated with the "Sunshine Project" was the "3-5-8-1 Project" in Beijing which set annual income ceilings for the various levels of the civil service corps in the capital. At the time these ceilings were 30,000 yuan in annual salary for sections heads; 50,000 yuan for division heads; 80,000 for bureau heads; and 100,000 for ministers. However in many localities the "Sunshine Project" has met with opposition as it has reduced bonus payments.

Cadre transfer

As civil servants also are cadres they are part of the so-called cadre transfer system (Dangzheng lingdao ganbu xuanba renyong gongzuo tiaoli 2003). For leading cadres below ministerial and vice-ministerial level, the rules are that they have to be transferred after their second term, i.e., after a maximum period of ten years. They will either be transferred to a new higher-ranked job or stay at the same level, but without leadership responsibility. Recently a new form of rotation has been introduced according to which central officials are rotated to local levels in order to take up local top positions (*di yiba shou*) as mayor or county head (Xin yi lun zheng siji zhongyang he defang guanyuan jiaoliu renzhi qidong 2011). In the same way local leaders are transferred to central positions. It is reported that local officials' enthusiasm to take positions at the central level is quite high, but the same enthusiasm is not reached among officials at the central level. The problem seems to be that you are not transferred temporarily while maintaining employment (*bianzhi*) in your original work unit (*guazhi*), but actually are assuming a leadership position at the local level (*renzhi*) and are not guaranteed a return to the central level.

Rotation increasingly takes place between big business and the civil service system. Thus government officials can be transferred to take up leading positions in the state-owned companies and vice versa. This kind of rotation has certain parallels to the French system of appointing members of the civil service elite to one of the country's top business positions after having spent a decade or so working for the state, often in a ministerial private office—a practice known as *pantouflage* (literally "shuffling across") (MacLean *et al.* 2001). These civil servants are all educated at French prestigious *grandes écoles* which gives access to the *grands corps* and from there they are "parachuted" into top business.

In China there are even more examples of the reverse process, i.e., top business leaders moving into state and Party leading positions. Examples include Xiao Yaqing who worked as President of Aluminum Corporation of China before he was transferred in February 2009 to the post of Deputy General Secretary of the State Council; Wei Liucheng who in 2003 was transferred from a position as General Manager of CNOOC to Hainan to become governor of the province; Chairman of Taiyuan Steel Company Chen Chuanping who in 2009 was transferred to the provincial government of Shanxi to serve as vice-governor; and recently the appointment of Sinopec CEO Song Shulin to governor of Fujian. A number of additional examples could be mentioned. They all show that Party and state organs increasingly use the large business groups as a recruitment base for filling important state and Party positions. The advantage of such a system is to bring new experience into the core bureaucracy. Many Chinese business leaders have an international exposure and have acquired knowledge of international management practices. The ability to tap into this reservoir of expertise can only strengthen the Chinese public sector.

Reforming PSUs[6]

China's large and diverse sector of PSUs (*shiye danwei*) is a constellation of public service providers alongside core government and separate from other state-owned or state-sponsored organizations such as state-owned enterprises (SOEs), state-owned financial institutions and state-sponsored "social organizations" (OECD 2005: 81). Today, there are more than one million PSUs, employing 27.4 million people (*China Statistical Yearbook* 2008: 115). According to Article 2 of the Interim Regulation on the Registration and Management of Public Sector Units revised in 2004, a PSU is "an organization with the provision of social services in nature, established by the governmental agencies or other organizations with state-owned assets, working for the public good in activities such as education, science and technology, culture and health" (China's State Council 2004). Whereas PSUs are characterized by their diversity in terms of services provided, governance structure, financing arrangements and relationship with the government, education (schools, universities) and health (primary care centers, hospitals) account for more than 60 percent of PSU total employment. About 60 percent of China's intellectuals are working for all sorts of PSUs, consuming about one third of the government's total fiscal expenditure (Cheng 2000: 3–5).

Early effort to marketize PSUs

Until the 1980s almost all the staff in PSUs had been on the state payroll. The PSU reform started in a piecemeal fashion more than 20 years ago and was accelerated from the mid-1990s, when the country speeded up reform on debt-laden SOEs and tried to streamline civil service systems. The tripartite reforms addressing respectively SOEs, PSUs and the civil service system compose the main story of China's long-lasting efforts to restructure its public sectors. However, the almost-simultaneous start of these reforms does not mean the same pace of advancement in all three sectors. SOE restructuring and reform began in earnest around 1995, with more than 50 million workers laid off afterwards. The politically risky reform on SOEs proved to be a success in dismantling the emblematic iron rice bowl in China's state firms. The transformation (*gaizhi*) of most SOEs into privatized or state-owned shareholding companies has produced a new personnel management system featuring contract-based employment. Correspondingly, the previous employer-guaranteed medical care and pension system for SOE staff has been transformed into a new mechanism in which most of the welfare is "socialized" (*shehuihua*) and provided on the basis of insurances funded by the individual, the employer and the state altogether.

At the initial stage of PSU reform in 1990s when Chinese decision-makers were dominated by the marketization mindset, many PSUs were "pushed into the market" like SOEs and asked to make profit to cover their own expenses. According to a World Bank report published in 2005, nearly half of PSU's funding is raised through charging fees, which often cross-subsidize the public service delivery of the unit, but also allow for bonuses and welfare for staff on top of formal salaries (World Bank 2005: 77). The reform resulted in a much more variable salary system in PSUs than that in the civil service, although this does not necessarily mean that average wage of PSU staff is higher than civil servants. On the contrary, the average wage of civil servants has been the highest among all (civil servants, PSU staff and employees in enterprises) for many years. In 2007, for example, the average yearly wage of staff in *jiguan* (government organizations) was 28,763 yuan, higher than that for PSUs (25,805 yuan) and enterprises (24,046 yuan) (*China Statistical Yearbook* 2008: 153). Unlike SOEs, the rise in income inequality among PSU staff members nonetheless did not trigger an overall change of human resource management inside these organizations concerning tenure of employment, pension and medical care. The ownership of most PSUs and their relationship with the government remained unchanged, and almost all the regular staff members in PSUs are still managed under the rigid *shiye bianzhi* system, which refers to the number of established posts in public service organizations. Just like administrative *bianzhi* (*xingzheng bianzhi*) that stipulates the number of administrative organs and the number of personnel in the civil service, *shiye bianzhi* is also rigid and involves staff allocation as well as budget outlays in the form of salary and allowances.

Although most PSUs have been commercialized and forced to at least partly finance themselves and reduce reliance upon state budgetary revenues, their regular staff still enjoy the similar lifelong tenure, pension and medical package as their peers in the civil service due to the government's financial responsibility for the welfare of staff under the *xingzheng* or *shiye bianzhi*. When many PSUs were commercialized, they were also encouraged by the government to go beyond the *bianzhi* limitation and recruit more staff members on the basis of market principle to improve their efficiency and increase labor market competition. PSUs employ these people in the same way as companies hire their employees, giving them variable salaries and bonuses based on their performances and capabilities. No lifelong tenure is guaranteed in the labor contract, with most of the social welfare including pension and medical care being "socialized" and not the employer's sheer responsibility. Over the past few years, a significant number of PSUs, especially those "PSUs managed as enterprises" (*shiye danwei qiyehua guanli*), have increased their employment of these contract-based staff by large margins. In many heavily commercialized PSUs, such as local newspapers and publishing houses, these contract-based staff members have outnumbered those with *bianzhi* and de facto lifelong employment.

Further step to categorize PSUs

The government's continuous effort to push PSUs into the market has been controversial, because reliance on user charges for financing service delivery is increasingly becoming a barrier to access for the poor, and greater autonomy in revenue generation is often not accompanied by better performance management and stronger financial accountability (World Bank 2005: 77). Realizing the high degree of diversity and complexity of PSUs, the Chinese government has tried to classify (*fenleihua*) PSUs into categories such as administrative and law enforcement units, public benefit units and business-related units first before transforming or restructuring them.

Although the PSU reform at its initial stage was criticized by some as lacking a clear-cut overall strategy and described as "touching the stones to cross the river without knowing where the other side of the river is" (Cheng 2000: 3), reformers gradually came to a consensus that the separation of for-profit organizations from not-for-profit organizations is necessary and only those engaging in commercial activities need to be transformed into state-owned enterprises or private companies. PSU reform has been speeding up in the past decade when more and more PSUs that are suitable to be run as enterprises have been transformed into for-profit organizations and their staff are managed in the same way as company employees without *shiye bianzhi* or pension and medical care fully financed by the state. In the news and publishing industry where the reform has been advancing in the fastest pace, the majority of local publishing houses and tabloids have been restructured into market-oriented companies or groups. According to a circular released by the General Administration of Press and Publication (GAPP) in April 2009, existing publishing houses are divided into two categories, profit and non-profit (Xinhua 2009b). Excepting non-profitable ones, all publishing houses owned by local government departments, public institutions and universities had to restructure themselves into market-oriented companies by the end of 2009, while those owned by the central government departments finished restructuring by the end of 2010. Even for those not-suitable-for-marketization PSUs that have been classified as organizations with "public benefit relevance" or government-like organs with administrative functions, some of their subsidiary businesses have been peeled off and transformed into semi-independent for-profit organizations, with most of their staff having no *bianzhi* or state-financed pension.

Taking the Development Research Center of the State Council (DRC) as an example, all the three personnel management systems (civil service, PSU and enterprise) coexist in this Beijing-based top official think tank that should fall into the PSU category according to conventional way of classification. Over 160 regular research staff in the DRC's seven core research departments as well as the General Office and International Cooperation Department are managed under civil service regulations and enjoy the same remuneration, pension and medical service as civil servants, although most of them have the *shiye danwei bianzhi* instead of the administrative *bianzhi*.[7] Other semi-peripheral institutes, centers, the newspaper, magazine and publishing house affiliated to DRC are either partly or fully self-financed PSUs or purely for-profit enterprises. Under this triple-track mechanism of personnel management, the DRC is able to recruit suitable personnel to meet the policy consultancy need from the central government and the market demand from commercial users. In the next-step reform, even those PSUs that have been classified as not-for-profit organizations with "public benefit relevance" will probably witness their staff's pension and medical package gradually unified with that in enterprises (*China Business News* 2009), with those PSUs managed according to civil service regulations (*canzhao gongwuyuan guanli*) as an exception.

Ongoing attempt to change personnel management systems

Because of most PSUs' characteristic of "public benefit relevance" and controversies over the commercialization process, the government has been pushing forward the reform of PSUs more slowly and cautiously than that of SOEs. About half of the total funding of PSUs is still from state budgetary allocations, and millions of PSU staff members with *bianzhi* share the same personnel system with civil servants in terms of lifelong tenure, pension, medical care and basic remuneration, which differ from those for SOE employees. Their nominal basic salary scales are set in line with those in the civil service. This kind of quasi-civil service management over PSU staff has exacerbated the government's budgetary expenditure on pension and medical services as the aging problem is becoming salient. In 2000, the government's total expenditure on the pension of government and PSU retirees was 48 billion yuan, but in 2009 this figure had already quadrupled to 209 billion yuan (Figure 5.1).

Meanwhile the lack of unified pension and medical care systems for PSU and company employees hampers the free flow of human resources among public service sectors and commercial organizations. Just like civil service, the whole welfare package of PSU staff is tightly linked with the *bianzhi* one has in the organization, and without the *bianzhi* the government will not allocate corresponding budgetary fund for such social security needs. Therefore, if a PSU employee with *bianzhi* wants to leave his/her working unit and find another job in a private company or a *"minban* non-enterprise unit," the non-state sector counterpart of PSUs, he/she will find that the previous pension and medical scheme pertaining to the *bianzhi* becomes null and void and he/she has to contribute his/her portion to the public pension pooling and medical schemes from a new beginning. This not only means that the PSU staff in their forties or fifties therefore may feel reluctant to change their jobs due to the mismatch of the two different welfare schemes, but also means that it may be inconvenient and too costly for a PSU to hire people without *bianzhi* from the society due to their shortage of *bianzhi* and relevant quasi-civil servant pension and medical welfare pertaining to the *bianzhi*.

To solve the "dual-track" pension and medical systems, encourage free flow of human resources and reduce unfairness between state and non-state sectors, the Chinese government merged the Ministry of Personnel and Ministry of Labor and Social Security into one, called the Ministry of Human Resources and Social

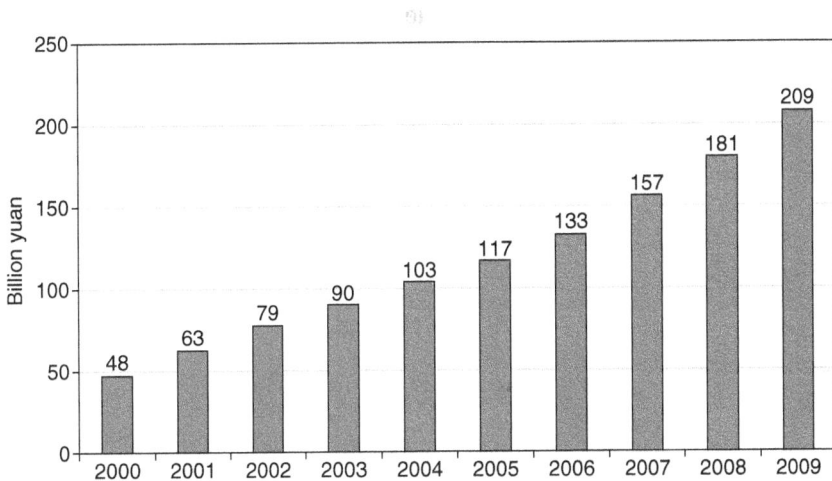

Figure 5.1 Pension expenditure on government and PSU retirees (billion yuan) (from 2000 to 2009) (source: China's Ministry of Finance 2010: 457–458).

Security (MHRSS), during its "super-ministry reform" (*dabuzhi gaige*) in 2008. The previous Ministry of Personnel used to be in charge of all personnel affairs related to state sector staff with *bianzhi* and "cadre" status, while the Ministry of Labor and Social Security had been responsible for the file and social security management over other employees that are out of the state system. In early 2009, the MHRSS issued an experimental reform scheme on the pension insurance system of PSUs (*shiyedanwei yanglao biaoxian zhidu gaige shidian fang'an*), trying to gradually abolish PSU staff's privilege of monthly retirement pay fully financed by the state and unify the pension schemes between PSUs and enterprises. According to the new initiatives aimed at alleviating budgetary expenditures, PSUs and their employees will have to jointly pay insurance premiums, with employers contributing an equivalent of at most 20 percent of the staff's monthly salary to the social pension pool and employees 8 percent of their salary to their individual pension accounts (China's State Council 2008). Instead of getting a regular pension from the state budget, PSU retirees will be qualified to withdraw monthly pensions after they have paid the premiums for at least 15 years. The pension level will be decided by how much and how long they have paid the insurance premiums as well as the average local salary level one year prior to their retirement. Those who started working before the implementation of this scheme will be paid a certain amount of additional pension as a kind of compensation. Some estimated the new scheme would slice in half the current pensions for such employees (Xinhua News 2009a). Five provincial areas, namely Shanghai, Guangdong, Chongqing, Zhejiang and Shanxi, were asked to experiment with the proposal since January 2009.

The reform initiative has been interpreted by influential media as a kind of PSU pension downgrading to the level of company employees (Xinhua News 2009a). This irritated many PSU staff especially those high-profile cadres who could represent their voices in the national and local parliamentary sessions. During the annual session of the People's Political Consultative Conference in March 2009, 77 representatives mainly from the education circle proposed a draft resolution that called for a suspension of the pension reform targeted at all teachers (*China Youth News* 2009). Public intellectuals like the president of Jiangsu Social Science Academy, Song Linfei, and Vice-President of Chinese Academy of Social Sciences (CASS), Zhu Jiamu, also gave their strong objections to the reform initiated by the MHRSS, saying the decision-makers had not listened to the opinions from the PSUs (*Nanfang dushibao* 2009). Qi Shanhong, a professor at Nankai University, admitted that the PSU pension reform had met formidable resistance, suggesting that civil servants' pension should also be downgraded to the level of enterprise employees (*Lianhe zaobao* 2009). It is too early to say whether strong objections from PSU staff will obstruct the reform, but the merger of two ministries into one MHRSS is a clear signal showing the government's decisiveness in integrating the dual-track human resource management and related welfare systems into a unified system for the sake of fairness and free flow of personnel. With the establishment of half-independent State Bureau of Civil Servants that reports to the MHRSS, the long-existing "cadre status" pertaining to the *bianzhi* will gradually be downplayed in the future and replaced by the concept of "civil servants," only referring to those working in the government or party organizations and excluding millions of staff members working for PSUs such as schools, hospitals and mass media.

In April 2012, the Chinese government publicized the guidelines on the PSU classification and reform, which classified (*fenlei*) PSUs into three categories, i.e., units with administrative functions, units engaged in "public benefit service" (*congshi gongyi fuwu*) and business-related units (*Xinhua News* 2012). PSUs with administrative functions will in the future be managed as a part of the civil service while business-related units will be fully commercialized and transformed into corporations. The most difficult part is the majority of PSUs that have been categorized as public service providers that include hospitals, schools and universities. According to the guidelines, these public service providers will continue to exist in the form of PSUs and further break down into two subgroups: Public Service Category I (*gongyi yilei*) and Public Service Category II (*gongyi erlei*) (*Xinhua News* 2012). Sectors in Category I provide basic public services like nine-year compulsory education, public health, basic research and grassroots medical services that should not be marketized at all while Category II units like universities and specialist clinics could be partially marketized. The guidelines demanded more governmental budgetary expenditure on all sorts of public services, saying that the government will provide the funding to the Category I sectors, and support the Category II sectors through financial subsidies and service purchase. An important part of the PSU reform is to change the personnel management systems relating to remuneration, pension and medical insurance of their employees. All PSUs (including those not-suitable-for-marketization sectors) are required to break the iron rice bowl features with guaranteed lifetime employment and government-paid pensions through signing contracts with employees whose pension, medical care and unemployment compensation are dependent on their contribution to the public pension pooling and medical schemes instead of government budgets. The administrative ranking of PSUs will be abolished while salaries and bonuses of their employees will fluctuate according to performance (*jixiao gongzi*).

Conclusions

The Chinese Party-state is engaged in substantive reform of the public sector in China. The aim is to create a less costly, but more efficient public sector, where a number of functions are being marketized or passed on to society. The process also involves partly privatizing certain welfare benefits (pension, health care etc.) which used to be the responsibility of the state. However, the process does not involve a loosening of Party control over the core bureaucracy. To fulfill the dual goals of power consolidation and efficiency improvement based on cost reductions, the Party had to take very different approaches to reform the personnel management systems pertaining to the SOEs, PSUs and the civil service. The core issue in China's public sector reform is closely related to the concept of the iron rice bowl, a socialist relic once provided for employees in all public sectors. Starting from the abolishment of iron rice bowls first in SOEs, the reform gradually tried to apply similar approaches to PSUs for the sake of efficiency, but since such reform could put the loyalty of civil servants at stake, the party-state finally had to retain iron rice bowls for its own officials. Despite being politically and economically efficient, such policies are perceived as morally incorrect and unfair. They have caused enormous implementation problems, especially in the reform of more vaguely defined PSUs. Employees in the sector have used the example of SOE employees having already suffered from previous reforms to boycott planned changes of their pension and medical schemes. The unfairness and discrimination in the initial reform design are major obstacles for the implementation of policies aimed at transforming PSUs. The new policies have caused widespread protest among PSU employees as they fear that they may suffer a downgrading of their status and economic benefits compared to civil servants. Special and privileged treatment reserved only for civil servants risks obstructing further reforms of other areas of the public sector. In the long run it may gradually erode the popularity of the ruling Party.

The aim of the reform seems to create a more clearly defined cadre corps primarily consisting of the civil servants and staff in some PSUs managed according to civil service regulations. These segments of public employees will have their economic and social status upgraded, whereas the majority of the staff employed in PSUs will lose in status and economic compensation and experience a marketization of their social and economic situation. The underlying goal of these reforms is to continuously improve the governing system, and the staff manning this system, in China. This requires clear regulations, improved working conditions, better economic compensation for those working in key positions, and a reform of welfare benefits such as pension and health insurances. A consequence of these reforms is a public sector that is less egalitarian in terms of status and income. The civil servants will benefit from the retained iron rice bowl, whereas staff in most PSUs will lose out and increasingly have difficulties attracting top talent.

Notes

1 Some studies mention a fourth public institution, state-sponsored social organizations (*tuanti*). In this context social organizations such as All-China Trade Federation, All China Federation of Women, All China Federation of Industry and Commerce and All China Federation of Returned Overseas Chinese are included in the category of Party and state organizations.

2 On occasion, a social organization *bianzhi* (*shehui tuanti bianzhi*) has been mentioned, but it is rarely used. Mostly the *bianzhi* of social organizations is categorized as *shiye bianzhi*.

3 Until 2002 the relevant category was called "government agencies, party agencies, and social organizations" (*guojia jiguan, zhengdang jiguan he shehui tuanti*).

4 The category of "public management and social organization" overlaps with the category of *jiguan* (agencies and organizations), which in 2007 included 10.86 million staff and workers. It is puzzling that these two categories do not correspond in terms of

number of employees, the category of *jiguan* having almost two million less staff and workers. The explanation seems to be that *jiguan* to a lessser degree include employees in *shiye danwei* who are managed by the civil service law. Even though they are strictly speaking not civil servants there is often an attempt to include in the "public management" category those who are managed, ranked and remunerated according to civil service regulations, and who perform key administrative functions, even though they may take place in *shiye danwei*.

5 Interview with official from the CCP Organizational Department, July 30, 2010.

6 China has had several high-level research teams working on the PSU reform, including one led by former Vice Chairman of National People's Congress Standing Committee Cheng Siwei (see Cheng 2000). Another was organized by the State Council Development and Research Center (see Ge 2003). A third was led by the National Development and Reform Commission (see Fan 2004). Some international organizations such as the World Bank, UNDP and OECD have also done intensive research on China's PSU reforms (World Bank 2005; OECD 2005; UNDP 2008).

7 Interview with Sun Lanlan, Director General of the International Cooperation Department of DRC in Singapore, June 16, 2009. Usually a civil servant in China should have the administrative *bianzhi*, but for those PSUs that are managed according to civil service regulations (*canzhao gongwuyuan guanli*), their staff may have the *shiye bianzhi* but are regarded as civil servants.

References

Brødsgaard, Kjeld Erik (2001) "China's Cadres: Professional Revolutionaries or State Bureaucrats? (I)," *EAI Background Brief* No. 94, Singapore: East Asian Institute.

Brødsgaard, Kjeld Erik (2002) "Institutional Reform and the *Bianzhi* System in China," *The China Quarterly* 170(June): 361–386.

Brødsgaard, Kjeld Erik (2009) *Hainan—State, Society, and Business in a Chinese Province*, Abingdon: Routledge.

Burns, John P. (2004) "Governance and Civil Service Reform," in Jude Howell (ed.) *Governance in China* Lanham, MD: Rowman & Littlefield, pp. 37–57.

Cabestan, Jean-Pierre (1991) "The Reform of the Civil Service," *China News Analysis* 1437(June 15): 1–8.

Chan, Hon S. and Edward Suizhou Li (2007) "Civil Service Law in the People's Republic of China: A Return to Cadre Personnel Management," *Public Administration Review* 67(3): 383–398.

Cheng, Siwei (ed.) (2000) *Zhongguo Shiye Danwei Gaige: Moshi Xuanze Yu Fenlei Yindao* (China's PSU Reform: Model Selection and Guidance Through Classification) Beijing: Minzhu yu jianshe chubanshe.

China Business News (2009) "Yanglao baoxian zhidu gaige jinxingshi: qishiye danwei zhidu xianjie" (Pension System on the Way: Unifying the System of Companies and PSUs), *China Business News*, January 21, available online: www.china-cbn.com/s/n/00 0002/20090121/020000098127.shtml (accessed January 22, 2009).

China Daily (2008) "770,000 sit exams for government jobs," *China Daily*, December 1, available online: www.chinadaily.com.cn/china/2008-12/01/ content_7255820.htm (accessed December 2, 2008).

China's Ministry of Finance (2010) *Zhongguo caizheng nianjian 2010* (*Finance Yearbook of China* 2010), Beijing: Zhongguo caizheng zazhishe.

China's Ministry of Personnel (2002) "Guanyu tiaozheng jiguan gongzu renyuan gongzi biaozhun de shishi fang'an" (Implementation Draft Concerning Adjusting the Wage

Salary System of Working Personnel in Administrative Organs), in *Renshi gongzuo wenjian xuanbian* (Selected Documents on Personnel Work), Vol. 24, Beijing: Renshibu zhengce faguisi, pp. 402–404.

China's State Council (2006) "Gongwuyuan gongzi zhidu gaige fang'an" (Reform Plan on Civil Service Salary System), available online: http://wenku.baidu.com/ view/5a6d046348d7c1c708a1450b.html (accessed January 3, 2014).

China's State Council (2008) "Shiye danwei yanglao biaoxian zhidu gaige fang'an" (Draft on the Reform of PSU Pension Insurance System), available online: www. sachina.edu.cn/Htmldata/news/2009/02/4909.html (accessed December 8, 2010).

China Statistical Yearbook (1996) (*Zhongguo tongji nianjian*), Beijing: China Statistics Press.

China Statistical Yearbook (2008) (*Zhongguo tongji nianjian*), Beijing: China Statistics Press.

China Youth News (2009) "Qishiqiming weiyuan lianming ti'an: zanting zai jiaoshi dui-wuzhong shishi shiyedanwei yanglaojin gaige" (Seventy-seven Members Jointly Propose the Suspension of PSU Pension Reform Targeted on Teachers), *China Youth News*, March 5, available online: www.cyol.net/zqb/content/2009-03/06/content_2567991.htm (accessed December 8, 2010).

Cooke, Fang Lee (2005) "Public-Sector Pay in China: 1949–2001," in Malcolm Warner (ed.) *Human Resource Management in China Revisited*, London: Routledge.

Dangzheng lingdao ganbu xuanba renyong gongzuo tiaoli (2003) (Regulations on Selection and Appointment of Party and Government Leading Cadres) *Renshi gongzuo wenjian xuanbian* (Selected Documents on Personnel Work), Beijing: Renshibu zhengce fagui si, pp. 8–27.

Fan Hengshan (2004) "Guanyu shiyedanwei gaige de sikao" (Some Thoughts on the Public Service Units Reform), *China Economic Times*, April 12, available online: www.51paper.net/free/2004523050934.htm (accessed December 10, 2011).

Ge Yanfeng (2003) "Reforming the Public Service Units and Related Systems: Progress and Problems" (*Shehui shiye tizhi he shiye danwei gaige de chengji he wenti*), *China Economic Times*, August 5, available online: www.china.com.cn/chinese/ zhuanti/ wmsyzy/382678.htm (accessed January 3, 2014).

Harasymiw, Bohdan (1969) "Nomenklatura: The Soviet Communist Party's Leadership Recruitment System," *Canadian Journal of Political Science* 2(4): 493–512.

Lam, Tao-Chiu and Hon S. Chang (1995) "The Civil Service System: Policy Formulation and Implementation," in Lo Chin Kin, Suzanne Pepper and Tsui Kai Yuenn (eds.), *China Review 1995*, Hong Kong: The Chinese University Press, pp. 2.3–2.43.

Lianhe zaobao (2009) "Shiyedanwei yanglaozhidu gaige yu chongchong zuli" (The PSU Pension Reform Confronted with Strong Resistence), *Lianhe zaobao*, February 17, available online: www.zaobao.com/special/china/cnpol/pages2/ cnpol090217.shtml (accessed May 9, 2012).

MacLean, Mairi, Charles Harvey and Jon Press (2001) "Elites, Ownership and the Internalisation of French Business," *Modern & Contemporary France* 9(3): 313–325.

Nanfang dushibao (2009) "Weiyuan tongchi shiye danwei yanglao gaige" (Delegates Attack PSU Pension Reform), *Nanfang dushibao*, March 10, available online: http://insurance. southcn.com/dygc/content/2009-03/10/content_4972711.htm (accessed May 9, 2012).

OECD (2005) "The Reform of Public Service Units: Challenges and Perspectives," in OECD (ed.) *Governance in China*, Paris: OECD, pp. 75–100.

Schurmann, Franz (1968) *Ideology and Organization in Communist China*, Berkeley, CA: University of California Press.

Shambaugh, David (2000) "The Chinese State in the Post-Mao Era," in David Shambaugh (ed.) *The Modern Chinese State*, Cambridge: Cambridge University Press, pp. 161–187.

UNDP (2008) *Access For All: Basic Public Services for 1.3 Billion People*, Beijing: China Translation and Publishing Corporation.

World Bank (Poverty Reduction and Economic Management Unit, East Asia and Pacific Region) (2005) *China: Deepening Public Service Unit Reform to Improve Service Delivery*, Beijing: CITIC Publishing House.

Xin yi lun zheng siji zhongyang he defang guanyuan jiaoliu renzhi qidong (2011) (A New Round of Rotation Between Central and Local Officials Starts), available online: http://news.sina.com.cn/c/2011-03-31/011122210698.shtml (accessed May 21, 2011).

Xinhua News (2009a) "Yangshi jiedu yanglao baoxian gaige, jiangdi shiye danwei daiyu baogongping" (China Central Television Interpreting Pension Reform: Downgrading PSU Treatment for the Sake of Fairness), *Xinhua News*, February 5, available online: http://news.xinhuanet.com/fortune/2009-02/05/ content_10767723.htm (accessed August 1, 2011).

Xinhua News (2009b) "China Encourages Shareholding Reform, Mergers of Publishing houses" April 6, available online: http://news.xinhuanet.com/english/2009-04/06/ content_11140050.htm (accessed November 1, 2011).

Xinhua News (2012) "CCP Central Committee and State Council's Guidelines on Pushing Forward PSU Reform by Category" (*zhonggong zhongyang guowuyuan guanyu fenlei tuijin shiyedanwei gaige de zhidaoyijian*) April 16, available online: http://news.xinhuanet.com/politics/2012-04/16/c_111785805.htm (accessed January 3, 2014).

Zhonghua Renmin Gongheguo gongwuyuan fa (2006) (China's Civil Service Law), in *Selected Documents on Personnel Work* (*Renshi gongzuo wenjian xuanbian*), Vol. 28, Beijing: Renshibu zhengce faguisi, pp. 56–77.

Zhu Guanglei (1998) *Dangdai Zhongguo shehui gejieceng fenxi* (Analysis of Social Strata in Contemporary China), Tianjian: Tianjin renmin chubanshe.

6 Health sector reforms in contemporary China

A political perspective

Daniele Brombal

> *Let us take the profit, the private economic profit, out of medicine,*
> *and purify our profession of rapacious individualism...*
> *Let us say to the people not 'How much have you got?'*
> *but 'How best can we serve you?'*
>
> Dr Norman Bethune (1936)[1]

Introduction

Since the mid-1980s, when it became clear that policies of reform and opening up were the dawn of a new, distinct phase in China's long pursuit of modernization, many scholars have attempted to provide a coherent explanation of the political processes characterizing policy making in transitional China. Although debate is still occasionally heated regarding the possible outcomes of China's transformation—ranging from elective democracy to the continuation of an authoritarian system dominated by the Party through a revival of either Confucian or revolutionary virtues—a broad consensus has finally emerged over the role played by market-oriented reforms in shaping a polity that is increasingly open to interaction between the private sphere and the political system (Zheng 2002: 64; Kennedy 2005: 160–186; Perry 2007).

A useful theoretical framework on which to develop the analysis of China's transitional system is that which focuses on the role played by interest groups, based on the assumption that an interest-based social order has emerged in the People's Republic. Applied to the study of US politics in the 1950s by David Truman, by the late 1960s the concept of interest group had already been widely utilized for analysing communist polities, with special reference to the Soviet Union.[2] While early works applying this approach to the study of communist regimes dealt primarily with the interests and conflicts within the bureaucracy, analyses focused on post-Mao China have described a context where the 'pursuit of economic expansion has led to the emergence of an interest-based social order' (Zheng 2002: 64) and a polity where the 'largest and most active interest groups are economically driven and have a great impact on ... political and social affairs' (Yang 2007: 2). Despite the profound influence of market-oriented reforms in the health care sector, this paradigm of increasing complexity and interaction has so far not been extensively applied to the study of health politics. Decision making in this area is still commonly considered the result of political processes taking place within a state's bureaucracy which is mainly concerned, at least at the centre, with national development priorities. Most efforts made by China scholars in investigating health care have focused on policy outputs, over-looking inputs from economically driven interests—in particular those of medical providers and pharmaceutical producers—to the political power, either in the form of resistance to the existing regulatory framework, or through the articulation of specific demands (on common narratives of health system change in China, see Bloom 2011: 1303–1305. Among the few studies focusing on rel-evant political processes, see Lampton 1977: 250–267; Huang 2006).

This paper attempts to investigate the processes which have led to the consti-tution of economically driven interests in post-Mao China's health care sector, how they have exerted their influence on the commitments made by the Hu–Wen leadership towards a more 'harmonious' pattern of socio-economic develop-ment, and which avenues they might follow in articulating demands upon the political system. Finally, we will introduce the coordinates of the most recent developments in health policies and the relevant debate involving the central leadership, health care providers and pharmaceutical producers.

Health care sector reforms 1980s–2000s

From patient to customer

In June 1982 the county of Yexian (Shandong province) hosted the 'Inter-Regional Seminar on Primary Health Care' (*chuji weisheng baojian qujian taol-unhui*). Officials from a dozen developing countries were invited by the Chinese Ministry of Health (MoH) and the World Health Organization (WHO) to learn from the Chinese 'outstanding example' of primary health care, as the then exec-utive director of the United Nations Children's Fund (UNICEF), Dr James P. Grant, defined it in a speech delivered during the seminar (WHO 1983: 11). Indeed, China had achieved remarkable improvements in the health status of its people. Between 1952 and 1982, average life expectancy rose from 35 to 68 years, while infant mortality was reduced from 250 to 40 deaths every 1,000 live births (Hsiao 1995: 1047). These achievements were possible thanks to a health care system focused on prevention, and financed through public resources—largely contributions of state-owned enterprises (SOEs) and communes—guar-anteeing universal access to primary healthcare. In brief, the Maoist system seemed to embody the spirit of the *Declaration of Alma Ata*, ensuring 'essential health care … made universally accessible to individuals and families in the community through their full participation and at a cost that the community and country can afford' (WHO 1978: 1).

Paradoxically, while the success of China's health care model was being celebrated, reforms in the economic realm were about to have a major impact on the health care sector. The dismantling of collectives in the countryside and the curtailment of workplace benefits in urban China were in fact to deeply affect health care financing and provision (Saich 2011: 300). The abolition of communes in the early 1980s caused the collapse of the Cooperative Medical Scheme (CMS) (*nongcun yiliao hezuo zhidu*), a community-based mutual insurance financed and operated at brigade and commune level. Between 1978 and 1985, the percentage of insured rural population dropped from 90 per cent to 5 per cent (Yip and Hsiao 2008: 461). In the 1990s, coverage also declined in the cities. In 1998, those insured constituted 56 per cent of the urban population, against 73 per cent in 1993 (MoH 1998: 23). Public financing of hospitals' current expenditures—salaries, maintenance, equipment—was greatly reduced, declining from an approximate 50 per cent to 5–10 per cent of the total budget of an average public hospital (WHO 1983: 66–67; Sun *et al.* 2008: 1046). Lacking public financing, providers turned to user fees. These, due to the shrinking insurance coverage, were largely paid out-of-pocket by patients. In 1985, hospitals were attributed substantial financial autonomy and allowed to retain the surplus generated through the sale of services (Meng 2006: 17). Although the government retained ownership of the majority of health providers, reliance on user fees and the attribution of financial autonomy resulted in a de facto privatization of health care.[3]

Scarce insurance coverage and rising costs caused huge difficulties in accessing treatments among the population, a phenomenon which in Chinese goes by the expression of *kan bing nan, kan bing gui*, 'seeking care is difficult and expensive'. In 1993, over 40 per cent of rural residents did not have access to hospital treatment when in need, in most cases due to unaffordability of services (MoH 2009a: 46). In the cities, although the situation was in comparison better, many could not access health care there either. In 1999, in Beijing and Lhasa, respectively 13 per cent and 26 per cent of the population had no access to emergency treatment (CAPM-NHI 2000: 19–20). Impoverishment due to medical expenditures became common, with health expenditures causing 45 per cent of the cases of impoverishment reported in the countryside in 1998 (Liu *et al.* 2003: 219). Because of its scarce profitability, public health was neglected, leading to a rise in the incidence of infectious diseases. In 2004, the reemergence of schistosomiasis was reported in seven provinces, while in recent years incidence rates of tuberculosis have been on the rise (Zhou *et al.* 2004: 555; MoH 2009a: 135).

Throughout the 1980s and most of the 1990s, Chinese leaders seemed convinced that, in the long run, market reform would work its magic, 'slowly raising all boats', despite the warnings periodically launched by MoH regarding the increasing inequality of the health care system (MoH 1993: 64–65; MoH 1998: 132–135). Although official medical ethics continued to be inspired by the ideological commitment to 'serve the people wholeheartedly' (*quan xin quan yi wei renmin fuwu*), and 'healing the wounded and rescuing the dying' (*qiu si fu shang*), by the mid-1980s the priorities of health care providers were already skewed towards maximization of profits (Yang 2008: 1, 9).

In those years, the shift towards market mechanisms was not peculiar only to China, but rather consistent with the neoliberal recipe advocated by international financial institutions, which defined 'global blueprints ... to promote privatization of health-service providers, and to increase private financing—via user fees—of public providers' (Whitehead *et al.* 2011: 833). The rationale of this approach is clearly stated in a policy document released by the World Bank in 1987 and intended to provide a vade mecum for health care system reforms in developing countries: 'the more common approach to health care provision in developing countries has been to treat health care as a right of the citizenry and ... provide free services to everyone. This approach does not usually work' (WB 1986: 4). The alternative consisted, according to the World Bank, in instituting charges at government facilities, encouraging the development of a competitive health insurance sector, decentralizing health service planning, budgeting and purchasing (WB 1986: 4–8).

Policies inspired to this approach were widely adopted, particularly where the implementation of the health package devised by the World Bank was included in programmes of economic structural adjustment for countries facing debt, as well as in those transitional economies where the political leadership clearly prioritized economic issues over social concerns. A memorable example of the latter is the answer that was given in the late 1990s by the then Chinese premier Zhu Rongji who, upon hearing of an MoH proposal to use an earmarked cigarette tax to finance health, stated: 'That's great—we can raise so much revenue from increasing the cigarette tax. That will help a great deal with our Three Gorges Dam Project!' (Liu and Rao 2006: 83).

Towards a more balanced approach

While health reform measures mentioned above were assumed to prevent overuse and increase quality of services, in fact they often caused severe negative consequences in terms of untreated morbidity, reduced access to care, irrational use of drugs and impoverishment due to medical expenditures (Whitehead *et al.* 2011: 833–834). As it has already been seen in this chapter, China was no exception, and in 2000 WHO ranked its health care system number 188 for equity among 191 countries and number 144 for overall performance (WHO 2000: 152). Impoverishment due to medical expenditures and high levels of precautionary savings were hampering economic development, while difficulties in accessing health care fuelled dissatisfaction among the populace. In late 2002, on the eve of the XVI Congress of the Chinese Communist Party (CCP), which was to designate Hu Jintao as general secretary, CCP Central Committee and State Council issued the 'Decision on Further Strengthening Rural Health Care'. This document redefined the rationale of the state's health policies in rural areas as 'promoting agricultural economy, protecting the development and stability of rural society' (Central Committee of the Chinese Communist Party—State Council 2002: Preamble). Although focused on rural health care, this document clearly outlined what would be the overall approach of the Hu–Wen administration over the next decade: health care is seen as instrument to ensure productivity and social peace, while the state's role is to guarantee that even disadvantaged strata of the population—such as peasants—are entitled to receive essential levels of care. The reform process was accelerated by the SARS crisis, which brought home to the leadership how the weaknesses of the medical system could lead to economic disaster (Saich 2011: 316; Gu 2004: 154).[4]

Although China's health expenditure as percentage of GDP and on a per-capita basis still remains comparatively low, the share of China's total health expenditure covered by public resources has been rising in the last few years, with a considerable increase in government subsidies to social health insurance (see Figures 6.1 and 6.2) (WHO 2011: 128–135; WHO 2009: China, Table A).[5] In 2008, the portion of insured people was 87 per cent of the total population, up from 22 per cent in 2003 (see Figure 6.3).

Wider insurance coverage was achieved largely thanks to the introduction, in 2002–2003, of the New Rural Cooperative Medical Scheme (NRCMS) (*xinxing nongcun hezuo yiliao zhidu*). By 2008, NRCMS was covering 93 per cent of rural residents, or 800 million people (MoH 2009a: 14). In urban areas the Urban Workers Basic Medical Insurance (UWBMI) (*chengzhen zhigong jiben yiliao baoxian*)—which, in 1998, had replaced the old LIS (Labour Insurance Scheme) (*laobao yiliao zhidu*)—was complemented in 2007 by the Urban Residents Basic Medical Insurance (URBMI) (*chengzhen jumin jiben yiliao baoxian*), targeting children, workers in the informal sector, the unemployed and the elderly.[6] By 2008, UWBMI and URBMI covered 57 per cent of the urban population (MoH 2009a: 14).

Although governance of the health care sector remains fragmented, efforts have been made to create consensus within the bureaucracy and to coordinate the process of policy formulation. In 2006 an ad hoc committee, the 'Health

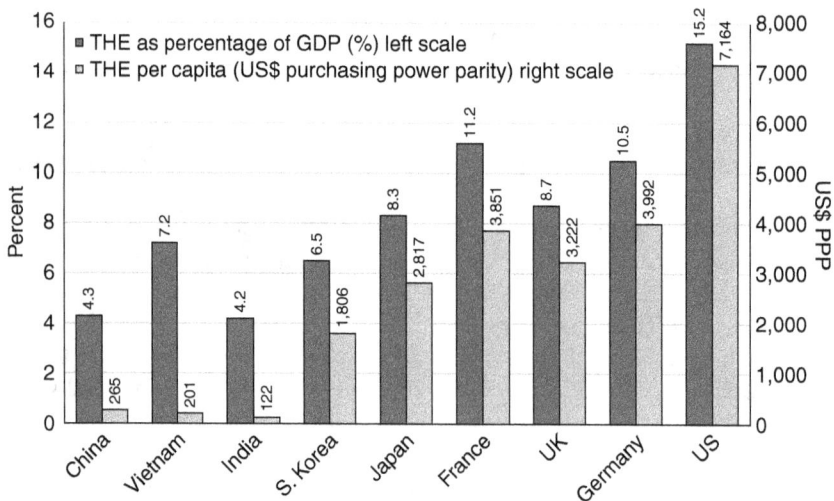

Figure 6.1 National Total Health Expenditure (THE) as a percentage of GDP and per capita THE in China and other countries, 2008 (source: WHO 2011: 128–135).

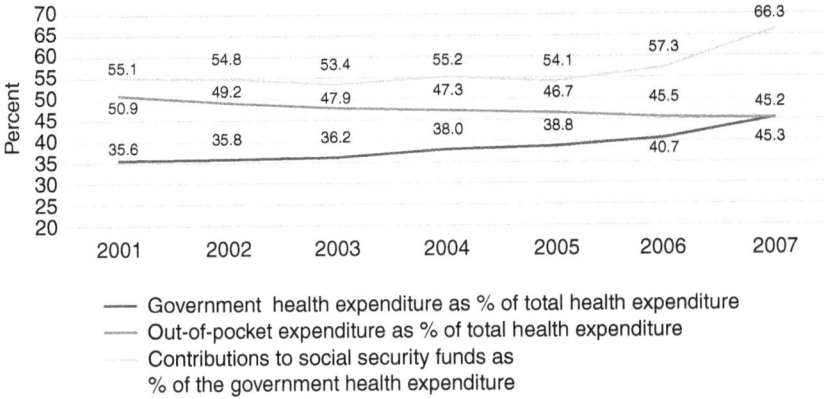

Figure 6.2 Composition of health expenditure and government investment in health, 2001–2007 (percentages) (source: WHO 2009: China, Table A).

Care Reform Coordinating Small Group' (*yiliao tizhi gaige xietiao xiaozu*) was created for this purpose. The 'Small Group' is supervised by the State Council and presided over by the MoH and the National Development and Reform Commission (NDRC). In 2009, the group comprised representatives of 14 ministries, departments and government agencies, including the Ministry of Finance (MoF), the Ministry of Human Resources and Social Security (MHRSS), the Ministry of Civil Affairs (MCA) and the State Food and Drug Administration (SFDA). Significantly, key domestic industry associations are not among the 'Small Group' members (Thompson 2009: 59, 67). The tendency towards more rational and centralized control over the core regulatory and administrative functions was confirmed in 2008, when the authorities decided to put the SFDA directly under the MoH's control. The general trend towards stronger coordination at the centre is accompanied by a certain degree of flexibility in policy implementation at a

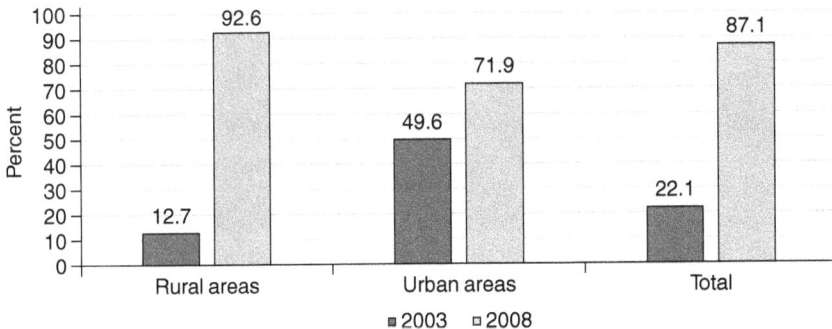

Figure 6.3 Insured population (percentages) (source: MoH 2009a: 14).

local level, with a tendency towards the harmonization of health policies—insurance plans, retail price regulation, characteristics of health information systems—at a provincial level.

Economically driven interests in the health sector

Payment system, price schedule and doctors' incentives

Payment of health services in China is commonly based on a 'fee-for-service' mechanism. The patient is charged for each item he/she consumes according to the relevant pricing schedule: a clearly inflationary system.[7] The Chinese medical price schedule is heavily distorted. Attempts made over the years by the authorities to curb rising medical expenditures have resulted in a situation where most prices for medical services are set at a level below cost, while providers are free to generate profits from the provision of hi-tech diagnostic procedures and from the mark-up added to the wholesale price of drugs. As a result, service provision is largely skewed towards prescribing the latter, so as to ensure high revenues.

To encourage service provision, hospitals provide monetary bonuses to physicians on the basis of the value and amount of drugs and treatments they prescribe. The more a doctor prescribes, the higher his/her income will be. According to the author's own investigation of a county hospital in northern China, bonuses are calculated and paid through a streamlined administrative procedure, supported by a hospital information system which records the items prescribed by each doctor and their price. In the hospital surveyed, bonuses often allowed doctors to double their basic salary—RMB2,500/month[8] for a clinical physician—provided by the government (Interview #0418, 2008).[9]

The combination of an inflationary payment system, a distorted price schedule and perverse incentives has led to rapid inflation in medical costs. Between 1980 and 2004, the average cost of OP and IP treatments increased respectively by 77 and 116 times—from 1.6 to 12.7 yuan for OP treatments; and from 40 to 4,662 yuan for IP treatments—an enormous increase considering that 2004 incomes were between 14 and 18 times those of 1980 (Zhang 2010: 5).

Selective provision of services and selective compliance with regulation

Incentives to provide curative treatments and a distorted price list heavily influence clinical practice, leading to selective provision of services, which manifests itself in: (1) over-provision of curative services and under-provision of preventive ones; and (2) therapy decisions taken on the basis of the profit margin. Over-provision of treatments in China—for those who can afford them—is well documented. A study conducted in 1998–1999 in four township health centres and eight village clinics concluded that less than 2 per cent of drug prescriptions were reasonable on medical grounds (Zhang *et al.* 2003, in Eggleston *et al.* 2006: 1). Another study found that 20 per cent of hospital expenditures associated with the treatment of appendicitis and pneumonia were clinically unnecessary (Liu and Mills 1999: 409). According to conservative estimates published in 2001, 20–30 per cent of China's overall health care expenditure was used for services and drugs whose prescription was either unreasonable or unnecessary (Zhong 2001, in Yu *et al.* 2010: 12). A particularly worrisome typology of selective provision concerns tuberculosis. Under the current regulatory framework, tuberculosis should be treated free of charge by local dispensaries of the Chinese Centre for Disease Prevention and Control. However, where local centres do not have the tools and equipment necessary to carry out the diagnosis—sputum examination, X-rays—patients suspected of having tuberculosis are referred to hospitals. In a village surveyed by the author in northern Shaanxi, patients had been treated for pneumonia in the nearby county hospital for months, before being diagnosed with tuberculosis. Needless to say, in the process thousands of yuan had already been spent on treatments which were probably not appropriate (Interview 0801, 2008).

Under Chinese regulations, medical personnel are forbidden to 'refuse emergency treatment' (NPC 1998: Art. 24). However, in Chinese hospitals treatment is often withheld when patients are incapable of providing an advance payment at the moment of IP admission. It is not uncommon to see patients receiving glucose infusions in the emergency room, after having been requested to provide an advance payment for IP treatments, which they found unaffordable. Among the 334 instances of hospitalization in critical condition analysed by the author, in 228 cases (68.3 per cent) an advance payment was required prior to hospital admission. In one case—multiple trauma in a car accident—the amount of the advance payment requested by the hospital was 30,000 yuan, ten times the local average per capita yearly income.[10] Similar situations often occur also *after* a patient has been admitted: once the advance payment has run out, medical personnel—generally a nurse—requires the patient's relatives to pay the 'deposit', which will usually be an amount set by the clinical physician in charge of the case. It has been estimated that in rural Central and Western China one-third of IP treatments are interrupted against medical advice, in most cases due to lack of money to continue the treatment (HCU-HHRDC 2009: 33–34). The problem is so widespread that, in 2009, the MoH issued specific regulations on the question, reiterating the principle of *xian jishi qiuzhi, hou bujiao feiyong* (first timely treat, then pay the fee) (MoH 2009b: Art. 23).

Hospitals and pharmaceutical companies

The interests of health providers are closely tied with those of the pharmaceutical industry. Hospitals account for more than four-fifths of all retail pharmaceutical sales, while on average 40–50 per cent of hospital revenues come from drug prescriptions. (Sun *et al.* 2008: 1046). Since the 1980s, the pharmaceutical sector has been developing rapidly. While, formerly, production plans—types of drugs and quantities—were planned by the government, economic reforms have allowed drug producers to define them on the basis of market demand. In 2005, there were 4,600 pharmaceutical manufacturers operating in China, up from 839 in the early 1980s, while the total value of domestic pharmaceutical production rose from 10 billion yuan in 1985 to over 446 billion in 2005 (Tang 2011: 3). The market is highly fragmented. In 2007, sales revenue of the top ten pharmaceutical firms accounted for only 10 per cent of total pharmaceutical sales, compared to the top ten international pharmaceutical companies, which accounted for about 42 per cent of global pharmaceutical sales revenue (Sun *et al.* 2008: 1043). Once distributed exclusively through government-controlled wholesalers, drugs can now be sold also directly to health providers (Yu *et al.* 2010: 10). Although Beijing in recent years has tried to put in place an efficient system for the wholesale purchase and distribution of pharmaceutical products at provincial level, sales agents still contact hospital managers and doctors directly, offering incentives—commissions, kickbacks, gifts—to encourage them to purchase or prescribe their products. Commercial promotion activities and networking are a fundamental part of the day-to-day operations of the Chinese pharmaceutical industry (Yu *et al.* 2010: 11; Interview 1130, 2011).

The impact of economically driven interests on Hu–Wen's policies

Access to health care and financial protection

Despite the increase in insurance coverage, the health care reform launched by the Hu–Wen administration has had poor results in terms of improving access to health care services and offering financial protection against medical expenditures. According to a study in which the author took part in 2008–2009, involving 11,000 individuals in rural areas of central and western China, more than 46 per cent of those who had been prescribed hospitalization in the 12 months prior to the survey had not been able to access treatment. In 89 per cent of cases, the reason was the lack of money to purchase the treatment (see Figure 6.4) (HCU-HHRDC 2009: 27).[11]

Interestingly, according to the same study, whether the patient was insured or not did not make much of a difference: there were no significant differences in levels of unmet health care needs between the insured and the uninsured. Where being insured *did* make a difference was in the amount of out-of-pocket expenditures a patient had to meet. Curiously, NRCMS insured patients were *more* likely to spend a large sum of money (≥10 per cent of the household annual income) on IP treatments than were the uninsured patients, although no evidence of adverse selection was found (HCU-HHRDC 2009: 20–40). This assessment is consistent with earlier findings of a World Bank research conducted in urban areas, which found a significantly higher probability of incurring catastrophic expenditures among insured patients than among uninsured ones (Wagstaff and Lindelow 2008: 990). A study conducted in Guangdong province similarly showed that the insured had spent, on average, 60 per cent more than the uninsured, largely due to higher costs and to the quantity of medicines prescribed for them (Pan *et al.* 2009: 1146). According to Professor Cheng, a health policy

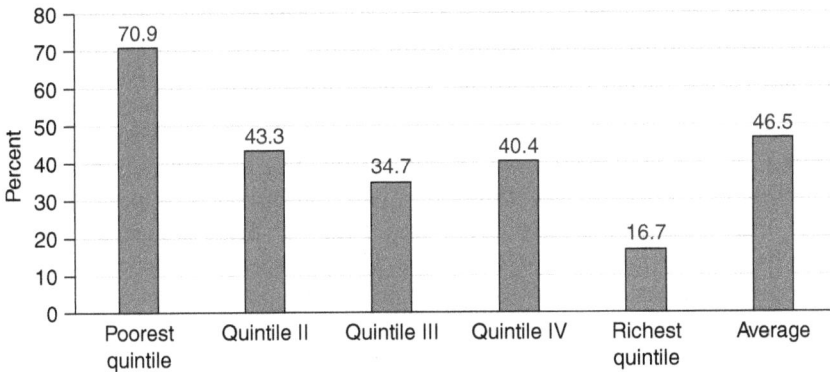

Figure 6.4 Unmet inpatient need in rural China (percentages) (source: HCU-HHRDC 2009: 27).

analyst based at Princeton University: 'out-of-pocket costs of inpatient care have risen, despite increased insurance from the government, which suggests it didn't make a difference ... hospitals and doctors help themselves by doing all sorts of additional tests and treatments' (Webster 2011: 1).

There is no doubt that, so far, the health reform has offered a good opportunity to pharmaceutical companies to increase their revenues. The value of the Chinese pharmaceutical market increased threefold between 2004 and 2009, with growth forecasts of around 20 per cent/year (*Partnering News* 2011a). According to estimates, the public resources allocated under the 2009–2011 Health Reform Plan— which will be discussed below— produced an 8 per cent expansion in the pharmaceutical market in 2010, for an estimated value of 53 billion yuan (Shen 2009: 3). The value of the drug market in China's county hospitals—which are located in rural areas, where the government's efforts to strengthen insurance coverage have been focused in the last decade—is reported to be expanding rapidly, attracting more and more attention from the marketing departments of both domestic and foreign pharmaceutical companies (*Interfax China* 2010).

Health care providers vis-à-vis society

Chinese citizens are aware of the contradiction between Beijing's commitments and the economic interests of the health industry and medical providers. In a comment posted on a web forum launched by NDRC in 2008 to collect the public's opinion on the health reform, Zhu Jianhong wrote:

> Before the adoption of New Rural Cooperative Medical Scheme, the cost of drugs prescribed for pneumonia was around 150 yuan a day [for IP treatment]. After its introduction, the same kind of pneumonia costs 300 yuan a

day. With a 50 percent reimbursement, the patient still has to pay 150 yuan. Looking at things from this perspective, who benefited from the scheme?[12]

Significantly, the frustration felt by patients and their families regarding the scarce affordability of services does not usually take the form of demonstrations against the local authorities—as is increasingly common over issues such as taxation, utilization of public soil, presence of polluting factories or plant, etc.— but is rather revealed by incidents of violence against medical personnel. In 2006, 10,000 cases of aggression were reported, with 5,500 wounded (*Xinhua News Agency* 2007). To prevent and deal with potentially violent episodes, in 2010 police officers were invited to become the vice-presidents of 27 hospitals in Shenyang, a large city in north-eastern China (*The Lancet* 2010: 657).

The words of a senior physician working in Beijing can help us understand the attitude and expectations of the medical personnel:

> I would be very glad if things could change. Nowadays, however, to be an idealist is useless. I just try to adapt to the current circumstances, doing a good job and avoiding troubles with patients' relatives. I want to build something for my own family. Besides my job at the hospital, I'm paid to enroll patients in clinical trials of new pharmaceutical products. My daughter is studying in the US, where I have bought a 200 sq. meters house in the suburbs of New York. Thank God at that time prices were quite low!
>
> (Interview 0920, 2010)

The words of Mr Li, cadre of a village located in a mountain area of Inner Mongolia, are equally indicative of the relationship between patients and doctors: 'Doctors prescribe us more medicines than what would be necessary. This way they can get higher salaries!' (Interview 0715a, 2008). The feeling is confirmed by Ms Sui, living in the same village:

> If we don't give a gift to doctors, it's almost like they won't take care of us. Last time I went to the hospital … I had to offer a 160 yuan dinner to my physician! Please tell this to senior officials in Beijing when you go back, so that they can do something!
>
> (Interview 0715c, 2008)

Resistance to regulatory pressures and interest articulation

Resistance as political input: selective provision of services and selective compliance with regulations

Market-oriented reforms in the health care sector have created the conditions for the emergence of economically driven interests, which share similar concerns over maximizing profits obtained by providing medical services. From a broad perspective, medical providers and pharmaceutical producers fit into the definition of an 'interest group', as they are 'a group of individuals who are linked by particular bonds of concern or advantage, and who have some awareness of these bonds' (Almond and Powell 1966: 75). To analyse the characteristics of this group from a political perspective requires identifying the route followed by its members in crossing the border between the pursuit of their particular interests and the attempt to influence political processes whose outcomes regulate—for better or worse—the development of China's health care system.

The capacity of single individuals and institutions to resist the policy and regulatory pressures put upon them in communist polities, and in China in particular, has been widely documented (Skilling 1966: 436; Burns 1988: 32; Hook 1996: 4). The aims and contents of such resistance vary hugely, as do the diverse historical, social-economic and political contexts they have emerged in and as do—of course—the interests involved. The selectivity with which services are provided and the selective compliance with regulations by Chinese health care providers offer clear examples of such resistance. Indeed, providing only those services which ensure high revenues and withholding appropriate treatments to patients unable to provide sufficient guarantees of their ability to pay, acquires a political connotation since it expresses a tendency that runs counter to the substance of the health care policies issued under the Hu–Wen leadership. Moreover, it has further political implications, as it is contributing to fuel a feeling of dissatisfaction within Chinese society, which is leading to the formation of anomic interest groups who may resort to violence to get their voice heard.

Interest articulation structures

Typically, interest groups will not limit their activities to supporting or opposing policies which have already been implemented. Rather, they will make demands 'through or upon any of the institutions of government', i.e. directly upon the decision makers (Truman 1951: 37). The dynamics of interest articulation within the Chinese health care sector have been little investigated. When inputs are taken into account, they are mostly described as the product of conflicts between central government agencies or of the articulation of anomic interests by the populace (Lampton 1977: 250–267; Liu 2008). Building on the existing literature, and analysing similar dynamics in other areas of China's economic, social and political life,[13] it is possible nonetheless to distinguish between three typologies of interest articulation platforms in the health care sector, characterized by different structures and constituencies: these are institutional, associational and corporate groups.

The major institutional group comprises managers and physicians working in public hospitals, parts of a bureaucratic structure tied to government authorities and to the party apparatus. These ties mean that hospital managers can be particularly effective in lobbying government departments at national and provincial level to gain access to financial resources, such as those allocated for the purchase of hi-tech biomedical equipment. At a broader level, hospitals have occasionally influenced the policy dialogue nationwide, mainly through MoH's institutional channels. Over the years there have been constant complaints from physicians about poor working conditions and low salaries, and the issue of how to ensure better working conditions and treatment of doctors has become an important issue in the debate on health care reform (Pye 1996: 38; Qiu 2009: 11). According to a well-informed source,

> when Zhang Wenkang, the ex-minister of health, sacked for the mismanagement of the SARS crisis, declared 'I'm not the CEO in charge of public hospitals, I'm the CEO in charge of the well-being of 1.3 billion people!' he was harshly criticised and was forced, a few months later, to correct his statement. This demonstrates how careful the MoH must be when dealing with doctors' interests!
>
> (Interview 0730, 2011)

As for associational groups, key actors in the Chinese health industry are grouped in various organizations, such as the Chinese Hospital Association, the Research and Development-based Pharmaceutical Association, the China Insurance Association, the China Pharmaceutical Commerce Association and the China Hospital Information Management Association. In general terms, these groupings seem to fit into the framework of state-corporatist organizations, working as a consultative arm of the government (Unger and Chan 1995: 37–51; Thompson 2009: 64). One example is the Chinese Hospital Information Management Association (CHIMA) which, over the past few years, has been working closely with the MoH to define hospital information systems (HIS) standards. Associations, however, can at times also be utilized as channels to convey demands and opinions upwards, formulated either by their own constituencies or by actors affected by the decisions being taken at higher levels. While introducing the characteristics of the new HIS national standards to a group of hospital managers in 2009, a CHIMA senior advisor was repeatedly questioned about the inclusion among the mandatory HIS modules of a new software, generating a DRG (Diagnosis Related Groups) code for each hospitalized patient.[14] The issue at stake was not the software itself, but rather the fact that its introduction would probably have led to closer controls over clinical and accounting practices. The scepticism expressed by hospital managers was subsequently the object of thorough discussion between the parties involved in a project promoting the adoption of efficient HIS systems, of which the gathering of hospital managers had been intended to be a start-up activity. To add more complexity to the analysis of these groupings is the fact that, although associations often appear to be 'monolithic' entities, the interests of individual members might not be. A glance at the board of advisors of Pharma China, an influential business media tied to the US consulting firm WiCON International, which advocates giving freer rein to the Chinese health care market, can help in giving a clearer picture of the links between government advisors, private consultancy firms and membership in key industry associations. Among the 12 people composing the board, five have a simultaneous involvement in government agencies and associations, as well as—in four cases—in the private sector.[15] This kind of multiple memberships reinforces the idea that the dynamics within associations might not be strictly controlled by government diktats and rather permeable to private interests.

Other than into institutional and associational groups, economically driven interests can coalesce into corporate interest groups. Corporate pressures, through either legal or illegal avenues—lobbying, kickbacks, bribes—have been widely documented in the pharmaceutical industry. In 2007, a scandal involved the Chinese SFDA, the government agency in charge of registering new drugs which can be sold on the Chinese market. The director of the agency, Zheng Xiaoyu, was executed after having been found guilty of receiving bribes to smooth the path for approving drugs that did not comply with mandatory quality and safety standards (*Xinhua News Agency* 2007; *BBC News* 2007). The dynamics of interest articulation in other key regulatory areas, such as setting indicative retail prices for drugs—for which NDRC is in charge—and the inclusion of drugs into the lists of items reimbursable by the government health insurances—NRCMS, URBMI and UWBMI, of which the MoH and the MoHRSS respectively are in charge—is more difficult to ascertain. However, in 2009 while new measures for drug pricing reform were being discussed by top leaders, 'intense discussions' reportedly went on behind the scenes (Shen 2009: 3). To understand the articulation of corporate interests in the pharmaceutical sector, the structure of the pharmaceutical market must also be taken into account. As has been seen, the pharmaceutical market in China is fragmented: none of the top ten pharmaceutical companies in China controls more than 2.5 per cent of the market. As such, neither international MNCs or the biggest domestic firms—most of which are state-related[16]—are in a monopolistic or quasi-monopolistic position, a condition which in other sectors allows major enterprises to press their interests successfully (KPMG Advisory (China) Ltd 2011: 20, 28; Naughton 2009: 7–8; Yang 2007: 2–5). However, in the near future the market structure will probably evolve towards increased concentration, as major mergers and acquisitions are occurring at a fast rate. In 2007, deals worth US$2.1 billion were finalised, up from US$1.1 billion in 2006 (PWC 2009: 22). In the first half of 2011 the trend was confirmed, when various collaborations were established between domestic producers and foreign MNCs.

Interest articulation avenues

In the Chinese context, the importance of direct contact between interested parties and their regulators has been recognised as being one of the most common forms of interest articulation (Kennedy 2005: 3). Considering the almost symbiotic ties that often exist between government and business, strengthened after Jiang Zemin opened the party ranks to entrepreneurs a decade ago, this finding is certainly not surprising. Interest articulation through personal connections and elite representation—i.e. presence of a group member in the policy-making structure or sympathetic representation by an elite figure (Almond and Powell 1966: 83)—seems to be the most likely pattern for putting demands upon the political system in the health sector. The fact that hospital managers are nominated by the CCP implies that they have a role in the political system, which they might be free to use to promote decisions serving their interests. Although excessive speculation over the issue should be carefully avoided, the links between political power and the interests of the health industry are also clear from the considerable presence of professionals involved in medical activities among the so-called 'princelings' (*taizidang*), the offspring of senior CCP leaders. In 2008, among 1,800 'princelings' whose names were posted on the web, 85 were reportedly employed in health-related activities (hospitals, research institutes, pharmaceutical companies, etc.).[17] Among others, the son of Li Ruihan,[18] Jeffrey Li, was for a long time employed by a multinational pharmaceutical company, before moving to a career in finance (*Financial Times* 2011).

The 2009–2011 reform plan: contents, debate and resistance

Contents of the reform plan

In 2009 Beijing launched a new phase of the health reform, identifying the following five priorities:

1   strengthen the government-run health insurance sector;
2   define an essential drug list to be adopted by public providers;
3   reinforce the health care provision network;
4   ensure equitable provision of public health services; and
5   reform the management of public hospitals (State Council 2009).

The government allocated 850 billion yuan over a period of three years (2009–2011), more than two-thirds of which were earmarked for subsidising premiums of government-run insurance schemes.

The MoH has, so far, listed over 300 'essential drugs'. According to the new regulations, physicians employed in the lower tiers of the health care provision network—village clinics (*cun weishengshi*), and township health centres (*xiang weishengyuan*) in the countryside, community health centres (*shequ weisheng fuwu zhongxin*) in urban areas—should only prescribe drugs on the list. The new measures also require that the mark-up on the price of drugs will be gradually abolished. Until now public hospitals were allowed to charge up to 15 per cent over the wholesale price in the case of 'Western' drugs and 30 per cent for traditional Chinese medicine (TCM) drugs. To compensate losses due to the implementation this policy, local authorities have been required to gradually increase their financial support for the current expenditures of hospitals.

As for hospital management, emphasis has been put on ensuring the cost-effectiveness of treatments, in order to rein in the increase in medical expenditures and stop over-prescription. Between 2009 and 2010, the MoH developed 112 clinical protocols, whose adoption is being piloted in over 100 public providers. Partial results show a decrease in average costs for IP treatments. In Jilin People's Hospital, average costs for IP treatments covered by the experimentation were reduced by 33.4 per cent (*Jiankang Bao* 2010a: 1).

Debate and resistance

Not surprisingly, the reaction of the pharmaceutical industry and medical providers to the new measures was negative. In January 2009, shortly before the reform measures were disclosed, Pharma China published a long editorial, whose central paragraph read 'Top priority of Chinese healthcare reform should not be cost containment' (Shen 2009: 2). In the first months of 2010, the debate went public. When commenting on the health reform plan during the Chinese People's Political Consultative Conference in March 2010, the delegate Zong Licheng, manager of a pharmaceutical company, criticized the measures which aimed to curb the rise in medical costs, and achieved some degree of media coverage for his argument (*Nanfang Zhoumo* 2010: B11). Public hospitals also expressed discomfort and began airing their views publicly. According to a hospital director surnamed Hu, 'even though the prescription of certain treatments isn't ethically justifiable, hospitals and doctors must find some way to survive' (*Nanfang Zhoumo* 2010: A6). When discussing the reform plan with the author, the director of a prefecture hospital located in Central China defined it as 'idealistic' (Interview 0520, 2010). Local authorities seem concerned too. When talking to the author, a representative of a provincial health department repeatedly expressed scepticism regarding both the economic sustainability of hospital operations under the new restrictive framework regulating drug prescription and regarding the introduction of standardized treatment protocols (Interview 0925, 2009). This scepticism could well be due to both the technical difficulties involved in coordinating the hospital management reform, and to the demands made on local authorities by the new reform plan regarding the increase in their financial support for the running costs of hospitals, a contribution designed to cover the losses hospitals would suffer through the abolition of the mark-up on drugs. The structure of the pharmaceutical industry could play a role too, since at local level drug manufacturing is often an important instrument of economic development and a chance for employment (Tang 2011: 3).

In such a context, it is hardly surprising that the progress of hospital management reform has been slow, due to tough opposition from physicians (Webster 2011: 1). Passive resistance to regulations seems likely to continue along patterns already introduced in this chapter. According to an former pharmaceutical marketing manager, 'hospitals will try to circumvent restrictions and continue to prescribe unnecessary treatments and/or newly introduced items, not yet subject to strict government regulations' (Interview 0221, 2011). According to another Chinese medical source,

> the proposed measures [on the abolition of the mark-up on drugs] could lead to informal arrangements between drug manufacturers and hospitals: the wholesale price of drugs could be artificially increased, so as to make up at least partially for the financial losses caused by the ban on mark ups
>
> (Interview 1014, 2009)

New perspectives for health reform?

New perspectives for health care reform are not likely to be unveiled until the new generation of Chinese leaders have consolidated their position. However, it is worth mentioning how recent policies seem oriented towards broadening the scope of non-public service provision. In late 2010, the State Council issued a circular aimed at 'eliminating policy barriers hindering the development of non-public medical institutions' (State Council 2010: Preamble). Only a few weeks before, the Minister of Health Chen Zhu released a statement praising the 'important social role' of non-public hospitals in 'protecting the common good' (*Jiankang Bao* 2010b: 3). Interestingly, the circular encourages the transformation of public hospitals into non-public, non-for-profit medical institutions (State Council 2010: Art. 4). The latter should, moreover, be given priority by local health authorities planning to expand service supply. The regulation also opens up to foreign investment, which will be allowed and encouraged, both in the form of joint ventures and wholly foreign ownership of medical institutions (State Council 2010: Art. 2).

While the intention of broadening the scope of non-public providers is consistent with the guidelines of the 2009–2011 Health Reform Plan (State Council 2009: Art. 10), the new regulation could herald a departure from the approach followed by the Hu–Wen leadership, as it states the importance of establishing 'mechanisms of competition, to improve efficiency and quality'. Indeed, these words resemble the motto 'let the better hospitals flourish!' which has been inspiring those advocating all-out privatization of China's health care (Chow 2006). It is too soon to predict possible concrete implications of the new regulations, and no detailed information is at present available on the approach the new leaders will take. One exception, however, could be constituted by Li Yuanchao, the new Chinese vice president and one of the most prominent figures of the new 'fifth generation of leaders'. Li served as CCP secretary of Jiangsu between 2002 and 2007, while in this province significant market-oriented experimentations were being conducted in the health sector.

Conclusions

The notion that private interests influence the development of health care systems worldwide is widely held among Western audiences (Chow 2006). Health is a constantly growing industry, with huge interests at stake. In China, during the 1980s and 1990s, economically driven interests in this area developed, when the retrenchment of the state from social sectors left vast areas ill-regulated and under-funded. During the Hu–Wen era, these interests have affected the capacity of the state to tackle the crisis of the health care system and the huge imbalances in terms of access to essential care, both of which have proved detrimental for the development of the economy and of society, as well as for the legitimacy of the party itself. Platforms and avenues through which demands upon the political system are made are already available to economically driven interest groups related to the Chinese health sector. Should these interests succeed in gaining even greater influence over the current health care reform process, the outcome of China's transition—at least in this area—may be different from the one advocated by many China scholars and observers. Policy-making could become responsive to powerful private interests, rather than accountable to society at large.

China faces enormous challenges in the field of health care and these are likely to become even more daunting in the coming years, due to the rapid ageing of the population. Whether China's health care system will be able to ensure equitable access to safe and effective health services will largely depend upon the interactions between social needs, political power and economic interests. These interactions deserve to be further investigated. When the author of this chapter recently asked for advice from a senior scholar of Chinese politics on how to approach the topic of this research, he received the prompt answer: 'Just follow the money!' While this might seem an oversimplification of the enormous issues affecting the development of the Chinese health care system, the preliminary findings introduced in this chapter show that his answer could indeed make sense.

Notes

1 Hannant (1998: 101). Known in China by the name of *bai qiuen*, Norman Bethune was a Canadian medical doctor and communist political activist. In 1938–1939 he was stationed in the Communist stronghold of Yan'An. He died in November 1939 of septicemia, probably contracted performing surgery on a wounded Chinese soldier. He is still remembered and celebrated in China among revolutionary heroes.

2 See in particular Skilling (1966).

3 The village is the only level of the health care provision network where privatization has gone to its fullest extent so far. By 1998, more than 40 per cent of village clinics were independent, private practices (Liu *et al.* 2006: 214). Village clinics are the first tier of the rural health care system and are usually staffed by one or two paramedics. Township health centres are the second tier of the government provision network in the countryside. While in the pre-reform period—when they were operated as commune hospitals—they also provided inpatient (IP) treatment for common diseases and deliveries, currently in most cases they provide only for outpatient (OP) care. The third tier consists of almost 3,000 county hospitals, which provide the bulk of curative IP services in rural areas.

4 The first cases of SARS (Severe Acute Respiratory Syndrome) were reported in Guangdong Province in November 2002. According to the WHO, between November 2002 and August 2003, confirmed SARS cases worldwide were 8,422, with 916 deaths (WHO 2003). The 'People's War on SARS' declared by President Hu Jintao in early 2003 (Perry 2007: 15), is often considered the watershed between the 'old', market-minded health policies and the 'new' path initiated with the so-called fourth generation of leaders, guided by Hu Jintao and Wen Jiabao.

5 Between 2000 and 2008, China's Total Health Expenditure (THE) as percentage of GDP remained substantially stable (4.5 per cent in 2000; 4.3 per cent in 2008) (WHO 2011: 128).

6 UWBMI was introduced in 1998. Unlike NRCMS and URBMI, whose premiums are heavily subsidized by the government with a flat rate contribution paid by the single

enrollee, UWBMI is financed by workers and employers. On average, UWBMI insurance premiums amount to 8 per cent of annual salary, of which 2 per cent is provided by the worker and 6 per cent by the employer. Portability of NRCMS' benefits has been an issue in the last few years with reference to the huge migrant population. Although most migrants are NRCMS enrollees, the rural insurance often cannot reimburse services purchased outside the county or province of residence. Since 2009, migrant workers have theoretically been allowed to enroll in either URBMI or UWBMI schemes, regardless of their residence status (*hukou*).

7 In most Western countries 'fee-for-service' mechanisms have been replaced by per-case based, forfeit payment systems. Among these systems, the most widely used to determine cost for IP services is based on Diagnosis Related Groups (DRGs). DRGs classify patients into major diagnostic categories. Each of these categories groups together diagnoses whose treatment should consume a similar amount of resources. DRGs were intended to offer a mechanism to encourage providers to economize and they have, to a large extent, proved effective. Since the real current costs incurred by the hospital are not taken into account, DRGs require the adoption of well-defined treatment protocols. Per-case payment mechanisms have been tested in many Chinese hospitals in the last few years, as the MoH called for the experimentation of payment mechanism based on patients' diagnoses. However, modalities through which pilots have been conducted raise suspicion about the abilities of per-case payment systems to reduce medical expenditures under the current Chinese institutional framework. In one area surveyed by the author, the local health bureau had set up a small unit to verify the consistency between diagnoses and treatments provided by a local county hospital, in order to prevent attempts to circumvent constraints imposed by the new payment system. When asked: 'how do you behave when there is evidence of some irregularity?' the young official coordinating the unit—who had no medical background—replied: 'we just ask the doctors [employed in the hospitals whose medical records were being checked] to clarify our doubts' [Interview 0817, 2008].

8 At the time of writing the first draft of this article (August 2011) RMB1 = US$0.16; EUR 0.11. In the same area, average income for peasants was around RMB3,000 per capita per year. In this chapter, reference is made to the Chinese currency also with the name 'yuan'.

9 Interviews used to draft this paper were collected during fieldwork carried out in six Chinese provinces between 2008 and 2011. A limited number of interviews were also conducted during a research stay in the US, in summer 2011. Data collection tolls included both unstructured and semi-structured in-depth interviews.

10 Data on advance payments required in case of IP treatment were calculated independently by the author, utilizing the database collected during the research project 'Impact of the New Rural Cooperative Medical Scheme on Health Care Services Accessibility in Central and Western China' (see HCU-HHRDC 2009).

11 The results of the study were published in 2009 at: http://saluteinternazionale. info/2009/09/riforma-sanitaria-in-cina-lo-stato-dellarte/ [in Italian].

12 At the time of writing the first draft of this article (August 2011), this comment was still accessible at: www.sdpc.gov.cn/ygyj/ygyj_detail.jsp?comId=29464.

13 See in particular Kennedy 2005: 1–24; Yang 2007: 2–5.

14 On DRGs' rationale and characteristics, see note 7.

15 See www.pharmachinaonline.com/AboutUs/advisoryboard.asp.

16 Among the top 11 Chinese pharmaceutical companies listed according to market capitalization in the first quarter of 2011, seven were state-related. They are: Sinopharm, Jiangsu Hengrui Medicine, Shanghai Pharmaceuticals, Yunnan Baiyao Group, Shandong-E E-Jiao, Harbin Pharmaceutical, Shanghai Fosun (KPMG Advisory (China) Ltd 2011: 28).

17 At the time of writing the first draft of this article (August 2011), the list was still accessible at: www.aboluowang.com/news/data/2008/0915/ article_58960_1.html. Since the source is unclear, information contained in the list must be referred to with care.
18 Member of the Standing Committee of the Political Bureau of CCP Central Committee until 2002.

References

Almond, G. and Powell, B. (1966) *Comparative Politics: A Developmental Approach*, Boston, MA: Little Brown and Company.

BBC News (2007) 'Death Penalty for China Official', 29 May, available online: http://news.bbc.co.uk/2/hi/6699441.stm (accessed 11 May 2011).

Bloom, Gerald (2011) 'Building Institutions for an Effective Health System: Lessons from China's Experience with Rural Health Reform', *Social Science and Medicine* 72(8): 1302–1309.

Burns, J. (1988) *Political Participation in Rural China*, Berkeley, CA: University of California Press.

Central Committee of the Chinese Communist Party (CCCCP)—State Council (2009) 'Zhonggong zhongyang, guowuyuan guanyu shenhua yiyao weisheng tizhi gaige de yijian', zhongfa, 6 hao (Suggestions of the Central Committee of the Communist Party of China and of the State Council on Further Strengthening Health Care System Reform) Central Circular 6, available online: http://gov.hzrb.cn/system/2009/04/06/010019487.shtml (accessed 22 March 2011).

CAPM-NHI (Chinese Academy of Preventive Medicine, Italian National Institute of Health) (2000) 'Emergency Care Services and Willingness to Pay in Three Areas of China: Results of a Survey Carried on in Lhasa, Jagedaqi and in the Dongcheng District of Beijing' (unpublished).

Chow, Gregory C. (2006) 'An Economic Analysis of Health Care in China', *Princeton University CEPS Working Paper* 132, available online: www.princeton.edu/ceps/workingpapers/132chow.pdf.

Easton, David (1957) 'An Approach to the Analysis of Political Systems', *World Politics* 9(3): 383–408.

Eggleston, Karen, Li Ling, Meng Qingyue, Magnus Lindelow and Adam Wagstaff (2006) 'Health Service Delivery in China: A Literature Review', *World Bank Policy Research Working Paper* 3978, Washington, DC: World Bank.

Financial Times (2011) 'To the Money Born', available online: www.ft.com/cms/s/0/e3e51a48-3b5d-11df-b622-00144feabdc0.html (accessed 10 June 2011).

Gu, Xin (2004) 'Health Care Regime Change and the SARS Outbreak in China', in Y. Zheng and J. Wong (eds) *The SARS Epidemic: Challenges to China's Health Management*, Singapore: World Scientific Publishing, pp. 123–155.

Hannant, L. (ed.) (1998) *The Politics of Passion: Norman Bethune's Writing and Art*, Toronto: University of Toronto Press.

HCU-HHRDC (Health Coordination Unit in Beijing—Italian Development Cooperation, Health Human Resources Development Center—Ministry of Health of People's Republic of China) (2009) 'Impact of the New Rural Cooperative Medical Scheme on Health Care Services Accessibility in Central and Western China', paper presented at the seminar 'The Chinese Health Care System at a Crossroads: The Issue of Accessibility and Reform Perspectives', Beijing, 19 June 2009.

Hook, B. (ed.) (1996) *The Individual and the State in China*, Oxford: Clarendon Press.

Hsiao, William C.L. (1995) 'The Chinese Health Care System: Lessons for Other Nations', *Social Science and Medicine* 41(8): 1047–1055.

Huang, Yanzhong (2006) 'From Bandwagoning to Buckpassing: The Political Logic of China's Healthcare Transition', paper prepared for the Annual Conference of Chinese Economists Society, Shanghai, 2 July, available online: http://202.121.142.130/conference/ces/paper/ces_pdf/6/6-1.pdf (accessed 20 October 2011).

Interfax China (2010) 'Health Care Reform Spurs County Hospitals' Pharma Market', available online: http://business.highbeam.com/407731/article-1G1-241197132/health-care-reform-spurs-county-hospitals-pharma-market (accessed 3 January 2014).

Jiankang Bao (2010a) 'Linchuang lujing shidian chujian chengxiao' (Experimentation of Clinical Protocols Achieves First Results), 26 October, available online: www.jkb.com.cn/document.jsp?docid=159796 (accessed 13 January 2014).

Jiankang Bao (2010b) 'Chen Zhu kanwang lao Zhen' (Chen Zhu Visits the Old Zhen), 18 October, available online: www.jkb.com.cn/document.jsp?docid=156807 (accessed 13 January 2014).

Kennedy, S. (2005) *The Business of Lobbying in China*, Cambridge, MA: Harvard University Press.

KMPG Advisory (China) Limited (2011) *China's Pharmaceutical Industry—Poised for the Giant Leap*, available online: www.kpmg.com/cn/en/issuesandinsights/ articlespublications/pages/china-pharmaceutical-201106.aspx (accessed 25 August 2011).

Lampton, D.M. (1977) *The Politics of Medicine in China: The Policy Process, 1949–1977*, London: Dawson & Sons.

Liu, Xingzhu and Mills, Anne (1999) 'Evaluating Payment Mechanisms: How Can We Measure Unnecessary Care?' *Health Policy and Planning* 14(4): 409–13.

Liu, Xingzhu and Rao, Keqing (2006) 'Providing Health Insurance in Rural China: From Research to Policy', *Journal of Health Policy and Law* 31(1): 71–92.

Liu, Yuanli (2008) 'Reforming China's Health Care System: The Balancing Act', paper presented at the seminar 'Where Is China Headed?', Boston, 8 December.

Liu, Yuanli, Berman, Peter, Yip, Winnie, Liang, Haocai, Meng, Qingyue, Qu, Jiangbin and Li, Zhonghe (2006) 'Health Care in China: The Role of Non-Government Providers', *Health Policy* 77(2): 212–220.

Liu, Yuanli, Rao, Keqing and Hsiao, William C.L. (2003) 'Medical Expenditure and Rural Impoverishment in China', *Journal of Health, Population and Nutrition* 21(3): 216–222.

Meng, Q. (2006) *Health Care Pricing and Payment Reforms in China: The Implications for Health Service Delivery and Cost Containment*, Stockholm: Karolinska University Press.

MoH (Ministry of Health) (1993) *1993 nian di yi ci guojia weisheng fuwu diaocha fenxi baogao* (Research on National Health Services—An Analysis Report of the First National Health Services Survey in 1993), available online: www.nhfpc.gov.cn/ cmsresources/mohwsbwstjxxzx/cmsrsdocument/doc9906.pdf (accessed 4 January 2014).

MoH (Ministry of Health) (1998) *Guojia weisheng fuwu yanjiu—1998 nian di'er ci guojia weisheng fuwu diaocha fenxi baogao* (Research on National Health Services—An Analysis Report of the Second National Health Services Survey in 1998), available online: www.nhfpc.gov.cn/cmsresources/mohwsbwstjxxzx/ cmsrsdocument/doc9907.pdf (accessed 4 January 2014).

MoH (Ministry of Health) (2009a) *Guojia weisheng fuwu yanjiu—2008 nian di si ci guojia weisheng fuwu diaocha fenxi baogao* (Research on National Health Services—

An Analysis Report of the Second National Health Services Survey in 2008), document presented at the conference 'The Senior Level Seminar on National Health Services Survey and Health Reform Monitoring and Evaluation of China', 2–3 December 2009, Beijing.

MoH (Ministry of Health) (2009b) *Jizhenke jianshe yu guanli zhinan (shixing)* (Instructions on Establishment and Management of Emergency Departments), available online: www.moh.gov.cn/mohbgt/s9509/200906/41146.shtml (accessed 4 January 2014).

Nanfang Zhoumo (2010) 'Yao yang de yiyuan' (Hospitals Depending on Drugs Sales), 11 March, available online: www.infzm.com/content/4244 (accessed 4 January 2014).

NPC (National People's Congress of the People's Republic of China) (1998) *Zhonghua renmin gongheguo zhiye yishi fa* (Law on Licensed Doctors of the People's Republic of China), available online: www.gov.cn/banshi/2005-08/01/ content_18970.htm (accessed 16 August 2011).

Naughton, Barry (2008) 'SASAC and Rising Corporate Power in China', *China Leadership Monitor* 24, available online: http://media.hoover.org/sites/default/ files/documents/CLM24BN.pdf (accessed 20 July 2011).

Pan, Xilong, Dib, H.H., Zhu, M., Zhang, Y. and Fan, Y. (2009) 'Absence of Appropriate Hospitalization Cost Control for Patients with Medical Insurance: A Comparative Analysis Study', *Health Economics* 18(10): 1146–1162.

Partnering News (2011a) 'AstraZeneca Sees Double-digit Growth in China into the Future'. Available online: http://ebdgroup.com/partneringnews/2011/05/ astrazeneca-sees-double-digit-growth-in-china-into-the-future/ (accessed 26 May 2011).

Perry, Elizabeth J. (2007) 'Studying Chinese Politics: Bidding Farewell to Revolution?', *The China Journal* 57: 1–22.

PWC (PricewaterhouseCoopers) (2009) *Investing in China's Pharmaceutical* Industry, 2nd edition, available online: www.pwc.com/gx/en/pharma-life-sciences/ investing-china (accessed 23 July 2011).

Pye, W. Lucian (1996) 'The State and the Individual: An Overview Interpretation', in B. Hook (ed.) *The Individual and the State in China*, Oxford: Clarendon Press, pp. 16–42.

Qiu, Zexi (2009) 'Towards a Harmonious relationship Between Yi and Huan', report presented at the conference 'The Senior Level Seminar on National Health Services Survey and Health Reform Monitoring and Evaluation of China', 2–3 December 2009, Beijing.

Saich, T. (2011) *Governance and Politics of China*, Basingstoke: Palgrave Macmillan.

Shen, James (2009) 'Wheels of Healthcare Reform Begins to Roll', *PharmaChina* 35: 2–4.

Skilling, Gordon (1966) 'Interest Groups and Communist Politics', *World Politics* 18(3): 435–451.

State Council (2009) 'Guowuyuan guanyu yinfa yiyao weisheng tizhi gaige jinqi zhongdian shishi fang'an 2009–2011 nian de tongzhi guofa, 2009 nian 12 hao' (Circular No. 12, 2009 of the State Council on the Implementation Plan for the Recent Priorities of the Health Care System Reform 2009–2011), available online: www.gov.cn/ zwgk/2009-04/07/content_1279256.htm (accessed 11 June 2011).

State Council (2010) 'Guowuyuan bangongting zhuanfa fazhan gaige weiyuanhui weishengbu beng bumen guanyu jin yi bu guli he yindao shehui ziben juban yiliao jigou yijian de tongzhi, 2010 nian 58 hao' (Circular No. 58, 2010 of the General Office of the State Council Forwarding the Opinions of NDRC, MoH and Other Ministries on Further Encouraging and Guiding Medical Facilities Established by Social Capitals), available online: www.gov.cn/zwgk/2010-12/03/ content_1759091.htm (accessed 18 August 2011).

Sun, Qiang, Santoro, Michael A., Meng, Qingyue, Liu, Caitlin and Eggleston, Karen (2008) 'Pharmaceutical Policy In China', *Health Affairs* 27(4): 1042–1050.

Tang, Shenglan, Sun, Jing, Qu, Gang and Chen Wen (2011)'Pharmaceutical Policy in China: Issues and Problems', available online: http://archives.who.int/tbs/ ChinesePharmaceuticalPolicy/English_Background_Documents/summarypapers/PPChinaIssuesProblemsShenglan.doc (accessed 30 August 2011).

The Lancet (2010) 'Chinese Doctors Are Under Threat', *The Lancet* 376: 657.

Thompson, Drew (2009) *China's Health Care Redux*, Washington, DC: Center for the National Interest, available online: www.cftni.org/Thompson-China-Health-Care-Reform-Redux2009.pdf (accessed 6 October 2011).

Truman, D. (1951) *The Governmental Process: Political Interests and Public Opinion*, New York: Alfred A. Knopf.

Unger, Jonathan and Chan, Anita (1995) 'China, Corporatism and the East Asian Model', *The Australian Journal of Chinese Affairs* 33: 29–53.

Wagstaff, Adam and Lindelow, Magnus (2008) 'Can Insurance Increase Financial Risk? The Curious Case of Health Insurance in China', *Journal of Health Economics* 27(4): 990–1005.

WB (World Bank) (1986) *Financing Health Services in Developing Countries: An Agenda for Reform*, available online: http://go.worldbank.org/I3YX1MJGZ0 (accessed 20 November 2011).

Webster, Paul (2011) 'Roadblocks to Health Reform in China', *Canadian Medical Association Journal* 183(12): E771–E772, available online: http://connection.ebscohost.com/c/articles/65924270/roadblocks-health-reform-china (accessed 3 January 2014).

Whitehead, Margaret, Dahlgren, Göran and Evans, Timothy (2011) 'Equity and Health Sector Reforms: Can Low-Income Countries Escape the Medical Poverty Trap?' *The Lancet* 358: 833–836.

WHO (World Health Organization) (1978) *Declaration of Alma Ata*, Geneva: WHO, available online: www.who.int/publications/almaata_declaration_en.pdf (accessed 3 January 2014).

WHO (World Health Organization) (1983) *Primary Health Care: The Chinese Experience*, Geneva: WHO.

WHO (World Health Organization) (2000) *The WHO Health Report 2000—Health Systems: Improving Performance*, Geneva: WHO.

WHO (World Health Organization) (2003) *Summary Table of SARS Cases by Country, 1 November 2002–7 August 2003*, available online: www.who.int/csr/sars/country/2003_08_15/en/index.html (accessed 10 June 2011).

WHO (World Health Organization) (2009) *National Health Accounts Series—March 2009*, available online: www.who.int/nha/en/ (accessed 10 October 2010).

WHO (World Health Organization) (2011) *World Health Statistics 2011*, available online: www.who.int/whosis/whostat/2011/en/index.html (accessed 25 November 2011).

Xinhua News Agency (2007) 'Doctor Face Growing Risks of Violent Medical Disputes'. Available online: www.chinagate.cn/english/medicare/50839.htm (accessed 20 April 2011).

Yang, Guangbin (2007) 'Interest Groups in China's Politics and Governance', *East Asian Institute Background Brief* 361, available online: www.eai.nus.edu.sg/BB361.pdf (accessed 3 January 2014).

Yang, Jinqing (2008) 'Serve the People: Communist Ideology and Professional Ethics of Medicine in China', paper prepared for the East Asian Social Policy (EASP) 5th International Conference, Taipei, 3–4 November, available online: www.welfareasia.

org/5thconference/papers/Yang%20J_communist%20ideology%20and%20profes-
sional%20ethics.pdf (accessed 4 January 2013)

Yip, Winnie and Hsiao, William (2008) 'The Chinese Health System at a Crossroads',
Health Affairs 27(2): 460–468.

Yu, Xuan, Li, C., Shi, Y. and Yu, M. (2010) 'Pharmaceutical Supply Chain in China:
Current Issues and Implications for Health System Reform', *Health Policy* 97(1): 8–15.

Zhang, Junhua (2010) 'The Progress of Chinese Health Reform', paper presented at the
workshop 'Developing Welfare Intruments for the Health Care Sector: Reform Perspectives from the P.R. China', Venice, 31 May 2010.

Zheng, Yongnian (2002) 'Interest Representation and the Transformation of the Chinese
Communist Party', *Copenhagen Journal of Asian Studies* 16: 57–85.

Zhou Xiaonong, Wang T.P., Wang L.Y., Guo J.G., Yu Q., Xu J., Wang R.B., Chen Z.
and Jia T.W. (2004) 'The Current Status of Schistosomiasis Epidemics in China',
National Institute of Parasitic Diseases 25(7): 555–558 (in Chinese).

7 China's centrally managed state-owned enterprises

Dilemma and reform

Huang Yanjie and Zheng Yongnian

Reform and the making of centrally managed SOEs

China's reform was initiated in the late 1970s. At that time, state-run enterprises (precursor of state-owned enterprises, the SOEs) were mired in inefficiency and low profitability while burdened with the provision of basic social welfare and employment. From managers to individual workers, there was little incentive to make a full effort and perform well. Starting in 1978, the first round of the SOE reforms were mostly characterized by the so-called *fangquan rangli* (decentralizing powers and sharing profits), where central ministries gradually transferred some decision-making powers to the SOEs. Similar to the household responsibility system, the SOEs managers were granted powers to make key decisions regarding production, investment and personnel appointments and the responsibility for the performance of their firms. The reforms were generally unsuccessful. Instead of improvements in productivity and profitability, the incentive scheme did not work properly to encourage productivity and the retained profits were often channeled to the wages and welfare of their employees (Holz 2006: 63–64; Walder 1981: 228–229).

Since 1984, with the onset of full-fledged urban economic reforms, the focus of SOE reforms shifted to fiscal and financial aspects. Reformers in this period aimed to transform the SOEs into more autonomous, self-disciplined, but still strictly state-run economic entities. These efforts included the so-called *li gai shui* (turning profits to tax revenues) reforms, which restructured the fiscal relations between SOEs and governments. In addition, SOEs were urged to wean themselves off budgetary supports and depend on bank loans. In 1987, another milestone in SOE reform was reached with the introduction of a responsibility system. Under the new system, SOE managers were given full scope to manage their enterprises on the condition that they turned in a contracted amount of taxes to the government. But these reforms were generally unsuccessful as well. Although the central ministries had weakened their control of SOEs, the powerful local governments had every reason to support local state enterprises under their jurisdictions by forcing banks to back them. The financial situation of the SOEs deteriorated during the bank loan boom in 1993 and 1996. The result was ill-enforced financial discipline, continued loss-making and the accumulation of huge bank loans (Naughton 1996: 64).

Beginning in 1993, the second phase of reforms was carried out under Premier Zhu Rongji, after the Fourteenth Party Congress formally renamed state-run enterprises (*guoying qiye*) state-owned enterprises (*guoyou qiye*, or SOEs). In November 1993, at the Third Plenary Session of the Fourteenth Party Congress, the objective of SOE reform was redefined formally as building a modern enterprise system. In 1995, the central government put forth a new basic principle of *zhuada fangxiao* (grasping the large and letting go of the small) to streamline the whole SOE sector through consolidation of the large state-owned enterprises and selective privatization of small- and medium-sized state-owned enterprises.

The *zhuada* strategy concerned large enterprise groups in strategic and heavy-industry sectors. Newly created enterprises were typically formed from former industrial ministries, their major departments, subsidiaries and affiliated research institutes. These enterprises were regrouped according to their core businesses and recapitalized through a variety of ways, in particular, shareholding reforms that transformed them into stockholding companies. A new system was established where the parent companies held controlling shares over their provincial, regional and functional subsidiaries. The petroleum, nuclear and telecommunication industries provided the best examples. The results of the reform were a few hundred large state-owned enterprise groups in the capital-intensive sectors in the manufacturing industries that had established significant administrative as well as economic barriers to entry.

The later strategy aimed to pull the state out of competitive sectors, especially businesses where private entrepreneurs enjoyed a clear comparative advantage. The best example was the tens of thousands loss-making small- and medium-sized enterprises under the local branches of the Ministry of Light Industry and Ministry of Textile Industry. Private entrepreneurs, most significantly former managers of these enterprises, were given the opportunity to acquire these enterprises through the selling and buying of state assets at very low prices. This strategy spawned a leap forward in the number of private and joint-stock companies. At the same time, much of the task of restructuring was decentralized to local governments, which for their own fiscal motives usually kept the more efficient and profitable firms and sold the inefficient and loss-making ones, in the spirit of the *zhuada fangxiao* policy of the center in Beijing. The resultant industrial ownership structure was a highly capital-intensive state sector vis-à-vis a much less capital intensive private sector. In 2009, the average assets of state sector enterprises were 16 times the average for non-state enterprises, up from about three times in 1998 (see Figure 7.1). In other words, within just a decade, the assets of the state sector expanded more than five times relative to non-state sector.

Since the mid-1990s the reforms have achieved considerable success in some of their key objectives. Above all, they have improved the profitability and efficiency of the SOEs. By downsizing the employment of the whole sector and beefing up the capital outlays of average individual enterprises, they have strengthened the financial position of the remaining SOEs. As indicated in Figure 7.2, within ten years, the total output of the remaining SOEs increased more than

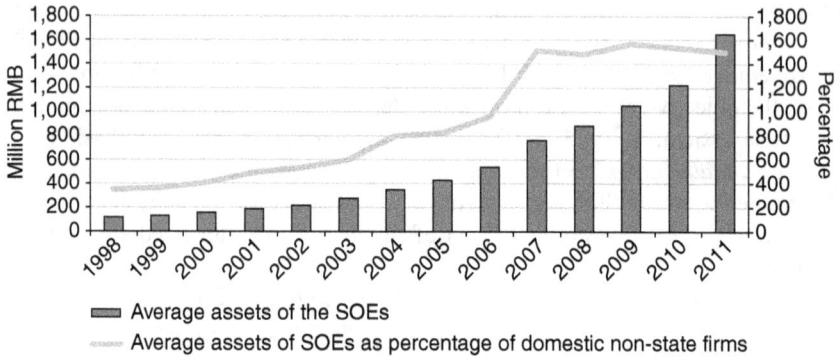

Figure 7.1 The average assets of the SOEs (source: China National Bureau of Statistics 1999–2011, 2012b).

600 percent, when the total national manufacturing output only expanded 250 percent (National Bureau of Statistics 2010: 256–257), whereas the employment has decreased more than half. In addition, there is an immense increase in per-capita productivity as indicated in Figure 7.2.

There have also been significant structural changes in the overall macro-management system. In the late 1990s, almost all the industrial ministries (except the Ministry of Railways) were either abolished or corporatized into ministerial-ranking SOEs. Both centrally and locally managed SOEs became autonomous corporate actors, at least on paper.

In 2003 a new macro-architecture was finally in place. In that year, all remaining SOEs were placed under the supervision of either central or local (provincial, municipal and county) branches of the State-owned Assets Supervision and Administration Commission (SASAC), a newly created agency under

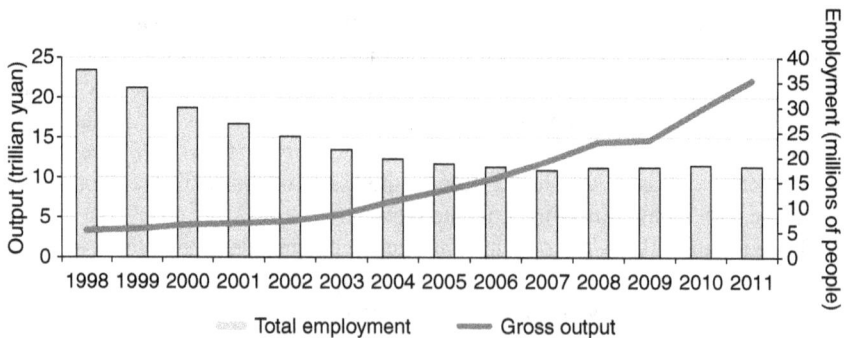

Figure 7.2 Gross output and total employment of the SOEs (source: China National Bureau of Statistics 1999–2011, 2012b).

the State Council. The centrally managed SOEs (central SOEs) were defined as enterprises under the direct supervision of the central SASAC in Beijing. There are both political-administrative and economic dimensions in their identity. In political-administrative terms, they are owned by all people and politically managed by the Party. At least equivalent to the municipality in administrative rankings, some of these enterprises were corporatized from industrial ministries. In an economic sense, they are the largest and most dominant enterprises in the economy, with huge resources and monopoly positions in their respective sectors. As shown in Figure 7.3, total profits of central SOEs have been constantly higher than local SOEs in the past decade.

The rise of central SOEs also arose from a weak state regulatory framework. Compared with the large enterprises under its nominal jurisdiction, the SASAC system is a much weaker bureaucratic system of supervision and administration. Although it has a very large nominal jurisdiction, it lacked the political authority and administrative resources to exert significant influence over rich and powerful large SOEs. The former head of the SASAC, Wang Yong, for instance, was not even an alternate member of the Chinese Communist Party Central Committee upon his initial appointment, with the consequence that his political and administrative ranks were even lower than that of the Party-appointed bosses of several of the largest SOEs.

The SASAC is often characterized as a weak regulator, but on the other hand, it is a successful promoter, when its interests in "keeping state assets steadily growing" neatly coincide with the central SOEs' drive for investment and expansion. Not only are the central SOEs the greatest profit-makers, they are also consistently the largest enterprises in terms of sales revenues, total assets, value-added and almost in all other quantitative indicators.[1] Measured in net assets, China's most powerful SOEs have consolidated their position on the Fortune 500 list of the largest global corporations in 2011, pushing the number

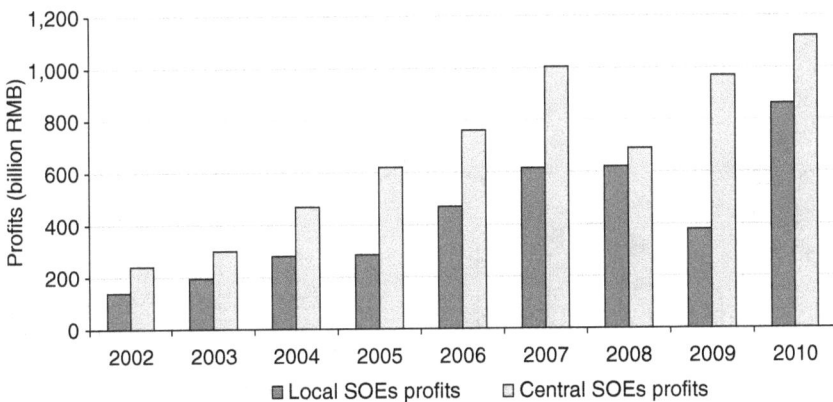

Figure 7.3 Profits of centrally managed and locally managed SOEs (source: SASAC 2009: 194, 2011a).

of Chinese firms on the list to an unprecedented 61.[2] Most of these giant SOEs, not surprisingly, are centrally managed monopolies in the most profitable and strategic state-dominated sectors such as banking, energy, electricity and insurance. Sinopec, China National Petroleum Corporation (CNPC) and State Grid, the three largest centrally managed SOEs, are ranked among the top ten largest enterprises in the world.

The centrally managed SOEs in the financial crisis

The expansion of centrally managed SOEs had become evident long before the global financial crisis. Since 2003, both the profits and gross assets of the centrally managed SOEs have increased fivefold (Figure 7.4). This was during a period when the GDP rose only by 200 percent and the total assets for all manufacturing enterprises increased by only 400 percent. In 2013, the 115 centrally managed SOEs routinely took more than one-third and the ten top profit-makers within this group more than a quarter of all profits made by the country's 400,000–450,000 above-scale manufacturing enterprises (revenues from main business above the scale of RMB20 million).

While other enterprises regard the global financial crisis as a great woe, China's centrally managed SOEs must have seen it as a great opportunity in retrospect. Although their profit did experience a temporary sharp dip in 2008, their relentless assets accumulation continued unabated. Under China's new economic system, central SOEs as an economic arm of state power have an inbuilt obligation to implement the key macroeconomic objectives of the central government, in particular, economic growth and structural adjustment.

Although 2009 was the big year of large investment projects funded by the RMB4 trillion rescue package, the central SOEs were in fact not the leading actors in the investment spree. In 2009, their gross investment only increased 15 percent, far below the 30 percent increase at the national level. Furthermore, 61 percent of these investments were funded by their own profits rather than bank loans (SASAC 2011b: 7). Rather, the central SOEs expanded structurally. The

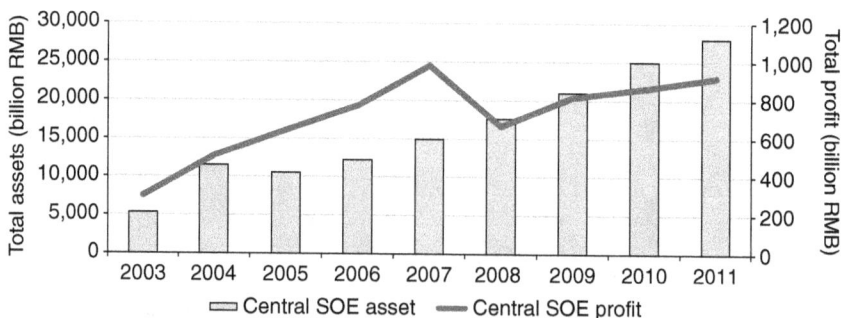

Figure 7.4 Performance of centrally managed SOEs (source: SASAC 2009, 2011a, 2012; National Bureau of Statistics 2004–2011, 2012a).

crisis helped the central SOEs in two ways. First, the central SOEs strengthened their relative positions vis-à-vis other players facing an immediate worsening of financial and economic conditions in the immediate aftermath of the crisis. Second, the financial position of central SOE were further strengthened since the Chinese government was forced to pursue a painful policy of credit squeeze to quench inflation as a result of its loose credit policy in the preceding two years. In both cases, the small- and medium-sized enterprises were the major casualty, followed by smaller state firms and even the financial positions of local governments. The central SOEs had managed to take full advantage of their strong financial position ensured by monopoly over key sectors.

While almost all large central SOEs have tightened their grip on their respective markets and explored new territories outside their main businesses, the most telling example is perhaps State Grid. According to an investigative article by the *Business Watch Magazine*, the general manager of State Grid, Liu Zhenya, who had a vision of building a Chinese Siemens, has sped up the corporation's forceful expansion into control manufacturing of power transmission and distribution machinery, small hydropower stations and even wind power (Wang 2011: 35). In particular, State Grid was able to push forward, despite protests from the China Machinery Industry Federation, the take-over of Xuji Group and Gaoping Group, two leading electrical manufacturers, after they suffered large losses when the crisis broke out in late 2008 (Fan 2011). En route to achieving a grand monopoly, State Grid adopted a range of aggressive practices to ensure its control and profits, including barring external wind generators access to its grid, procrastinating further reforms to separate transmission and distribution, and conducting strong price bargaining with the major five power plants to achieve a handsome profit. This practice inadvertently caused a severe power shortage. (*Guangming Daily* 2009). Meanwhile, the core system of the electrical grid is undergoing a rapid ultra-high voltage transmission, in preparation for a planned nationally integrated smart power grid, a visionary idea for the next generation power grid that only came out five years ago.

In every aspect, State Grid, now ranked seventh in Fortune Global 500, is rapidly reshaping the whole power sector. In a high-profile display of the political might of State Grid, *Business Watch Magazine* was banned from circulation for a month for its alleged "false report," but there was no further statement detailing which part of the report was indeed flawed until the magazine itself was discontinued in May 2011. But political clout and market monopoly was no guarantee of good economic performance. Although the State Grid was able to secure 42 percent of the profits and 65 percent of the sale revenues of the whole sector (including State Grid, Southern Grid and all the power plants), the return of capital was only 2 percent, a low achievement even among the central SOEs (ABOUND 2011: 2–3).

If State Grid had directed its expansionary strategy at a system centering on its own turf, some other larger central SOEs have explicitly crossed over to naked profit maximizations. The best example is the central SOEs expansion in the real estate sector in the past two years, which saw the most rapid increases in revenues and profits of all major sectors. It was reported in 2010, for instance, that seven of the ten most expensive land lease deeds were made between the centrally managed SOEs and the local government. The news came at a time when the central government and the media were seriously concerned about rising land and property bubbles, which have caused many severe economic and social issues (*China Youth Daily* 2010).

The coal-mining sector was another field where central SOEs crushed their private rivals in a series of high-profile mergers and integrations.[3] In the steel sector, the state has consolidated its control on the larger manufacturers and recovered some formerly privately owned steel mills. In the coal sector, the state revoked the permits previously issued to private individuals and firms operating in hundreds of small coal mines in an effort to "rationalize" the sector through renationalization. Spearheading this de facto nationalization were China's largest central and provincial SOEs in the coal sector, such as the Shenhua Group. Similarly, in Inner Mongolia, coal-sector restructuring had precluded private investors and the redistribution of the mines went to about 20 large SOEs, led by Shenhua and Huadian International (*Shanghai Security Daily* 2010).

Now it has become clear that China has seen the rise of a new SOE paradigm which is decidedly different from the old SOEs during the planning period as well as in early reforms. As a new type of economic organization, the new SOE paradigm carries much less social responsibility, but no less political and economic weight. More importantly, the new SOEs are distinguished from the old SOEs by a very high degree of autonomy from both the economic force of the market and the fiscal and administrative control of the central government. In this sense, they no longer represent even a vague sense of national interests, but rather their own corporate interests. This arises partly from a relationship of autonomy and interdependence which the new SOEs have developed with the other significant economic interests within the state.

The rise of new SOEs presented a significant challenge to the leadership in China. Since the second half of 2009, centrally managed SOEs were subjected to severe media criticism. In the opinions of some liberal economists and observers, the SOEs were criticized as de facto non-state owned in the sense of being controlled by a bureaucratic capitalist class.[4] Recently, a number of SOE-related policy directives have been released as a symbolic gesture to rein in the central SOEs, but no concrete reform has so far been forcefully carried out. As this chapter will discuss further, a more systemic approach, either through tightened regulatory or legal frameworks, may also suffer major shortcomings. More specifically, there seems to be a lack of policy enforcement power on the part of regulatory and legal authorities, vis-à-vis the politically vocal large SOEs.

Centrally managed SOEs and the state

The rise of new SOEs was part and parcel of perhaps the most profound structural change in China's political economy, that of a resurgent state in the economic life of China. In many ways, this is the consequence of Zhu Rongji's mid-1990s reforms, albeit an unintended one. Indeed, what makes the new state economy different to the Communist economic system since mid-1950s is the fact that, despite a grand design to make it an efficient growth-promoting and centrally coordinated system that complements and supports the market by the reformers, as in the case of the developmental state of East Asian newly industrialized economies, the outcome is a system that is only efficient in a narrow sense and far from well coordinated from the Centre, in spite of its many growth-promoting features.

As Figure 7.5 illustrates, a striking development since 1998 has been the rise of non-regular and non-budgetary fiscal base, chiefly the after-tax profits of the SOEs and land transfer receipts of the local government. As the centrally managed SOEs routinely take 60–70 percent of the profits of all SOEs, they are the dominant actors in control of the first non-budgetary fiscal base. For the second non-budgetary fiscal base, the revenues of land sales, the major vice-provincial and municipal-level cities in coastal areas and the four directly controlled municipalities took the lion's share. Together, these two independent sources of revenues reached 12 percent of the GDP and 35 percent of the gross government revenues in 2011 (Figure 7.5).

The rise of autonomous fiscal bases for the SOEs and powerful local governments beg a reconsideration of the role of state in China's economy. The conventional wisdom, of referring the economic powers of the state to its tax and administrative revenues, tends to ignore the fact that the expansionary process involves multiple autonomous state actors and far exceeds the rise in government budgetary revenues. As Figure 7.5 shows, the size of the gross government revenue (including regular government revenue, land transfer receipts and after-tax profits of the SOEs) is approximately one third of the whole economy

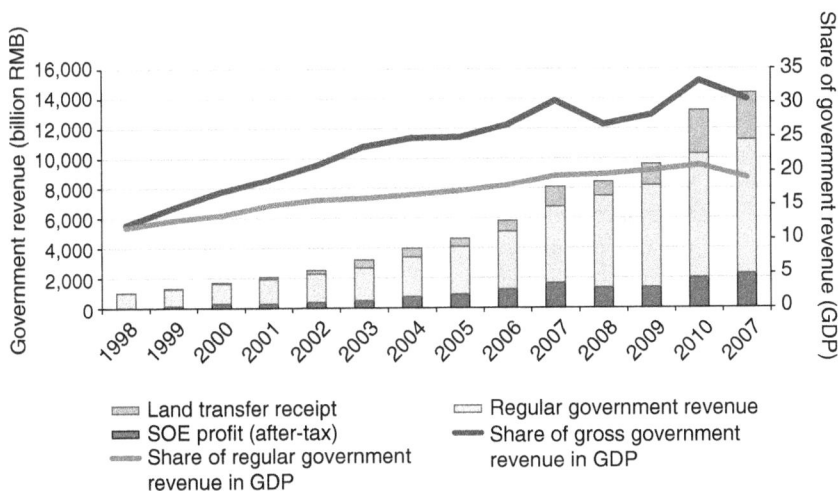

Figure 7.5 Structure and share of government revenue (source: China National Bureau of Statistics 1999–2011, 2012a).

in recent years. The rate of increase of non-budgetary state revenue has well exceeded that of government revenue.

The expansion of centrally managed SOEs is both the outcome of and an important driver for this decade-long state expansion. Since the SOEs started to make profit in 1998, the one-way dependency of the 1990s, where the loss-making SOEs depend on government bail-out, has been reversed. Since the early 2000s, it is now the government counting on the centrally managed SOEs for the most stable and secure source of tax revenue. In 2010, for example, all SOEs accounted for 31 percent of the total tax revenue and centrally managed SOEs alone contributed 19 percent. The continuously rising tax revenues from the centrally managed SOEs add new force to the fiscal bonds binding central SOEs and central government. Under the existing tax-sharing system the central government claims all corporate taxes and about 75 percent of value-added taxes of central SOEs, and tax revenues from these SOEs routinely account for 30 percent of central government revenue.[5] This mechanism, which links the performance of centrally managed SOEs directly to the state coffers, provides strong incentive for the central state to control the SOEs in whatever ways fiscally optimal. Ironically, the current practice of minimum state control and lax regulatory framework for the autonomous monopolies and oligopolies serves the state coffers best, as taxes from the SOEs have continued to outstrip other important tax bases in the last decade. This is a classic case of the recurrent pattern in China, where the closest bond of fiscal interests of the central authority leads to the highest degree of autonomy.

The central SOEs also appear to have played a dominant role in their interactions with local governments. Compared with central government and centrally managed SOEs, local governments have relatively strained budgets and arguably the highest incentive for economic growth. Under this prevailing incentive structure, the centrally managed SOEs have played the game to their advantages by making use of their political autonomy and economic monopoly.

In recent years, the number of cooperative projects involving centrally managed SOEs and local government (*yangdi hezuo*) has been on the rise. Just like courting Hong Kong and Taiwan companies in the 1990s and large foreign enterprises in the early 2000s, it is now the centrally managed SOEs awash with cash that are heatedly courted by local governments to play the role of lead investors. A cooperation contract in this category often involves local government offering cheap land, infrastructure and, sometimes, loosening of environmental standards. Centrally managed SOEs have been more successful than foreign enterprises in securing local markets at low entrance cost and almost zero political risk (*Twenty-First Century Economic Review* 2009).

Until now, the most active recipients of investment from centrally managed SOEs were initially provinces in central China, regions that are placed in middle range in terms of economic size, including Anhui, Henan, Hunan, Jiangxi, Liaoning, Hubei and Chongqing. But since late 2008, developed economies like Guangdong, Zhejiang, Shandong and Jiangsu have also joined the race. For example, Anhui, one of the most significant recipients of investment from centrally managed SOEs, has concluded 585 investment agreements with centrally managed SOEs with a total value of RMB1.6 trillion by May 2011.[6] At least 20 of these investment projects exceeded US$10 billion. The record set by Anhui was soon broken by Guangdong, which signed RMB2.5 trillion-worth of contracts with 71 central SOEs during the annual session of National People's Congress, when local, central and industrial and other elites of the Party got together in Beijing (Li 2011). As the monopoly profits and potential financial might of the centrally owned SOEs and growth fever of the local governments joined hands, these emergent relationships of structural interdependency will likely emerge as new pattern in China's state economy.

The rise of centrally managed SOEs as powerful players in the economy with strong bonds of interdependence with other state players has produced many unexpected outcomes in recent years. For one thing, the centrally managed SOEs have gained so much autonomy that they were beginning to change the functional division on which the system was based, as some of the most powerful SOEs expanded their subsidiaries in the real-estate sector. From late 2009 to early 2010, when real-estate fever was on the rise, 78 of 122 centrally managed SOEs took part in the fervent expansion (Xinhua News Agency 2010a). Although they were not the main force in the real estate sector, they nevertheless flexed their muscles by producing seven of the ten most expensive land transfer deals. In recent months, it has been reported that some central SOEs are creating their own "internal banks," a move signifying further financial autonomy of the central SOEs as self-sufficient corporate groups in the shape of industrial–financial conglomerates (Japanese Keiretsu). In the foreseeable future, the corporatization and conglomeratization of central SOEs are likely to further delink them from the economic and fiscal control of the central government.

While the SASAC may lack the authority to exercise regular administrative control on the centrally managed SOEs, there are always the central organs of the Chinese Communist Party, which appoints and manages the top managers of the central SOEs. The corporatization of the SOEs has not weakened their links to the Party as has been the case in relation to the state. Instead, in terms of elite representation and circulation, centrally managed SOEs seem to have acquired a new importance, as the Party tends to reward economic performances and recognize actors with autonomous sources of powers. In 2009, 17 alternative members and two full members of the Central Committee came from the central SOEs (Brødsgaard 2012). In recent years, as cadre promotion through the circulation of elites between the center (ministries and departments), local government (provinces and municipalities) and the industrial sector (centrally managed SOEs) gradually became the norm of the nomenklatura, many top managers in the centrally managed SOEs have become regional or national leaders. By the end of August 2011, 43 of China's 263 current provincial Party secretaries, governors and vice governors had SOE background, mostly central SOE affiliations (Gore 2011). Good performance in the central SOEs could well offer an ideal stepping stone to a career in local leadership. In 2010, for instance, the Party promoted Su Shulin, the general manager of Sinopec to govern the province of Fujian, making him the youngest governor in China.

Centrally managed SOEs and the economy

Despite their huge amount of revenues and profits, China's central SOEs, in particular the centrally managed SOEs are often criticized as a major source of resource misallocation, hotbeds of poor corporate governance, and a chief culprit for the widening income gap. While all these criticisms could stand further examination to a certain degree, the solutions are nevertheless not straightforward, as the fundamental problems of the SOEs are inextricably linked to more profound structural problems in the Chinese political economy. The rest of this section will look into these major problems.

Corruption, inefficiency and lack of responsibility

While the economic performance of central as well as local SOEs have improved significantly since 1998, they still lag behind in all other indicators of competitiveness, such as unit job creation, investment efficiency, productivity, and value-added and technological innovation, considering the financial resources they control.[7] Despite the rapid rise in the amount of profits and assets, central SOEs' profit-to-asset ratio has been dismal at best, achieving either negative or slightly positive growth for recent years (*Economic News Daily* 2010b). While some of these inefficiencies might be justified as the cost for the provision of public goods, the lack of competition and poor corporate governance are more likely to have caused poor performance.

According to the recent study by the Unirule Institute of Economics, China's leading private economic think tank, the state sector lags far behind the non-state sector in its overall economic performance as measured in terms of average rate of return on equity (Figure 7.6). Since 2011, nominally, the gap between SOEs and non-SOEs seems quite narrow, but if the full scale of subsidy, including subsidized capital, land and energy, is accounted for, the gap increases to a

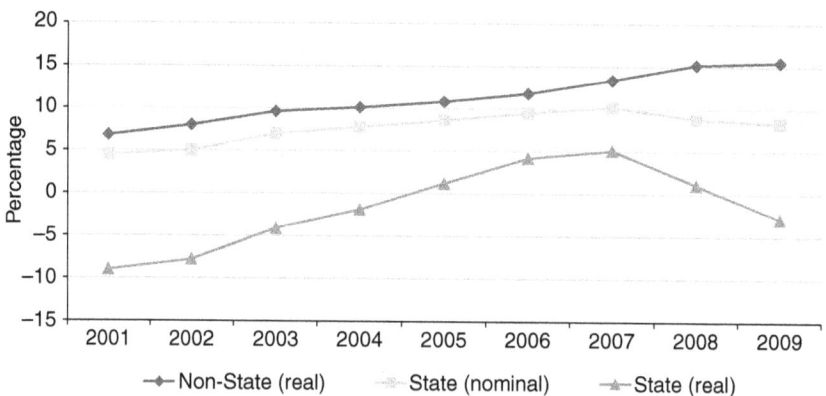

Figure 7.6 The rate of return to equity for state and non-state owned enterprises (source: Sheng and Zhao 2012: 81).

staggering 10–15 percent. The worst year was 2009, when the efficiency gap went back to the pre-2005 level of more than 15 percent. In particular, sectors where centrally managed SOEs dominate were the least efficient and contributed the most towards this efficiency gap (Sheng and Zhao 2012: 79–80). Even though this measuring method might understate the efficiency of the more capital-intensive state sectors vis-à-vis non-state sector, there is no doubt a huge efficiency gap between the two sectors' use of capital.

Besides inefficiency, poor corporate governance and the high incidence of corruption in the state sector have also long attracted much attention from both domestic and overseas analysts. High-profile corruption cases often broke out in the top management of the largest centrally managed SOEs. In 2009 alone, two ministerial-ranking SOEs magnates, Kang Rixin (former CEO of the China Nuclear Corporation) and Chen Tonghai (former CEO of Sinopec), were both arrested for embezzling hundreds of millions in state assets. Another recent investigation into Wuliangye, a leading state-owned wine manufacturer, was carried out by China's Securities Regulatory Commission (SRC), for serious financial misconduct, which led to heavy losses in state assets.[8] In the light of numerous cases of SOE financial fraud in the past few years, this is hardly an isolated case.

Effects on income distribution

Based on a 2008 income survey, the average wage rate in the state sector is 63 percent higher than in the private sector and 17 percent higher than national average wage rate, including government organizations and public service providing institutions (public education and health care sector) (Sheng and Zhao 2012: 101–102). A province-wide survey by Zhejiang Statistical Bureau in 2009 found that the two sectors dominated by central SOEs—energy and telecommunication— were among the top earners across all sectors, with a wage income about 200 percent higher than average wages in the private sector and for workers in manufacture in general (Figure 7.7). Since real income levels and welfare provisions for employees of the SOEs far exceed published salary, the actual income gaps between employees of the SOEs in the monopoly sectors and those in other enterprises and sectors are likely to be even larger than reflected by these published formal studies (Ren and Zhou 2005: 27–28).

A more worrying development is the fast increasing hidden income, better known as gray income, which does not appear on state statistical surveys on income. Two studies by a team of researchers led by Wang Xiaolu, a leading specialist in the study of China's income distribution, listed SOE monopoly as one of the top five factors contributing to China's dangerously high level of income inequality through a myriad of "gray" sources, such as housing subsidy and miscellaneous welfare benefits (Wang 2010: 75–76). In 2007, observers were alerted to the striking fact that Sinopec and CNPC, the two largest state-owned oil companies, alone garnered and retained a total profit of RMB100 billion, almost five times the amount China spent in minimum livelihood supports for both rural and urban areas, which was just over RMB20 billion (*Southern Daily* 2011).

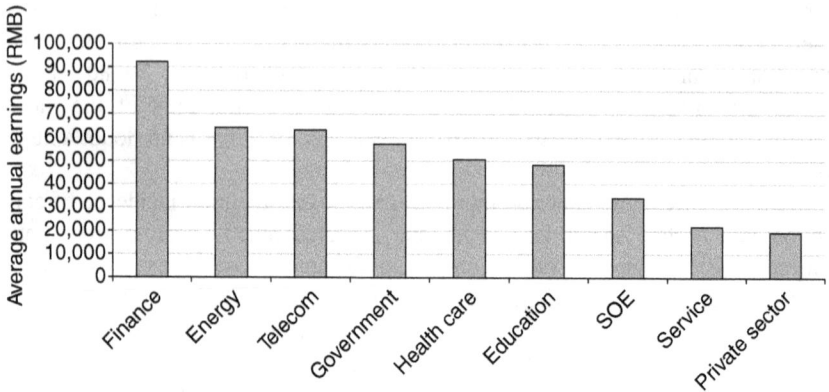

Figure 7.7 Inter-sectoral wage differentials (source: Zhejiang Statistical Bureau 2009).

The State Council has long urged the SOEs to turn in part of their profits as national social security contribution. In 2007, the State Council ordered the centrally managed SOEs to turn in a minimum 5 percent of their profits to the Ministry of Finance to contribute to China's social security fund. But in the last three out of four years, the SOEs failed to meet even the 5 percent minimum requirement as a simple token of their social responsibility. Except for the year 2009, the profits turned in on average only accounted for 2 percent of the total profits of the central SOEs. Since even the minimum was often not met, it is doubtful that the SOEs would turn in 15 percent of their profits to meet the State Council's requirement from 2012 onwards.

The distributional consequence of the SOEs has a critical political dimension. As economists from the Unirule Institute of Economics rightly argued, since SOEs are nominally state-owned entities, they should contribute to the welfare of *all* the people, instead of distributing the after-tax profits internally, in the form of high welfare payment and other non-monetary returns to its own management and employees (Sheng and Zhao 2012: 95–107). Unless the government find some mechanisms to redistribute the after-tax profits of SOEs to society, the SOEs are bound to suffer more critical criticisms on social and political grounds.

Price distortions

Monopoly pricing behavior by the centrally owned SOEs has been a particular concern over the last few years. Some centrally managed SOEs, as sole suppliers of energy and transportation services, were frequently reported as exploiting their monopoly position by marking-up the prices of key products. Sinopec and CNPC, for example, reportedly decreased the supply of natural gas supplies when there was a seasonal hike in the demand for heating during the winter months from 2007 to 2010. It was widely regarded as a means to ask for a higher fixed price, or policy support from the state in the form of more price subsidies administered by the National Development and Reform Commission (NDRC) (*Economic Observer Daily* 2010).

Similarly irregular and monopolistic pricing behaviors were also widely observed across the state-owned telecommunication sector, when China Netcom and China Telecom priced internet broadband to over 300 percent its operation costs.[9] According to the initial result of a joint study on mobile communication and Chinese society, the average Chinese spent 5.4 percent of their income on mobile telecommunication and for those who earn less than RMB10,000; the share is as high as 10.3 percent, whereas the similar estimated share in developed countries is about 1–2 percent (*Qujing Daily* 2011). The underlying implication is that the price of necessities provided by the central SOEs act likes a regressive indirect tax. Although price hikes for monopoly enterprises usually go through public hearings, most of the hearings have only been a matter of formality.

Dilemma of further SOEs reforms

Amidst many criticisms leveled against the SOEs, in particular the centrally managed large SOEs, the central government's response was lukewarm at best. On the one hand, the government clearly realizes the critical nature of the problems and has repeatedly reaffirmed the commitment to future reform. A recent State Council policy directive argued for more policy support for the largely privately owned small- and medium-sized enterprises. The new policies include, among others, more equal access to bank loans and opening of more sectors previously dominated by the SOEs to domestic private capital.[10] But there is little sign of a systemic reform, which entails an overhaul of the whole system. Observers and critics put forward three approaches, namely the regulatory approach, economic approach and the legislative approach.

The regulatory approach aims to strengthen the current regulatory and supervisory systems. This will require the current supervisory body, the SASAC, to exercise tight control and carry out necessary reforms of the SOEs. But the SASAC in its current design appears more likely to be an obstacle rather than vehicle for further SOE reform. It is noticeable that while the NDRC and other ministries are becoming more concerned with the problems associated with the centrally-managed SOEs, the governing body itself seems reluctant to lay more blame on its supervisees. Recent five-year reviews of SASAC consistently stressed its achievement in increasing the assets it administered from RMB7.3 to 21 trillion, while hardly addressing any critical issues like income inequality and excessive SOE involvements in the real estate markets (SASAC 2011b: 26).

In fostering the growth of state assets, the SASAC has established a symbiotic relationship with all the SOEs and tapped many political benefits from its swelling size and apparent prosperity. Although aggressive expansion of SOEs has attracted many criticisms in the last decade, the SASAC tend to strongly defend the internal governance practice of SOEs instead of chastising them for malpractice and mismanagement. For instance, in response to the criticism on super-high bonuses for central SOE management based on their monopolistic profits, Li Rongrong, former head of the SASAC, claimed in a speech in August 2009 that he would "feel sorry for not awarding them (top management of centrally managed SOEs) appropriate bonuses given such spectacular surges in SOE profits" (*Guangdong Daily* 2009).

With the erosion of regulatory controls, large central SOEs have largely spun out of the orbit of the government's macroeconomic management. In the past two years the feeble control of the central government of the centrally managed SOEs was vividly demonstrated by the failure to control the involvement of these expansionary SOEs in the real-estate sector. In view of rising real-estate bubbles, the SASAC ordered 78 centrally managed SOEs whose principal business was not real estate to withdraw their investment in real estate by March 2010 (*Economic News Daily* 2010a). But as late as in early December 2010, it was reported that only seven out of the 78 centrally managed SOEs had actually divested their subsidiary real-estate business. In view of the ineffective orders, the government has lately ordered state banking to refuse lending to the real-estate businesses under these SOEs. But this policy is unlikely to constrain the SOEs as well, since most centrally managed SOEs could simply fund the real-estate investment out of their own profits (Xinhua News Agency 2010b).

While the regulatory approach towards the SOEs may not be very effective, since the central managing authority might easily turn from regulator to the protector of vested interests, the legislative approach towards monopoly and corporate governance are not much better. Even before China enacted a very inclusive anti-trust law in June 2007, scholars in the West had cast serious doubts on the applicability of the proposed anti-trust laws to China's larger SOEs (Owen 2009: 37–38). Since then, there have been so few successful cases that few legal scholars judged it an enforceable legal tool to tame the large centrally managed SOEs. A legal scholar has also pointed out other fatal weakness in its application of laws, in terms of the murkily defined state interests, lack of enforcement mechanisms and strong legislative backings (Huo 2011: 60).

Although the law was supposed to regulate monopolistic practices for both domestic and foreign firms, it has been rarely applied to the state monopolies. The first high-profile case came in May 2009, when the Ministry of Commerce (MoC) warned China Unicom and China Netcom of breaching the Anti-Trust Law in their planned merger (*Economic Observer Daily* 2009). However, a closer look at the issue would suggest that this was the exception rather than the rule. And even for this specific case where the MoC dared to stand out, the SASAC promptly stepped in to exonerate the two telecom giants under its aegis, arguing that merging and restructuring of state assets were not under the jurisdiction of the Anti-Trust Bureau of the MoC. Therefore, there is very little space for a legal approach to SOEs regulation, especially for the largest centrally managed SOEs as their CEOs are often concurrently high party officials who are not directly subject to the rule of law.

Another, more radical, approach, as proposed by some liberals, is to make SOEs accountable to the central and local National People's Congress (NPC), China's nominal legislative body, just like the government and the judicial establishment. For example, the Unirule Institute proposed to set up a "State Asset Governance Committee" under the NPC to supervise and administer the SOEs. It is hoped that by transferring the authority of state assets from governments to the NPC, SOE management will be more accountable to the people (Sheng and Zhao 2012: 224–230). This legislative approach is even more far-fetched and impractical than the legal approach, as it requires fundamental changes in the political system.

Any political moves against the vested interests of SOEs certainly run against strong political resistance. Ultimately, the central SOEs are the cream of the economic system that embodies "public ownership" and represents "advanced productive powers" in the "Three Represents," written in both the State and Party Constitutions. As in many previous cases, recent policy directives that suggest moves against SOEs have largely remained on paper. This has to do with the remarkable political power and influence of central SOE management. According to the Unirule research report, 31 percent of ministers and vice-ministers under the State Council have working experiences in the SOEs (Sheng and Zhao 2012: 182–183). Furthermore, CEOs of top SOEs usually hold important political offices in the CCP Central Committee as high-ranking Party officials. The political capitals of large SOEs are a formidable hurdle for any reform of the SOEs.

Conclusion

As an important institutional phenomenon in China's state-led development, the phenomenal yet problematic rise of SOEs after the outbreak of the Global Financial Crisis underlines a serious conundrum faced by the Chinese development model in general. The state, which enlisted the SOEs as its top economic agents, has become reliant on the SOEs while exercising little effective control over them, in particular, concerning the state's share in the monopoly profits. This is an interesting development, since it was the loss-making large SOEs who turned to the state for protection only slightly more than a decade ago.

While the impact of an aggressive state sector on economic growth prospects still remains debatable, the quality of such growth is certainly worrying. It requires much political determination as well as institutional innovation to resolve the issue in a systematic way. In this respect, even the most comprehensive policy directive aimed at increasing the private capital in sectors previously dominated by the state requires new political dynamics to be realized. Unfortunately, the financial crisis, which could have provided an opportunity for generating such a dynamics, proves to have produced exactly the opposite effect. As for now, the SOE reform seems to be in a stalemate. It is unlikely there will be any significant breakthrough in reform unless the regime manages to push through a clear division between the Party-state apparatus and the operation and management of the central SOEs, thereby keeping the vested interests of Party-business relations in check.

Notes

1 The number of centrally managed SOEs has been constantly decreasing over time. There used to be over 190 such SOEs in 2003 when SASAC was set up; currently (2013) there are only 115 of them left. See SASAC Five-Year Review, available online at www.SASAC.gov.cn, for a summary of their overall performance.

2 In 2011, of the 61 Chinese firms from mainland China and Hong Kong on the Global Fortune 500 list, there are 54 centrally managed SOEs, one locally managed SOE, two private enterprises based in mainland China and four private enterprises based in Hong Kong. The detailed list is available online at: http://money.cnn.com/magazines/fortune/fortune500/2011/full_list/.

3 For a full review of the debate on expansion of the state sector, see *Southern Weekly* (2009).

4 There are hundreds of articles on this topic. The representative articles include: Wu (2010), Zheng and Huang (2009) and Xu (2009). The most pertinent English paper on the subject is Yang and Jiang (2010).

5 According to a SASAC report (SASAC 2011b), total tax collected from centrally SOEs reached RMB1.4 trillion. This amounted to about 19 percent of the total government tax revenues. Within this 1.4 trillion, more than 1.1 trillion were central taxes, contributing about 35 percent of central government tax revenues.

6 The full report is available online at: http://ah.anhuinews.com/system/2011/09/26/004452339.shtml (accessed January 7, 2014).

7 The *China Statistical Yearbook*s provide much information on the overall average performance.

8 The first news about the scandal was covered by a Shanghai-based newspaper, *Diyi Caijing Ribao* (The First Financial News) on September 24, 2009. But the next report on the progress only comes 20 months later in the same paper, on May 27, 2011. The indictments and punishments appear to be much less than public expectation.

9 Interestingly, this criticism first came from top state media, in the form of a letter from a reader. See *People's Daily* (2010). But in a more interesting episode, China Central Television launched an attack over two state telecom companies' monopoly pricing of broadband internet service through one of its more popular social investigative programs on November 9, 2011. This time, the state telecoms fought back through the state-run ministerial-level China Telecommunication News. Later, the *People's Daily* and Xinhua News Agency joined on the side of China Central Television. It is widely speculated that the criticism came from major state media and its Party boss, the Department of Propaganda's growing dissatisfaction with the China Telecom and China Unicom's monopoly over Internet and the obstacles to its own ambitions. The later had the possible backing of the Ministry of Trade and Information and the SASAC. The state media seemed to have enjoyed the upper hand in the political struggle for now, since China's highest economic regulator, National Development and Reform Commission (NDRC) had filed a case of monopoly pricing against the two state telecom operators. But according to the *First Finance News* (2011), the three sides seemed to have reached an agreement as the two central-owned enterprises admitted their wrongdoings and agreed to lower the internet access price.

10 See "Policy Directives on Further Promoting the Development of the Small and Medium-Sized Enterprises," available online: www.gov.cn/zwgk/2009-09/22/content_1423510.htm.

References

ABOUND (2011) *Daily Economic Analysis*, 3943, June 14.

Brødsgaard, Kjeld Erik (2012) "Politics and Business Group Formation in China: The Party in Control?" *The China Quarterly* 212: 624–648.

China Youth Daily (2010) "Weishenme dongduan yangqi yonguanshi diwang" (Why the Centrally managed SOEs always Play the Lead Bidder in Land Market), *China Youth Daily*, March 15.

Economic News Daily (2010a) "Yangqi chehui de zuihou qixian" (Timetable for Centrally Managed SOEs Withdrawal), *Economic News Daily*, July 13.

Economic News Daily (2010b) "Guanzhu yangqi" (A Special Report on Centrally Managed SOEs), *Economic News Daily*, December 29.

Economic Observer Daily (2009) "Shangwubu guangyuan cheng liantong wangtong hebing bingwei shenbao" (Ministry of Commerce Official Said There Is No Merger Application From Unicom and Netcom), *Economic Observer Daily*, May 1.

Economic Observer Daily (2010), "Qihuang shi longduan de shouduan" (Gas Panic as the Means to Achieve Monopoly Pricing), *Economic Observer Daily*, December 24.

Fan, Ting (2011) "Guojia dianwang longduan kuozhang" (The Expansion of State Grid Monopoly), *Economy & State Weekly* 2(1).

First Financial News (2009) "Wuanliangye zheng jieshou zhengjianhui diaocha" (Wuliangye Under Investigation by SRC), *The First Financial News*, September 24.

First Financial News (2011) "Longduan zhizhan" (The War against Monopolies), *The First Financial News*, November 21, 2011.

Gore, Lance L. P. (2011) "China Recruits Top SOE Executives to the Government," *EAI Background Brief* 661, September 30, Singapore: East Asian Institute.

Guangming Daily (2009) "Guoqi duiyu guojia jingji de juese" (On the Role of SOEs in the National Economy), *Guangming Daily*, August 4.

Holz, Carsten A. (2006) *China's Industrial State-owned Enterprises: Between Profitability and Bankruptcy*, Singapore: World Scientific.

Huo, Zhengxin (2011) "A Tiger without Teeth: The Anti-Trust Law of the People's Republic of China," *Asian Pacific Law & Policy Journal* 10(1): 32–60.

Li Peng (2011) "Difang zhengfu bang yangqi chaoyong" (Local Government Rushing to Embrace Central SOEs), *Economy & Nation Weekly* 2(9): 17–20.

National Bureau of Statistics (1999) *China Statistical Yearbook 1998*, Beijing: China Statistics Press.

National Bureau of Statistics (2000) *China Statistical Yearbook 1999*, Beijing: China Statistics Press.

National Bureau of Statistics (2001) *China Statistical Yearbook 2000*, Beijing: China Statistics Press.

National Bureau of Statistics (2002) *China Statistical Yearbook 2001*, Beijing: China Statistics Press.

National Bureau of Statistics (2003) *China Statistical Yearbook 2002*, Beijing: China Statistics Press.

National Bureau of Statistics (2004) *China Statistical Yearbook 2003*, Beijing: China Statistics Press.

National Bureau of Statistics (2005) *China Statistical Yearbook 2004*, Beijing: China Statistics Press.

National Bureau of Statistics (2006) *China Statistical Yearbook 2005*, Beijing: China Statistics Press.

National Bureau of Statistics (2007) *China Statistical Yearbook 2006*, Beijing: China Statistics Press.

National Bureau of Statistics (2008) *China Statistical Yearbook 2007*, Beijing: China Statistics Press.

National Bureau of Statistics (2009) *China Statistical Yearbook 2008*, Beijing: China Statistics Press.

National Bureau of Statistics (2010) *China Statistical Yearbook 2009*, Beijing: China Statistics Press.

National Bureau of Statistics (2011) *China Statistical Yearbook 2010*, Beijing: China Statistics Press.

National Bureau of Statistics (2012a) *China Fiscal Yearbook 2011*, Beijing: China Statistics Press.

National Bureau of Statistics (2012b) *China Statistical Yearbook 2011*, Beijing: China Statistics Press.

Naughton, Barry (1996) *Growing out of the Plan*, New York, NY: University of Cambridge Press.

Owen, M. Bruce (2005) "Anti-Trust in China: The Problem of Incentive Incompatibility," *SIER Paper 340*, Stanford, CA: Stanford Institute of Economic Research.

People's Daily (2010) "Zenyang gaige guoyou dianxinye" (How to Reform the State Telecom Sector), *People's Daily*, September 21.

Qujing Daily (2011) "Shouji feiyong shuoming pinfu fenhua wenti" (Costs of Mobile Phone Fees Explain China's Income Gap), *Qujing Daily*, January 12.

Ren Zhong and Zhou Yunbo (2005) "Longduan dui woguo hangye nei shouru chaju yingxiang daodi you duoda" (How Much Does Monopoly Influence China's Industrial Income Gap?), *Jingji Lilun yu Guanli* (Journal of Economic Theory and Management) 29(4): 25–30.

SASAC (State-owned Assets Supervision and Administration Commission) (2009) *SASAC Five-Year Review*, December 2009, available online: www.sasac.gov.cn/2009rdzt/yjj/wzn.pdf (accessed June 15, 2011).

SASAC (State-owned Assets Supervision and Administration Commission) (2011a) *SASAC Annual Report for 2010*, available online: www.SASAC.gov.cn (accessed June 15, 2011).

SASAC (State-owned Assets Supervision and Administration Commission) (2011b) *Zhongyang qiye yingdui jingrong weiji baogao* (Report of Centrally SOEs in the Financial Crisis), Beijing: Zhongguo jingji chubanshe.

SASAC (State-owned Assets Supervision and Administration Commission) (2012) *SASAC Annual Report for 2011*, available online: www.SASAC.gov.cn (accessed August 15, 2012).

Shanghai Security Daily (2010) "Huadianguoji quandi Neimengu meitan jinsanjiao" (Huadian International's Land Grab in Inner Mongolia's Gold Triangle of Coal Mines), *Shanghai Security Daily*, September 1.

Sheng, Hong and Zhao, Nong (2012) *China's State-owned Enterprises: Nature, Performance and Reform*, Singapore: World Scientific.

Southern Daily (2011) "Ruhe shi yangqi zhenzheng guoyou" (How to Make Centrally managed SOEs Truly State-owned), *Southern Daily*, January 2.

Southern Weekly (2009) "Guojin mintui: yangqi kuozhang yinfa reyi" (The Advance of State Capital and the Retreat of Private Capital: Debating Boundless Expansion of Centrally Managed SOEs), *Southern Weekly*, August 20.

Twenty-First Century Economic Review (2009) "Bangyangqi jiangyifa guozi xinbuju" (Local Dependency on Central SOEs Inducing a Change in the Distribution of State Capital), December 7.

Wang Qiang (2011) "Guowang diguo" (The Empire of the State Grid), *Shangwu Zhoukan* (Business Watch Magazine), 11(3): 31–37.

Wang, Xiaolu (2010) *Grey Income and Income Inequality in China*, Beijing: National Economic Research Institute of China Reform Foundation.

Walder, Andrew (1988) *Communist Neo-Traditionalism: Work and Authority in Chinese Industry*, Berkeley, CA: University of California Press.

Wu Jinglian (2010) "Tiaozhan quangui zibenzhuyi: Zhongguo gaige jinru shenhuichu" (China's Reform into Deep Waters: Challenging Crony Capitalism), *Green Leaves* 21(1/2): 90–95.

Xinhua News Agency (2010a) "Yangqi tuishu fangdichan zhimi" (The Myth of Central SOEs Exit from Real Estate), March 25.

Xinhua News Agency (2010b) "Yangqi tuichu fangdichan meiyou zuihou qixian" (No Deadline for Centrally Managed SOEs' Real Estate Business), December 6.

Xu Xiaonian (2010) "Guojin mintui beili gaige fangxiang" (The Advance of State and the Retreat of Private Capital Derails the Economic Reform), *Shang Zhoukan* (Business Weekly) 8(22): 22–23.

Yang Dali and Jiang Yunyan (2010) "*Guojin Mintui:* The Great Recession and Changing State-Economy Relations in China," conference paper presented at the International Conference China and the Great Recession: The Global Financial Crisis and China's Development, Beijing, July 31.

Zhejiang Statistical Bureau (2009) Inter-sector Income Disparity Survey 2009, available at www.zj.stats.gov.cn (accessed July 15, 2011).

Zheng Yongnian and Huang Yanjie (2009) "Zhongguo guojiazhuyi jingji moshi hechuqu" (Whither China's Statist Economic Model), *China Entrepreneurs* 8: 16–19.

8 Creating corporate groups to strengthen China's state owned enterprises

Jean C. Oi and Zhang Xiaowen

Introduction

China stands out among the former socialist planned economies as taking the gradual, less risky political road of reform that eschewed full privatization of its state owned enterprises (SOEs). Some dismissed China's piecemeal reforms as a recipe for failure (Sachs and Woo 1997; Steinfeld 1998; Woo 1999), others noted problems of corruption (Manion 2004; Wedeman 2004; Ding 2000). Accompanying high rates of non-performing loans and an ever-troubled banking sector only added to the pessimistic forecasts.

Yet, surprisingly, even though the process was slow, by the mid-2000s, a new day seemingly dawned for China's SOEs. Not all problems have been solved, but economists agree that China managed a turnaround in its SOEs (*China Economic Quarterly* 2008; Naughton 2008). Many of the worst performing SOEs have either been closed or sold. China culled thousands of firms from its SOE ranks. Overall, after 30-plus years of reform and restructuring, deep change has occurred in the state economy.

As Table 8.1 shows, from 1978 to 2008, the number of SOEs declined by 33.13 percent; the total number of workers decreased by 23.8 percent; total state assets increased 59 fold; SOE income increased 35 fold; realized profits

Table 8.1 Thirty years of change in SOEs

	Firms (number)	Workers (million)	Core revenue (billion)	Total assets (billion)	Total profits (billion)
1978	170,087	46.362	662.92	723.39	66.54
1983	269,552	56.274	983.34	1,005.67	54.03
1988	231,818	61.650	1,792.49	2,103.52	80.55
1993	190,780	66.138	4,300.27	5,380.23	114.20
1998	238,152	65.652	6,468.51	14,865.00	21.37
2003	149,988	43.112	10,733.97	19,710.33	495.12
2008	113,731	35.307	22,936.35	42,547.28	1,330.74

Sources: 2008 figures are from *Zhongguo guoyou zichan jiandu guanli nianjian* (2009). The remaining figures are from SASAC's website: www.sasac.gov.cn/n1180/n4175042/n5405123/index.html.

increased 20 fold. Improvements are most evident in the biggest and most important state owned enterprises—those under central control—have reported large increases in production, profits, and taxes paid to the state (SASAC 2006; Naughton 2008). Moreover, and perhaps most important, rather than declining in importance, the remaining SOEs have become more dominant and have grown in size with the formation of corporate groups (*jituan*). The decline in the number of SOEs masks an advance, not retreat, of the state in certain sectors of the economy.

To understand the nature of China's current SOEs, both their strengths and their weaknesses, we look back at the restructuring process itself. It is especially important to understand how and why the corporate groups were created. China is now actively trying to grow the scale of firms to create internationally competitive national champions, but the origins of these complex corporate groups can be found in the political and economic logic of the restructuring process.

Reducing the number but growing the size of SOEs

The number of SOEs at all levels has been cut drastically and continues to decline. The state has shed large numbers of its firms. However, there are other cases where large numbers of SOEs are subsumed under massive industrial entities organized as corporate groups, which are then counted as one enterprise. The *jituan*, which is sometimes called a holding company, is considered the parent company and a wholly state-owned enterprise. Under the holding company, there are individual firms, which are called second level companies. These are likely to have been independent companies before the consolidation. They are sometimes also wholly state-owned, but other times only state controlled, meaning that the state has a controlling share holding in the company. Under these second level companies are third level companies that are subsidiaries of the second level companies. Within some of these third level companies the state may have shares, but not controlling shares.

The dominance of the corporate groups reflects an aspect of China's corporate restructuring that is sometimes missed by those who only focus on the decrease in the number of SOEs. While the state has reduced the number of SOEs, it also has tried to increase the strength and size of its remaining SOEs. The State-owned Assets Supervision and Administration Commission (SASAC) of the State Council was created in 2003 to represent the state as the investor of state-owned assets in advancing reform and reorganization. The most important goals of this state asset supervisory and management agency are to: (1) protect and increase state assets; (2) to increase and strengthen SOEs to bring into play their power, influence, and ability to lead; and (3) foster the international competitiveness of large enterprises and corporate groups. But the emergence of corporate groups took place long before the creation of SASAC. As we shall show below, SASAC must deal with firms and groupings that have roots in China's gradual and politically constrained system of restructuring.

Roots of China's corporate group system

In the Former Soviet Bloc countries, corporate restructuring is commonly associated with privatization, which was the most common form of property rights reform. Privatization is usually understood as one-step restructuring that changes property rights. The assumption is that ownership of the means of production immediately changes directly from state to private hands. SOEs are presumed to become fully privately owned as a result of restructuring. In contrast, China's corporate restructuring has been a multi-step process.[1] Earlier studies have documented how forms of restructuring changed over time and varied by region and firm. What we want to stress in this work is that, in the end, in spite of reform and restructuring, many of the most important restructured firms remain state owned or state controlled. As we suggested above, the decrease in the number of state-owned firms is deceptive. Over the course of the restructuring process, during each of the different phases of reform, the state consistently put firms together, rather than closing weaker firms, to solve a variety of problems.

1980s–1990s

During the 1980s into the early 1990s, the state attempted to stimulate individual enterprises through management reform. More authority and a larger share of profits were granted to firms while adjusting the financial burdens, rights, and benefits between the state and firms to strengthen the vitality of SOEs, giving them more autonomy to spur initiative. However, it was difficult for the state to completely let go. It is well known that during this stage, SOE reforms were in a halfway state, with the result that relatively few workers lost their jobs and firms stayed mired in red ink. What needs to be stressed is that one way the state managed to keep ailing SOEs open was to have them form alliances with stronger firms.

Beginning in the 1980s, during the early stages of reform, instead of using the new bankruptcy option, there were consecutive pushes for horizontal alliances of firms; in some cases, firms merged, as the state attempted to stay within the original management framework, through adjusting the organization and structure of the enterprise.

During this same period, as part of the drive to streamline government administration, the state reshuffled and allied industrial sectors, to strengthen the degree of specialization and cooperation between industries. In practice, this also pushed firms together as SOEs were reorganized and formed horizontal economic unions (*lianhe*). Initially, these were not formal mergers, but firms working closely together. Eventually, this gave rise to the industrial *jituan*, the form that dominates the state sector today. By the end of 1988, nationally, there were already 1,630 *jituan*.

In some cases the state went a step further to keeping factories open by actually merging firms. These consolidation strategies allowed the state to address the problems of inferior enterprises riddled with deficits but it also allowed the stronger enterprises to become larger. In 1984 some areas, such as Baoding, Hebei and Wuhan, Hubei, took the lead in piloting firm mergers. By 1988, nationally, 2,856 firms took in and merged with 3,424 other firms.

1990s–early 2000s

The late 1990s is the watershed in China's corporate restructuring (Oi 2005; Oi and Han 2011). Nationally, the pattern and speed of reform is markedly different before and after this period. A distinct upward tick occurs, as a whole, in restructuring beginning around 1995 and reaching a peak around 1998. The year 1997 was a crucial turning point. The 15th Party Congress gave the official green light to privatization. The legitimacy of the private sector was reaffirmed and its importance expanded for the development of China's economy (Heilmann 2011; Jung 2011).

But the difference was not just in the speed of restructuring. Significant shifts also occurred in the forms of restructuring adopted, the number of workers laid off, constraints on privatization, and the distribution of shares within restructured firms. During the first part of the 1990s to the early 2000s, SOE reform and restructuring moved beyond management reform to address the need for institutional change and innovation, most importantly property rights reform. With the explicit goal of fixing the entire state economy, China made use of the principle of "advance and retreat," i.e., pulling out of certain areas of the economy but strengthening its role in others. With regard to SOEs this translated into the "grasp the large and let go of the small" strategy.

Much has been made of the "letting go" aspect of this policy where the state sold the smaller SOEs, turning all property rights over to the new, private owners. But "letting go" was only half of the reform strategy. After 1997 more large SOEs were also restructured, but for them the policy was not to have the state let them go, but to hold them. In fact, these firms were held and given special treatment to strengthen them—a more accurate meaning of the term *zhua* is to "grasp," in this case, by the state.

To understand how these larger SOE firms were handled, a distinction needs to be made between privatization and corporatization. When large firms were restructured they were corporatized not privatized. Corporatization meant that the state no longer was the sole owner but simply one of a number of owners.[2] In a corporatized firm, shares are sold to others, some to the workers and managers of the firm, but often the state held a controlling number of shares. In a privatized firm, the state owns no shares. For the large SOEs that the state decided to "grasp," limited changes in property rights were made through the process of corporatization. A firm's assets were assessed and then divided into shares so that it could diversify ownership. The state kept controlling shares but allowed workers and managers to hold shares in shareholding systems.

Much attention has been focused on the state's letting go, i.e., privatization, but it is the state's grasp of those SOEs that it kept that explains the dramatic turnaround we see today. China's two prong, dual-track method for dealing with different types of firms took root in the first phase of restructuring (Oi 2005). Even during the earlier periods, when the government generally moved cautiously, China left room for a select group of strategically important enterprises—the biggest and most important enterprises in various key sectors, those that are now considered the strategic sectors, such as energy, communications, and heavy industry, such as steel mills—to adopt much bolder reforms. For some of these large, important firms, the best portions of their assets were spun off to form a new, financially attractive entity. This new firm could then be listed on the stock market while the parent firm remains a state-owned entity, which is now often called an enterprise group.

China's strategy to spin off a new firm is not unique. In the US, in an effort to restructure ailing firms like GM, a part of the old firm was spun off into a new entity during the global financial crisis. This was the best part of the firm—the portion with the best chances of survival. Similarly, in China, the best assets of a big state firm were spun off to form a new company, which then tried to get listed. But unlike what has happened to GM, where the worse parts were sold off, in China the worse parts remain with the original owner, in China's case the state. The original firm, what can be considered the parent company, still is a state-owned enterprise. China wants and expects the parent company to reform as well, but it is given a much longer timeline to become profitable. The parent company is encouraged to adopt new measures to make it more profitable, but all the while it continues to carry the burden of the old debt, the least productive workers and many of the non-economic costs that have characterized China's SOEs—the *danwei* system. These burdens include the funding of schools, hospitals, and other public goods that would in the US be the responsibility of local government. Even as late as 2008 some SOEs were still responsible for schools and hospitals, which are considered public goods in other countries. This burden is on top of holding debt and having to support the less skilled workers, who also are likely to be stuck with older equipment that was left in the parent firm.[3] These various strategies resulted in a complex property rights mix within one single enterprise group that contains really good as well as really weak firms.

The double-pronged strategy, while not the most economically effective way to reform, allowed China to pursue a dual agenda to improve economic efficiency and move forward with reform while maintaining political stability in some of its most important SOEs in strategic sectors. This strategy reflected the need to create as little dislocation as possible, but at the same time allow substantive reform to occur. For example, for big steel firms, like Wuhan Iron and Steel or Baogang Steel, each with thousands of workers, it was possible to have only a portion of the firm undergo radical change—not all of the company had to be reformed at the same rate, at the same time. In these instances radical reforms could result in new ownership forms appearing within an unreformed SOE.

By distinguishing between firms based on size and importance, reform of SOE property rights achieved some headway during this period. While property rights change was still gradual during this period, based on a five-city survey, we know that the state moved faster to change some types of firms than others.[4] In the 1990s firms that were privatized or declared bankruptcy were limited while adopting shareholding was common.[5] Across the five cities, the data shows that privatization was the last form of restructuring adopted. However, the firms that were privatized were collectively owned enterprises, which tended to be the less important and smaller firms. The survey found that collective firms were more likely to be sold or leased than state-owned firms during the earlier phases of reform. For state-owned firms the most popular form of restructuring was share-holding, which became the most common form of restructuring as China attempted to establish a modern corporate system. By the end of 1996, according to statistics from the State Commission on Reform of the Economic System (*tigaiwai*), 4,300 plus firms were registered as recognized shareholding companies that complied with regulations in the company law, with 356.5 billion yuan of capital.

More importantly for the purpose of this chapter, as part of the "grasping the large" strategy, the state pushed to a new stage the familiar strategy of putting SOEs together. From 1991 to 1997 the state, in two successive batches, selected 163 large *jituan* as experimental points to perfect the *jituan* system and make them more competitive. Some firms that were not part of these experiments were simply merged as a form of restructuring.

These steps were taken in response to goals set in 1997 at the 15th Party Congress to deepen and move to a new phase of SOE reform. The problems of SOEs had already become acute and the situation was grim for different industrial sectors. Textiles, coal, and military works and many other sectors were seriously in the red. Again, the state had to devise strategies to help those firms that it had decided to "grasp." At this point, the state's grasp resulted in taking shares of firms through a system of debt equity swaps, where the state relieved a SOE of its debt but in return the state was given an equivalent amount of equity shares. In 1999 the state approved the debt equity swap reform measure and assumed 405 billion yuan of debt as equity from 580 firms. Moreover, in the three years following 1997, when the state tried to get its SOEs out of difficulties, 126.1 billion of bad loans were canceled. Moreover, mergers again became a common solution to help struggling firms. Nationally, 1,718 approvals were given for firm mergers and bankruptcies.

However, even though significant progress has been made in reforming SOEs, during the late 1990s and into early 2003, because the identity of the state as the investor was still undefined and no clear representative of the state as the shareholder existed, it was difficult to protect state rights and interests. As a result, this period of reform and restructuring saw asset stripping. It was during this time that managers were able to gain increased shares and control over firms. Based on the results of two CASS surveys, we see a significant percentage increase between 2000 and 2004 in managers as controlling shareholders. Whereas in 2000 only a little over 4 percent of the managers were the controlling shareholders, after later restructuring in these same factories, by 2004 more than half of the managers had become new controlling shareholders.[6] Managers holding a controlling share or buying the entire enterprise were the most frequent type of firm restructuring (26.4 percent) according to the 2005 survey.[7]

Interviews in 2005 suggest that in some parts of the country manager buyouts were being instituted in enterprises as soon as the decision to restructure was made, without allowing workers to hold shares, which happened earlier elsewhere during the reforms. Local officials explained that this was necessary because effective corporate governance requires a major hands-on stakeholder to have the necessary incentive to manage the firm effectively (Oi June–July 2005).

Current organization and system of state asset management of SOEs

In 2003 a new system of state asset management was established. SASAC was created to oversee the strategic readjustment and reorganization of SOEs in the national economy. SASAC became an explicit state body that would have "legal person" status to push SOEs forward to reorganize, restructure, and renovate.

The chain of the state asset management includes people's congress, government, and SASAC, which is the authorized agency that represents the government as the state investor and carries out its responsibilities. Set up by the State Council, SASAC is the organization that oversees state assets in SOEs—those that are wholly state owned, those that are state controlled, and those in which the state only has minority shares.

Under the new asset management system state-owned firms are accordingly divided into two major categories—central state owned and local state owned, which means those owned by the provincial, municipal, or county levels. The stated logic of the division of firms is as follows: The central state owned firms are those large firms that are at the core of the national economy and affect security and those involving infrastructure and natural resources (natural monopolies such as water, oil, gas, and coal), public goods and services, and those deemed the pillar industries, and key enterprises within the high-tech sector. This category also includes those industries that supply competitive products such as processing, construction, and trade. In short, the centrally owned SOEs are the best and the most important firms. It is not surprising that many have argued that these are essentially monopolies, and comparatively speaking, they were the better performers. All other firms still under state control are left to local levels.

The responsibility of SASAC included the right to select managers of SOEs. The party organization and the head of the central-level SOEs are usually selected by and appointed by the central organization department; the party organization and head of local SOEs are selected and appointed by the local party organization, and their economic achievements are assessed by the relevant asset management agencies. Protection and growth of state assets are the most important quotas in each review. The term for the leading cadre in each enterprise is usually three years. The firm manager signs a contract with the asset management agency with specified targets. According to this agreement, the asset management agency engages in annual assessments and reviews at the end of each term, and then uses the results as an incentive policy for the managers.

Strategic adjustment to create national champions

The establishment of SASAC quickened the strategic adjustment of the central level SOEs. By the end of 2006, nationally there were 4,251 firms that were allowed to go bankrupt, 8,370,000 people were laid off. Within these, bankruptcy in three key point sectors—coal, non-ferrous metals, and munitions—was basically completed.

More broadly, from 2002–2007 the number of SOEs have decreased almost by 10,000 firms. In 2007 nationally, sales revenues added up to 18 trillion yuan, which represents a 20.1 percent increase over this period. Realized profits were 1.62 trillion yuan, which was a 31.6 percent increase. Taxes paid were up 1.57 trillion yuan, which was a 21.8 percent increase. For the central level SOEs, over this same period, 2002–2007, total assets of central level SOEs reached 14.8 trillion yuan, which is a 20.5 percent increase. In 2007, their realized sales revenue was 9.84 trillion yuan, which is a 19.3 percent increase; while realized profits were 996.85 billion yuan, which is a 30.3 percent increase over this period from 2002; and taxes paid equaled 830 billion yuan, which is a 23.8 percent increase.

In 2003 when SASAC was established, there were 196 companies under its control. But within that year, the number was cut to 189. Table 8.2 shows the continued decrease in the number of firms directly under central control since that time. The stated goal, issued in 2006, was to only have somewhere between 80–100 firms by 2010 (Office of the State Council 2006). So even though this target has yet to be reached the state is working to limit the number of central level SOEs.

As in the overall number of SOEs, the decline in the number of central SOEs should not be understood as the state selling its firms. Some are sold, but again, some are simply being merged into other SOEs to form a larger firm, which is similar to the strategy that we described for the earlier periods of reform. SASAC is carrying out its task of increasing state assets by developing firms that have the ability to dominate market share. The state has been trying to create a batch of outstanding firms—large companies, large corporations, and corporate groups—that have advanced technology, good organization, and nimbleness. The goal is to take between 80–100 of such firms and forge them into 30–50

Table 8.2 Number of centrally controlled state-owned enterprises (unit: individual firms)

Year	2003	2004	2005	2006	2007	2008	2009	2010
No. of firms	189	178	169	159	151	142	129	122

Source: *Zhongguo guoyou zichan jiandu guanli nianjian* (2003–11).

large firms that would have the ability to compete internationally. The corporate group is the vehicle for achieving this. These corporate groups now dominate any sector in which they participate, especially those that the state has identified as "strategic." They are accorded preferential treatment by the state and thus have access to key inputs, especially low-cost credit. Managers of these privileged SOEs firms have come under increasingly strict performance criteria as well as lucrative incentives given for good performance. Apparently, one of the incentives that drive managers is that if they fall behind and are not able to be among the very top performers, their firm may be acquired by a better performing firm. Competition has been injected within these sectors but often it is only other SOEs that are allowed to compete.

While the dominance of the restructured and newly strengthened SOEs may be disappointing to those who thought corporate restructuring would result in marketization of the economy, China's goal in restructuring was never to fully privatize or marketize its industrial sector. Rather, the overarching goal was to unburden the state, most importantly, the central state, of the costs of supporting all SOEs. Ultimately, this meant trying to reduce the burdens of having an "iron rice bowl" economy that kept millions employed, regardless of profits and performance. Political constraints necessitated a go-slow approach that minimized layoffs, but the regime also tried to maximize growth. The solution was to adopt a dual-prong approach to reform. Rid the central state of the burdens of the poor performers, let the market do the culling and growing, but keep the best and the most important firms and focus resources on these firms.

China, as Nolan argued over a decade ago, is intent on creating national champions (Nolan 2001). These are the state firms that dominate today but these were also the firms that from an early stage of restructuring were allowed to do the most radical forms of restructuring even as the reforms overall were still moving at a slower, less disruptive rate. These are among the firms that are under the control of SASAC under the State Council. The best and most profitable among those are controlled by Beijing. This is not to say that all within the centrally controlled SASAC group are star performers. Remaining political problems have prevented the completion of reforms. Some of those under central SASAC control have not been able to be reformed.

Why SOE reform remains incomplete

By 2006 China declared the process of corporate restructuring complete. The majority of SOEs had changed from public to private ownership. The state managed to cull the majority of its SOEs, privatizing many problem firms, but the reform process remains unfinished. A key part of the problem is that the state managed to sidestep the thorniest issues of reform during the earlier phases of corporate restructuring in the 1990s, taking politically easier steps that delayed privatization and minimized layoffs. Because the state was constrained politically and used the strategy of mergers, it built up a system where some weak firms remained under the state umbrella. Some were kept as independent firms, while others were simply given over to stronger state firms. This diversity among firms remains to this day. The consequences of earlier politically expedient steps are coming back to hinder current efforts to push reforms of SOEs to the next stage.

As we have shown earlier, after 1997, when restructuring increasingly took the form of privatization under the slogan "grasp the large and let go of the small," the letting-go policy was intended primarily for small- and medium-sized firms. Even for these smaller firms, when firms were sold, strings were attached. Before a sale was made, the new owners had to agree to either provide an acceptable severance package or keep all the workers for at least a certain amount of time. Only later were the tails removed. For the larger, more important SOEs the state never let go but tried to keep them alive, not always in their original form but often by subsuming them under or merging them with stronger firms.

Shareholding was a useful political tool for moving forward corporate restructuring during the early stages of the process. Diversification of ownership through shareholding changed the state's role and responsibilities with regard to SOEs—the state went from being the sole proprietor to being simply one of many investors in SOEs. The process of corporatization allowed for a clarification of state assets as well as property rights. Even though the state often still held a controlling share, this change in the state's ownership status meant that the state was no longer responsible for profits and losses—it no longer had to guarantee earlier levels of support. This hardened enterprise budget constraints and made the firm, not the state, responsible for taking care of workers. It opened the door for factories to be shut down or sold and workers to be fired or laid-off—but that was a process that the state delayed.

Prolonging the restructuring process and thereby minimizing worker dislocation also paved the way for future restructuring options. Shareholding eventually opened the door for the state to end its implicit social contract with state workers. Allowing workers to be investors through the shareholding system allowed the state to claim that workers had become or had the right to become owners in the public firms to which they have devoted their working lives.

In part because of the lack of social security institutions, the CCP needed to go through what was a political as much as an economic process. As shareholders, workers became part owners of the public assets that they had worked hard to develop. This was a necessary and important political act. Shares were distributed as political payoff to state workers for their previous service to the firm and the state. Such distribution would thus help thwart charges of asset stripping and maintain political stability to appease workers. Making workers shareholders changed the status of state workers. The state could then say that workers had the right to either remain "owners" in the firm or sell their shares for immediate cash and leave the firm—at which point their relationship with the firm (and the state) would be terminated. The decision belonged to the workers. Obviously one can say that it was nothing more than ritual, but such acts were necessary in China to pave the way politically for the transformation from public to private ownership of once state-owned assets.

However, as firms have moved into second or third phases of restructuring, the political concerns that originally steered the state to favor relatively equal worker–manager shareholding started to hinder further change. Interviews in 2004 and 2005 suggest that enterprise managers were increasingly frustrated by the power of employee shareholder associations that were blocking opportunities for sales or joint ventures.[8] What started out primarily as schemes to raise money through the sale of shares to workers under the shareholding system has turned into a means by which workers can block further restructuring, including sales to both domestic and international companies.[9]

Interviews reveal that some local authorities were so anxious to ensure that a firm could be sold that they gave workers money based on years of service to buy extra shares but then immediately turned around and offered to buy back all the workers' shares—allowing workers an opportunity to get a quick cash return. One might ask why not just give workers the extra money? When asked, the local authorities explained that it was a necessary step in the restructuring process to give shares to the firms' long-time workers and then buy back shares to mark an end to one stage in China's history and the beginning of another— from a socialist planned economy to a capitalist market economy.

This was also a time when local governments realized that a big stakeholder was necessary for effective corporate management. Consequently, local governments shifted strategy away from equal distribution to encouraging managers to increase their shareholdings, which resulted in an increasing number of manager buyouts.

Conclusion: obstacles to further SOE reform

China took the politically more expedient road of SOE reform, culminating in the creation of corporate groups to reduce layoffs and absorb weaker firms. While this politically expedient strategy bought the CCP time, there is an economic price that the regime must pay. The state now faces two sets of obstacles that may prove increasingly costly as it attempts to move to the next stage in its industrial development. First, the state still has more SOEs than it wants. The state has been criticized for not retreating from some sectors of the industrial system. But in some cases, continued state presence is not by choice. Policy groups within the government have recommended that the state get out of non-strategic sectors. While the state overall improved its management of SOEs and the state economy continues to improve, reform of the state monopoly sectors still lags behind. The distribution of SOEs across industries remains irrational, not strong enough in sectors where it would make sense for the state to dominate, but too dominant in those sectors where it should exit. The problem is that the political costs for the state to exit are too high.

The state, surprising as it may seem, is still constrained by some of the same politics from two decades earlier, which we described above. The state still fears reaction to the sale of SOEs, if not worker layoffs. About the same time that SASAC was created, in the early to mid-2000s, opposition to further privatization developed after the rush of manager buyouts. Segments of the population, cadres and workers alike, remain opposed to more radical restructuring, including manager buyouts and privatization more generally (Oi 2010). Press reports of steel workers in Jilin who beat to death a private factory owner who was planning to buy a majority stake in a state owned steel factory are indications of lingering strong opposition to privatization (Bradsher 2009; Branigan 2009).

In 2007, political backlash to manager buyouts rose to a point where the central state had to halt the practice. This prohibition remains in effect today along with that against giving out shares to workers. These political constraints have in the end prevented the state from finishing the process of SOE reform. The consequence of such opposition is that the state has been forced to keep firms that it would otherwise want to sell at low prices simply to get rid of them. But selling these SOEs at low prices would attract charges of asset stripping.

The second and related obstacle to further reform is centered on the competitiveness of China's corporate groups, even those that are to be the national champions. This problem similarly stems from the inability to cut unwanted firms. In the mid-2000s SASAC, under Li Rongrong, ordered the centrally controlled SOEs, i.e., the corporate groups, to shed themselves of all non-core industries to make the strategic sectors stronger and more profitable. However, this order has turned out to be nearly impossible to implement.

As we stressed above, *jituan* were formed in the beginning of the 1990s to try to save as many SOEs and minimize layoffs as much as possible by consolidating them under one strong enterprise, whose task was to help its brothers turn into effective firms. The resulting *jituan* often encompassed all firms within one sector in a city, such as steel. A key example of this was Baosteel. All the steel firms in the Shanghai area became part of the Baosteel corporate group. In some localities, the problems of consolidation of SOEs into corporate groups were further compounded when firms from different sectors were put under the strongest local firm, regardless of whether they were in the same industry or not.

Eventually, some of these corporate groups, including strong ones like Baosteel, were able to pay workers the necessary severance and layoff many of the workers. They eventually also closed firms under their group and restructured others. But not all corporate groups were able to completely rid themselves of weak and inefficient firms. Thus, there was a need for SASAC to clean house and order the sale of non-core industries.

For a time it was unclear whether the consolidation strategy of forming corporate groups would continue. It was not a given that SOEs would eventually emerge as corporate groups. Well-performing firms resented and resisted taking in all the other firms within their sector simply to keep workers in those firms from being laid off. As one might imagine, such a policy would drag down the achievement of the efficient firm. The idea that bigger is better, especially in a global context, rules the day, but this idea has also been bolstered by political constraints and the need to keep workers. The idea was that merging firms was the most politically and economically feasible way to keep the maximum number of workers employed until policies or funds became available to layoff workers.

But the forced marriage of weak and strong firms into *jituan* has no doubt created inefficiencies and problems that would hinder the emergence of true competitive national champions.

Now when the state may want to actually sell some of these firms that are part of the big corporate groups, the way forward to that reform has been muddied because the state cannot sell these firms cheaply lest there be charges of asset stripping in the wake of negative reactions to and eventual prohibitions against manager buyouts. Yet, no one wants to buy problem-ridden firms at high prices. The state is thus left holding on to more state-owned firms than it wants. Remember that SASAC has failed to reduce the number of centrally controlled firms to the earlier stated 80–100 firms.

In an attempt to clear the log jam and further reform its SOEs, the central authorities have created a new asset management company, not unlike the four that were created in the late 1990s. However, whereas asset management companies like Huarong and Cinda were for the banks to clean up their problems, the state has now created one for enterprises called Guoxin, under SASAC. Centrally owned SOEs that need to be restructured will be moved into Guoxin. Guoxin then will have the authority and leeway to sell these firms or to reorganize and restructure them. Its sole purpose is to restructure, sell, or turn around problems of these SOEs.[10] The firms to be moved into Guoxin will be selected by SASAC but must be approved by the State Council. It remains to be seen how successful this entity will be in overcoming lingering opposition to property rights reform in China's large SOEs. In the meantime, the state must continue to carry these poorly performing firms and their burdens. This is the economic price for political stability. The longer-term question is how such strategies will hold back the state's efforts to create truly internationally competitive national champions.

Notes

1 For a useful volume that puts China's corporate restructuring in a comparative perspective see Green and Liu (2005).
2 See Walter (2011) for more details on this distinction.
3 On the one hand, this might seem like an untenable situation but the parent–child relationship provides the old firm some assistance. This strategy opens the door for the parent company to benefit from its child both through shares in the newly spun off firm as well as in less legal transactions. See Zheng and Kim (2011) for further details on how this works.
4 This study draws from the national statistics as well as on the empirical findings of two specially designed surveys implemented in 2000 and 2005 by the Chinese Academy of Social Sciences (CASS). The 2000 survey studied 451 firms and obtained information dating back to 1994. The 2005 survey covered 1000 firms. The industrial sectors sampled in both surveys were machine building, chemical, electronics, electrical equipment, and textiles. The 2000 survey covered Wuxi, Zhengzhou, Jiangmen, Yangcheng, and Hangzhou. The 2005 survey returned to Wuxi, Zhengzhou, Jiangmen, and added two new sites, Chengdu and Shenyang.
5 In spite of the policy of "grasp the large and let go of the small" the numbers let go were limited. Even when we disaggregate our data, we find that, regardless of firm

size, sales totaled no more than 7 percent of total firms as of 2000 in our sample. Further discussion of the 1990s can be found in Oi (2005).

6 Survey I.

7 Survey II, Q2.

8 For a different perspective on whether the employee shareholder associations have any influence at all, see Sargeson and Zhang (1999), especially pp. 91–92.

9 A small percentage of our respondents answered that worker shares should be abolished.

10 One centrally owned enterprise, Huaxing, has been slated to be transferred to Guoxin. See *Economic Observer* (2011).

References

Bradsher, K. (2009) "Bowing to Protests, China Halts Sale of Steel Mill," *New York Times*, August 16, available online: www.nytimes.com/2009/08/17/business/ global/17yuan. html?_r=0 (accessed April 16, 2012).

Branigan, T. (2009) "Chinese State Steel Workers Beat Private Firm Boss to Death," *Guardian*, July 26, available online: www.guardian.co.uk/world/2009/jul/26/ china-steel-workers-riot (accessed April 16, 2012).

China Economic Quarterly (2008) Special Issue 12(2).

Ding, X. L. (2000) "The Illicit Asset Stripping of Chinese State Firms," *China Journal* 43: 1–28.

Economic Observer (2011) "Huaxing Group Likely to Become First COE to be Incorporated into Guoxin Asset Ma," available online: www.eeo.com.cn/ens/ 2011/0516/201441.shtml (accessed April 16, 2012).

Green, S. P. and Liu, G. S. (2005) *Exit the Dragon? Privatization and State Control in China*, London: Chatham House.

Heilmann, S. (2011) "Experience First, Laws Later: Experimentation and Breakthroughs in the Restructuring of China's State Sector," in J. C. Oi (ed.) *Going Private in China: The Politics of Corporate Restructuring and System Reform in the PRC*, Stanford, CA: Stanford University, The Walter H. Shorenstein Pacific Research Center, pp. 95–118.

Jung, J.-Y. (2011) "Reinvented Intervention: The Chinese Central State and State-Owned Enterprise Reform in the WTO Era," in J. C. Oi (ed.) *Going Private in China: The Politics of Corporate Restructuring and System Reform in the PRC*. Stanford, CA: Stanford University, The Walter H. Shorenstein Pacific Research Center, pp. 119–134.

Manion, M. (2004) *Corruption by Design: Building Clean Government in Mainland China and Hong Kong*, Cambridge, MA: Harvard University Press.

Naughton, B. (2008) "SOE Policy: Profiting the SASAC Way," *China Economic Quarterly* 12(2): 19–26.

Nolan, P. (2001) *China and the Global Economy: National Champions, Industrial Policy, and the Big Business Revolution*, Basingstoke/New York: Palgrave.

Office of State Council (2006) "Guanyu tuijin guoyuo ziben tiaozheng he guoyou qieye chongzu de zhidao yijian" (Guiding Opinion Concerning the Promotion of the Readjustment of State Assets and the Restructuring of State Enterprises), State Council Directive 97, available online: www.gov.cn/gongbao/content/2007/ content_503385. htm (accessed April 16, 2012).

Oi, J. C. (2005) "Patterns of Corporate Restructuring in China: Political Constrains on Privatization," *China Journal* 53: 115–136.

Oi, J. C. (June–July 2005) "China Interviews," Shandong.

Oi, J. C. (2010) "Political Cross Currents in Chinas's Corporate Restructuring," in J. C. Oi, S. Rozelle, and X. Zhou (eds.) *Growing Pains: Tensions and Opportunity in China's Transformation*, Washington, DC: Brookings Institution Press.

Oi, J. C. and Han, C. (2011) "China's Corporate Restructuring: A Multi-Step Process," in J. C. Oi (ed.) *Going Private in China: The Politics of Corporate Restructuring and System Reform in the PRC*, Stanford, CA: Stanford University, The Walter H. Shorenstein Pacific Research Center, pp. 19–38.

Sachs, J. and Woo, W. T. (1997) *Understanding China's Economic Performance*, NBER Working Paper No. 5935, Cambridge, MA: National Bureau of Economic Research.

Sargeson, S. and Zhang, J. (1999) "Reassessing the Role of the Local State: A Case Study of Local Gorvernment Interventions in Property Rights Reform in a Hangzhou District," *China Journal* 42: 77–99.

SASAC (State-owned Assets Supervision and Administration Commission) (2006) "General Information on Reform and Development of Central SOEs and Development of State-Owned Assets Management System Reform," available online: www.sasac. gov.cn/n2963340/n2964712/3059894.html (accessed September 10, 2012).

Steinfeld, E. S. (1998) *Forging Reform in China: The Fate of State-Owned Industry*, Cambridge: Cambridge University Press.

Walter, C. E. (2011) "Stock Markets and Corporate Reform: A Pandora's Box of Unintended Consequences," in J. C. Oi (ed.) *Going Private in China: The Politics of Corporate Restructuring and System Reform in the PRC*, Stanford, CA: Stanford University, The Walter H. Shorenstein Pacific Research Centre, pp. 203–240.

Wedeman, A. (2004) "The Intensification of Corruption in China," *China Quarterly* 180: 895–921.

Woo, W. T. (1999) "The Real Reasons for China's Growth," *The China Journal* 41: 115–137.

Zheng, Lu and Kim, Byung-Soo (2011) "Spin-offs and Corporate Governance: Listed Firms in China's Stock Markets," in Jean C. Oi, (ed.) *Going Private in China: The Politics of Corporate Restructuring and System Reform*, Stanford, CA: Stanford University, The Walter H. Shorenstein Pacific Research Center, pp. 241–268.

Zhongguo guoyou zichan jiandu guanli nianjian (China State-Owned Supervision and Management Yearbook) (2003–2011) Beijing: Zhongguo jingji chubanshe.

Zhongguo guoyou zichan jiandu guanli nianjian (China State-Owned Supervision and Management Yearbook) (2008) Beijing: Zhongguo jingji chubanshe.

9　China's bureaucratic capitalism

Creating the corporate steel sector

Andrew G. Walder

By the 1980s the flaws of Soviet-style central planning, and in particular the problems of the state socialist firm, were already clear.[1] The remedy also seemed clear. First, a procurement system that guaranteed sales of all output must be jettisoned in favor of a system of market allocation, which would put competitive pressures on firms for the first time. Second, firms should be given an incentive to produce efficiently (rather than hoard labor and supplies) by permitting them to retain profits. These retained profits—and not state subsidies—would become the source of wages, executive compensation, and welfare expenditures. Third, the "paternalistic" relationships between the state and the firm must be ended. The "regime of bargaining" whereby the bureaucrats who ran large state firms extracted concessions from planners in terms of taxes, investment, and concessionary loans, largely through lobbying in the halls of power, must be ended (Kornai 1980, 1992).

This last crucial condition was the most difficult of all. It was widely recognized that state firms and their government minders were in a situation of "dual dependence"—the state depended on the firms for output, revenues, employment, and welfare provisions, while the firms depended on the regulatory and tax concessions and financing that permitted them to succeed. One school of thought—represented by the architects of Hungary's "New Economic Mechanism" of the 1970s, and China's enterprise reforms of the 1980s which were deeply influenced by the Hungarian experience—was to gradually unleash market forces, but retain state ownership of firms. A second school of thought—articulated first by the influential Hungarian economist Janos Kornai and later by many Western economists who advised post-communist governments after 1989—insisted that the "mutual dependence" and "regime of bargaining" that undermined firm efficiency could not be changed significantly so long as state ownership was maintained (Kornai 1990). Early reforms in China in the 1980s, which were closely patterned after the Hungarian model, exhibited many of the same problems (Steinfeld 1998; Walder 1992a). Kornai argued persuasively that so long as the state owned the firm, government officials would always feel pressured to bail them out, or provide favorable circumstances to permit them to succeed. This, he argued famously, was a "soft budget constraint" that would eventually undermine any effort to place market pressures on firms. He spoke with great authority, because he could point to the ultimate failure of such reform in Hungary in the last years of communist rule (Kornai 1986).

The question, then, became privatization. Was it really necessary, and if so, how should it be carried out? In the years since 1989 there have been three broad approaches to the problem. The first is the post-Soviet experience. In former Soviet republics, especially Russia and Ukraine, the collapse of the Soviet party-state and its ensuing administrative disarray permitted incumbent state enterprise managers and planning officials to consolidate control over their enterprises. As the structures of the Soviet party-state collapsed, Russian managers seized de facto control over their firms, and in a process described as "spontaneous privatization," aided by the distribution of majority shares to employees, were able to assert control over the vast majority of state assets and resist control by outsiders who might restructure and downsize their operations (Åslund 2007; Blasi, *et al.* 1997; McFaul 1995; Shleifer and Treisman 2001). A second approach is the one taken in Poland and other post-communist electoral democracies on the borders of Central Europe. State enterprises were more slowly and systematically restructured and privatized by state agencies in conformity with prevailing international standards. This was part of an explicit aim of post-communist leaders to follow a model that provided prosperity and security in the European Union (Appel 2004; Hanley, *et al.* 2002; King and Sznajder 2006; Sachs 1993). Neither course was followed in China, where the leadership of an intact party dictatorship, committed both to its own survival and the revitalization of its economy, explicitly rejected the privatization of large state firms and maintained a rhetorical commitment to socialism in the context of market transition.

China's approach to this question since 1990 has revealed dimensions of reform that were scarcely considered in the 1980s. China no longer follows the same course pursued in Hungary in the last decades of communism. Instead, on the one hand, thousands of smaller state enterprises have been closed, merged, or privatized. On the other hand, the larger firms have been retained under state ownership, in many cases merged into even larger corporations, but restructured in other ways that are quite radical (Leng 2009; Oi 2011; Oi and Han 2011; Jung 2011; Walter 2011). These restructurings alter the boundaries of the traditional state socialist firm, indeed its very definition.

Discussions about reform in the 1980s took for granted that the "firm," or "enterprise" had to be granted greater autonomy. But what, after all, is the "firm"? Should the "firm" have the same boundaries as the companies that existed under state socialism? Should the independent plants of the socialist era maintain their identity and autonomy, or should they be merged into even larger corporations or "groups"? Should the boundaries of the "firm" include the housing estates, schools, clinics, and day-care centers of years past, or should these be carved out and put under the jurisdiction of local governments? Should the accumulated pension obligations, formerly funded directly out of current sales revenues, be shifted to other entities, and taken off the books of a restructured corporation? The Chinese approach has raised all of these issues, which were not even on the radar of the early reform agenda.

Reform and restructuring: two approaches

The steel sector was the heart of the socialist planned economy. Emblematic of modern industrial might, it was the foundation for forced-pace industrialization and received massive infusions of capital. The Soviet model emphasized large industrial complexes, and in China this was reflected in a series of celebrated giant enterprises, usually created or expanded in the 1950s with Soviet assistance. These were the famous socialist steel complexes of the 1960s: Anshan, Ma'anshan, Benxi, Wuhan, Capital Iron and Steel. They employed and housed tens of thousands of workers, providing extensive cradle-to-grave welfare: child care, schools, housing, clinics and hospitals, medical insurance, and pensions, all funded directly out of current enterprise revenues (Walder 1986, 1992b).

China's steel sector passed through two distinct phases of enterprise reform. The first, begun in the 1980s, followed the original script of "enterprise autonomy" reforms of the late socialist Hungarian experience. Managers of existing state enterprises were granted greater control over production, marketing, investment and expansion, and rights to share profits from their operations. The economic benefits of this increased enterprise autonomy, and the discipline of the market, were expected to revitalize state firms and permit them to maintain employment and benefits.

After more than a decade of experimentation with market incentives for existing state firms, it became clear that this approach was a failure. During the mid-1990s, instead of privatizing the firms in the manner of East-Central Europe or Russia, China's leaders embarked on a radical restructuring that reorganized and merged them into a smaller number of large state controlled corporations with much smaller labor forces and greatly reduced welfare obligations.

Like many older state socialist enterprises, China's large steel complexes began market transition with huge liabilities: outdated and run down physical plants, a labor force far in excess of actual needs, large housing and welfare costs, and a rapidly accumulating bill to fund pensions of successive generations of retired workers. Despite the enormous demand for steel products generated by sustained double-digit economic growth, the state steel complexes could not compete in an expanding market economy. Local governments established thousands of small new steel mills to meet local demand for basic steel products that did not have large social welfare obligations and employed newer technologies.

Restructuring of the state steel complexes was on the agenda from the beginning, but it was not initially clear what form it should take. It was generally agreed that control and income rights should be transferred downward to the level of the firm, which would be permitted to retain profits and have greater control over production and investment decisions. Privatization was ruled out on political grounds by the ruling Communist Party. From the 1980s through the mid-1990s, the preferred alternate strategy was decentralization—greater autonomy for the managers of existing plants, which would become autonomous companies forced by market competition to increase the efficiency of their operations and boost output (Steinfeld 1998). In other words, the old socialist giants—Anshan, Ma'anshan, and the others—would be transformed into market-oriented corporations.

By the mid-1990s, however, state steel complexes faced mounting debts. After a period of growth in fixed capital investment and technological upgrading, steel sector investment turned downward in 1995 (see Figure 9.1). Expected to increase output to meet burgeoning domestic demand for steel while maintaining employment and bearing large costs for their social service programs, firms resorted increasingly to short-term loans. At Capital Steel, then China's largest steel company, indebtedness reached such levels its high-profile manager was forced to resign in 1994 as the state bailed out the failing firm (Steinfeld 1998: 206–224). Other large state steel complexes had similar experiences (Liu *et al.* 2006: 43–46; Chiu and Lewis 2006).

The failure of this approach led to a second and more radical phase of restructuring. First, the state solidified its ownership and control of the steel sector, merging existing companies into larger corporations, and enlarging the scale of firms in an effort to make them more competitive both domestically and globally. Second, the state altered the scope of these firms, carving out productive assets and listing them separately as new companies on domestic and international stock exchanges. Labor forces were drastically downsized, and social welfare obligations were left with separate holding companies that exercised dominant stakes in the new listed firm (Chiu and Lewis 2006; Oi and Han 2011; Jung 2011).

In this second phase of restructuring, employment in the state sector plummeted. Despite a doubling of output in the decade after 1990, 1.1 million jobs

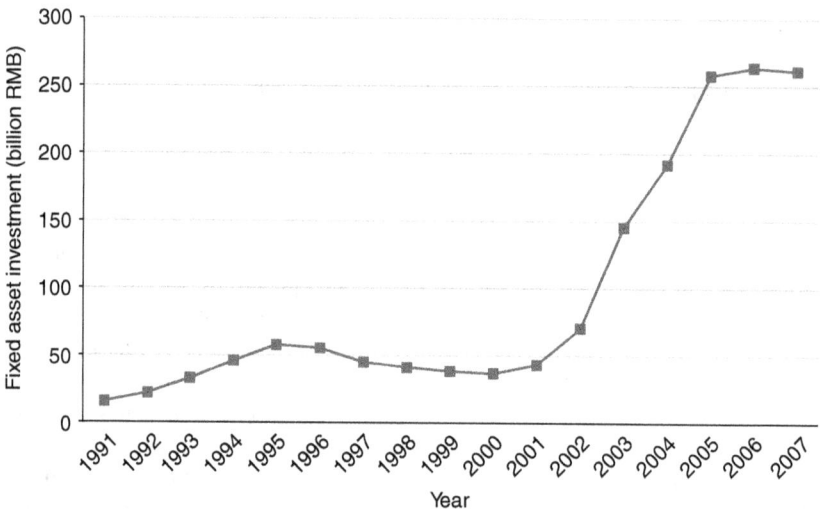

Figure 9.1 Fixed capital investment in the iron and steel sector, 1991–2007 (sources: *China Steel Yearbook* 1996: 79–84; 1999: 25–29; 2002: 85–87; 2005: 145; 2007: 103; 2009: 107).

were lost, with all of the job losses coming after 1995 (see Figure 9.2). During this period China's steel output moved from a distant fourth in global rankings (behind the United States, Japan, and the former Soviet Union) to become far and away the world's largest producer. Increasing total output eight-fold after 1989, China's 2007 output of 495 million metric tons was more than four times that of Japan, the next largest national producer (World Steel Association 2009: 3–5). Despite this spectacular output growth, hundreds of thousands were laid off as the older enterprises were downsized, closed, or merged, shedding the schools, housing estates, hospitals, and other social services that were the signature of state socialism (Chiu and Lewis 2006).

The cuts were deepest at the old steel complexes. During a six-year period from 1993 to 1999 employment in China's 12 largest steel companies shrunk by one quarter. China's largest, Capital Iron and Steel, cut almost 40 percent of its labor force, and Ma'anshan Iron and Steel, once a celebrated socialist enterprise, cut its labor force almost in half (see Table 9.1). Anshan Iron and Steel, a national model that employed more than 210,000 in 1975, was down to 166,000 by the end of the 1990s (*Anshan Steel Annals* 1994: 44–45). As steel output accelerated, layoffs continued. From 2001 to 2007, as output tripled, employment in the 80 largest steel companies fell further, from 1.85 to 1.65 million (*China Steel Statistics* 2002: 132, 2008: 158; *China Steel Yearbook* 2008: 162–167; World Steel Association 2009: 4). By 2007 Chongqing Steel's labor force of 25,000 was half the 1993 figure (*Chongqing Steel Yearbook* 1993: 292). The steel sector is emblematic of the overall downsizing of the traditional state sector in urban China after the mid-1990s, during which state employment dropped from more than 100 million to 65 million in a decade (Giles, *et al.* 2006).

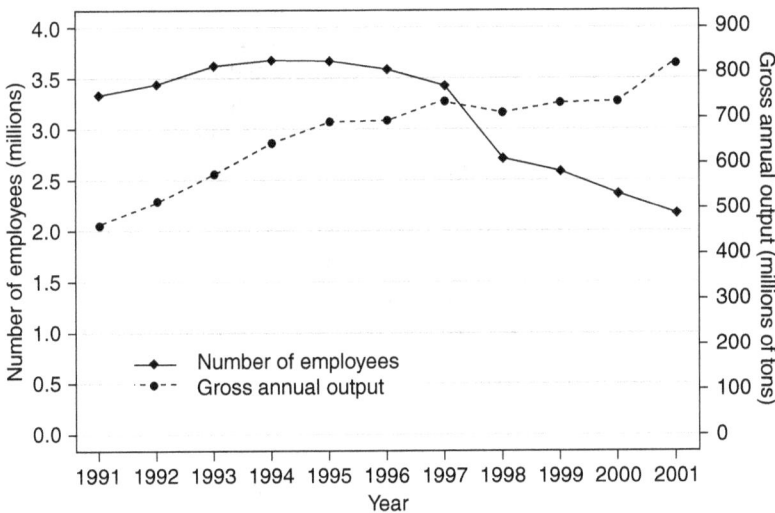

Figure 9.2 Output and employment in the iron and steel sector, 1991–2001 (source: *China Steel Yearbook* 1996: 79–84, 1999: 25–29, 2002: 85–87).

Table 9.1 Employment in largest Chinese steel complexes, 1993 and 1999

Enterprise name	1993 (thousands)	1999 (thousands)	% change
Capital Iron and Steel	262.3	160.9	−38.7
Anshan Iron and Steel	207.9	166.7	−19.8
Wuhan Iron and Steel	139.4	100.9	−27.6
Baotou Iron and Steel	105.1	87.1	−17.1
Panzihua Iron and Steel	102.5	77.6	−24.3
Benxi Iron and Steel	100.7	80.1	−20.5
Ma'anshan Iron and Steel	83.2	44.2	−46.9
Taiyuan Iron and Steel	69.4	72.3	+4.2
Tangshan Iron and Steel	55.9	44.9	−19.7
Jiangxi Xinye Iron and Steel	51.1	37.4	−26.8
Chongqing Iron and Steel	49.6	36.9	−25.6
Kunming Iron and Steel	43.2	33.3	−22.9
Total	1,270.3	942.2	−25.8

Source: *China Steel Statistics* (1994: 370–372, 2000: 262–264).

Ownership structures

Steel is a strategic national industry, and the Chinese state, still controlled by the Communist Party, remains unwilling to privatize the large firms. After a period of experimentation with enterprise autonomy, the state seized control back from the managers of floundering companies, merging and restructuring them while retaining dominant ownership stakes. State holding companies partitioned their productive assets as separate new firms, listing them on domestic or international stock exchanges (Leng 2009; Price *et al.* 2007; Walter 2011). Non-productive assets and social security obligations like schools, housing, hospitals, and so forth remain with the state holding company but no longer are funded directly by flows of income from the productive assets. Schools and hospitals were often transferred to local governments, housing stock sold to employees at a deep discount, and land and buildings sometimes sold to real estate companies (Walter 2010). State ownership was maintained, but the boundaries of the firm were redrawn.

As the old steel complexes were downsized and restructured they were merged into larger corporations. In recent years Baoshan Steel, China's largest, was merged with Guangzhou Steel and other state firms (Baosteel Group 2010). Tangshan and Handan Steel were merged into Hebei Steel; Anshan and Benxi Steel were merged into Anben Steel; Laiwu and Ji'nan Steel were merged into Shandong Steel; and Xiangtan, Lianyuan, and Hengyang Steel were merged into Hunan Valin (*Asia Times* 2005; *China Daily* 2008a; China.org 2008; *China Daily* 2012). All of these firms were among the ten largest in terms of output (Table 9.2). Meanwhile, fixed investment increased five-fold after 2001 (see Figure 9.1). Control, transfer, and income rights became more highly concentrated in a unitary state entity. The largest privately held firm, Rizhao Steel, was compelled to merge with state-owned Shandong Steel in 2008 (Reuters 2008).

Table 9.2 Ownership status of ten largest firms, steel and real estate, 2008

Iron and steel		Real estate	
Firm name	*Ownership status*	*Firm name*	*Ownership status*
Baosteel Group	Listed, state controlled	Vanke	Listed, private control
Hebei Iron and Steel	Listed, state controlled	China Overseas Development	Listed, state controlled
Wuhan Iron and Steel	Listed, state controlled	Poly Group	Listed, state controlled
Anben Iron and Steel	Listed, state controlled	Hopson Group	Listed, private control
Jiangsu Shagang Group	Listed, privately-controlled	Rich Force Property	Listed, private control
Shandong Iron and Steel Group	Listed, state controlled	Evergrande Group	Listed, private control
Maanshan Iron and Steel Group	Listed, state controlled	Wanda Group	Privately held by founder
Shougang Group	Listed, state controlled	Greentown Group	Listed, private control
Hunan Valin Iron and Steel Group	Listed, state controlled	Beijing Capital Development	Listed, private control
Baotou Iron and Steel Group	Listed, state controlled	Dahua Group	Listed, private control

Sources: *China Real Estate Statistics* (2008: 372); China Mining Association (2009).

By 2008, nine of China's ten largest steel corporations (by output) had listed their controlling shareholder as some branch of the State Council's Assets Supervision and Administration Commission (see Table 9.2). State entities were controlling shareholders of 74 percent of the steel industry's publicly listed firms in 2008, with highly concentrated share ownership in which the largest stake averaged 47.5 percent (see Table 9.3).

From a comparative perspective, what is most striking about these changes in the structure of the large state corporations is how radical they are. Postcommunist Russia became well known in the popular press for radical "shock therapy" that purportedly led to mass misery, which in turn led to academic denunciations of neo-liberal "market Bolshevism" and rapid privatization (Reddaway and Glinski 2001). In fact, however, the drastic restructuring of the Chinese state firms that began in the mid-1990s, reflected in the downsizing of the large steel complexes, eventually led to more extensive permanent layoffs than in rapidly privatized post-Soviet industrial sectors during the crisis-plagued decade of the 1990s. Russian firms delayed wage payments and cut wages in a period of severe inflation and stagnant economic growth, but employment declines were nonetheless relatively modest (Brown and Earle 2002; Brown, *et al.* 2010; Gerber 2002, 2006; Gimpelson and Kapeliushnikov 2011). Managers seized de facto control of most firms, and the Russian privatization program granted the majority of ownership shares to employees, which permitted managers to defend insider control and stave off new outside owners who would be likely to restructure and downsize the firms as the state did in China. Russia, after all, had regular elections in the 1990s, for both parliament and president, and mass layoffs during that period would have returned Communist candidates to power. China's leaders faced no such electoral constraints—and they had the luxury of a rapidly growing economy—and as a result orchestrated much more radical and rapid restructuring of state firms than the allegedly radical "neo-liberal" Russian reformers. It is ironic that state ownership and control in China fostered a radical restructuring of firms that was far more decisive than the much-reviled "neo-liberal" approach in Russia that privatized firms quickly.

Table 9.3 Ownership structure of publicly listed steel firms, 1999–2008

	State as largest shareholder (%)	*Average equity stake, largest shareholder (%)*
1999	93.9	57.1
2001	91.8	55.6
2003	86.8	54.4
2005	83.5	49.8
2007	67.9	46.2
2008	73.5	47.5

Source: CCER Database (Center for China Economic Research, Beijing: China Securities Market Database). Online proprietary database of historical and current data on China's security markets.

Ordinary Chinese did not accept these changes quietly. Popular protest has been called a "tracer" of social change, as groups expropriated by such macro-historical processes as the expansion of national states, the spread of markets, and proletarianization organize to resist (Tilly, *et al.* 1975; Tilly 1986). The massive job losses in state enterprises led to a large wave of worker protest in China's rust belt beginning in the mid-1990s. Whether the restructuring of a state firm involved outright closure or downsizing, protests initially were organized around the failure to deliver promised levels of compensation, or the failure to pay state-mandated pensions for those who were retired early (Chen 2000, 2006; Hurst and O'Brien 2002; Lee 2007). The most serious protests were organized in communities dominated by single industries, especially in smaller state firms that were closed or merged. Workers in these communities mobilized to charge managers and local officials with violation of state law, and charged them with corruption and self-enrichment in the course of privatization. These protests were met with a mixture of repression aimed at protest leaders and concessions to partially meet popular demands (Cai 2002, 2006, 2008). In recent years workers in firms targeted for mergers or reorganization have taken a more proactive stance, and have organized to protest plans for future changes that threaten their job security and incomes. Some of these protests have turned violent, including the taking of hostages and the murder of company officials (*New York Times* 2009a, 2009b). The rapid and drastic restructuring of the steel sector has bred conflicts that state officials view as potential threats to political stability, and it is this awareness of this danger that underlies the unremitting hostility of the Chinese state to any form of independent labor organization.

Corporate (not private) wealth

Because large steel enterprises remain overwhelmingly under state control, opportunities for the personal enrichment of corporate executives have been limited. The steel sector has not generated a large group of wealthy "oligarchs" of the kind popularly associated with Russia. The successful smaller companies that have grown up since the 1980s, not the restructured state-owned "national champions," have been the sources of vast accumulations of personal wealth. Many of China's wealthy private steel magnates have a common story—most have managerial experience in state-owned companies, and many have worked in local government agencies. For example, the founder of the private Yonggang Steel Group worked in a local steel mill and served as a village party secretary before establishing the firm in his native village (China Agriculture Newsnet 2008). Having local government connections enables entrepreneurs to find seed capital while knowledge of the industry proves vital to ensuring successful operation. The wealthiest steel magnate, the founder and owner of Rizhao Steel, was worth an estimated five billion US dollars in 2008 (*Hurun Report* 2009).[2] He was a former employee of Capital Iron and Steel who struck out on his own, forming partnerships with nearby rural governments in the 1980s to back his early ventures (Rizhao City Newsnet 2007). His Rizhao Steel grew to rival the state firms, but in 2008 he was compelled to merge it into the state-controlled Shandong Steel. Another leading steel entrepreneur took over a failing city-owned steel company in 1999 and eventually converted it into the highly successful Jianlong Iron and Steel Group (*Hurun Report* 2010). Another steel entrepreneur purchased the Bohai Metallurgy Industrial Group in Tianjin in 2001 for 280 million, and built it into Rongcheng Steel (*China Daily* 2008b). These individuals are among China's wealthiest people. The steel sector produced another ten individuals with assets in excess of US$730 million by 2007 (*Hurun Report* 2008). None of these fortunes were derived from state-owned entities.

The connection between the steel sector and private wealth becomes clearer if we contrast it with the real estate sector, which generates by far the largest concentration of private fortunes in China. The real estate sector differs from steel and other traditional sectors in one important way: there were no enterprises devoted to commercial real estate development under state socialism. Real estate development companies had to be formed from scratch: they did not have a prior labor force or existing business models. Local governments entered into a variety of partnerships with private and foreign capital to fuel this rapidly growing sector. As a result, the ownership structure of the largest real estate firms contrast almost completely with steel. Table 9.2 shows a stark contrast: only two of the top ten real estate development companies were state controlled by 2008, while nine of the top ten steel companies were. As a direct result, the number of wealthy individuals on the Hurun list from the steel sector has fluctuated between 2 and 5 percent after 2004, while the real estate sector has accounted for roughly one-third of all private fortunes (see Table 9.4).

Bureaucratic corporations

The end result of this long process of radical restructuring is a steel sector dominated by a relatively small number of very large steel producers. On a global scale, China's state steel corporations weigh heavily. In terms of physical output, ten of the largest 30 global steel producers in 2010 were Chinese state enterprises, and five of the top ten.[3] Six of these companies rank in the Fortune Global 500 for 2011.[4] While these companies now are ranked among world leaders and are listed on stock exchanges as if they are corporations equivalent to others around the world, there are a number of ways in which they are different from their international peers, and there are a number of ways in which they are not much different from their earlier incarnations in the state socialist era, despite the radical changes of the past two decades.

The primary way in which these corporations differ from their peers around the world is that they are fully integrated into the structure of the national party-state. These are not private companies that are independent of state control and run by professional managers who answer (at least in theory) to their boards of directors and shareholders, as is the model in mature market economies. Nor are these nominally private enterprises run by appointees of the executive branch, as in Putin's Russia, where the wealthy private oligarchs now tend to be former

Table 9.4 Wealth generation in steel and real estate sectors

Year	Iron and Steel			Real Estate			Average Wealth (all industries, in RMB billions)	N Cases
	% of individuals on Hurun Rich List	% of total wealth on Hurun Rich List	Average Wealth (in RMB billions)	% of individuals on Hurun Rich List	% of total wealth on Hurun Rich List	Average Wealth (in RMB billions)		
2004	5.0	2.6	1.82	42.0	48.0	2.81	2.47	100
2005	4.0	5.1	2.31	32.5	39.8	1.86	1.52	400
2006	5.8	8.5	3.26	26.0	34.7	2.72	2.21	500
2007	4.5	7.4	4.38	26.0	39.8	6.61	4.31	800
2008	4.3	6.9	4.80	28.6	37.2	3.88	2.98	999
2009	2.0	3.3	6.37	32.6	40.3	4.72	3.87	999

Source: *Hurun Report* (2009).

officials from the state security apparatus (Treisman 2007). In both of the above examples, it is not unheard of for state entities to hold significant stakes in companies. However, in the case of Chinese state firms, the state holds an overwhelmingly large ownership stake, and completely dominates boards of directors and the appointment of top executives.

Part of this dominance is due to a distinctive characteristic of shares in China's stock markets. Only a portion of the total shares in these state firms are traded on exchanges. More than half of the shares are "state shares," which are a legacy of past state socialist ownership and which at present cannot be converted to tradable shares. One implication of this is that rankings of firm sizes based on market valuation are essentially fictional in the Chinese case. Non-traded shares, which may make up the majority, are valued at the market rate for the traded shares. In essence this is a definition of book value that has little relationship to the actual value of these firms, and this is a polite fiction honored by the international investment banks that earn massive commissions for share placements and other businesses from these companies. This share overhang is difficult to resolve for two reasons. First, these state shares are defended politically as a bulwark of party-state control. Second, the release of these shares onto stock markets would depress the value of those entities that hold stakes of tradeable shares. The state shares falsely inflate the value of Chinese companies in certain kinds of international rankings, but the key point is that this is a direct expression to continuing state ownership and control (Leng 2009; Walter and Howie 2006; Walter 2010, 2011).

A second expression of the tight integration of these corporations into the party-state is the appointment system for top executives. Communist party organizations are alive and well in these firms, and indeed are a key mechanism of control over them. Party secretaries are often given euphemistic titles that sound very businesslike, but they are party secretaries all the same, and answerable to higher party organs. Top executives are part of the national "nomenklatura" system, whereby the organization departments of party organizations at the next higher level make all leadership appointments. Examination of the resumes of the executives of these firms reveals that they have had long careers in regional bureaus or national ministries related to the steel industry. The top executives of these largest state firms regularly are transferred in from, or out to, party secretary posts of large cities and provinces, or into ministerial positions in the national governments. These executives sit on provincial party committees and the Central Committee. They hold their posts at the pleasure of the party (Brødsgaard 2012).

It is clear that the top executives of these state corporations are an integral part of the state's bureaucratic appointment system. However, we should also consider the ways in which they have leverage over their reputed superiors. This small group of large steel corporations has been restructured at great social cost and some political risk by the national government as part of an explicit strategy to create "national champions" that can compete on a global scale. China's national leadership has a great deal at stake in ensuring the success of these firms—not just national pride, but also to supply a rapidly growing economy with a product that is essential for China's rapid economic expansion. At the same time, the ability of the executives of these firms to lobby the government for favorable treatment—access to iron ore at low cost, favorable tax treatment, and easy financing from state banks at concessionary terms—has been greatly enhanced. In the former state socialist economy, a much larger number of somewhat smaller firms competed for the favorable attention of their immediate superiors. These giant new corporations, by contrast, represent an enormous concentration of fixed investment and are carriers of national prestige. Their executives have high political rank in the party system and are represented at the highest levels of government (Brødsgaard 2012). One wonders whether these restructured steel corporations, and their counterparts in other strategic industries, have developed a much greater capacity than in years past to lobby effectively at the very centers of national power, creating "soft budget constraints" of a different variety and perhaps even much more consequential scale.

Conclusion

China's large state enterprises, as typified by the steel corporations, represent something of a paradox. On the one hand, they have been radically restructured, in many ways more radically and more effectively than enterprises in Russia that were long reviled as examples of excessively radical neo-liberal reforms. After an initial decade of hesitation, labor forces and their welfare obligations were excised much more rapidly and deeply than in the former Soviet Union. With the help of international investment banks, the firms were restructured financially and listed on domestic and foreign stock exchanges in creative ways. The old planning system, which guaranteed sales and led to a culture of hoarding resources, plant capacity, and labor, is a distant memory. China's state firms are treated internationally as if they are corporations analogous to other corporations listed publicly on international exchanges.

However, in other respects, very little has changed. The executives in these state corporations, while surely more capable and better trained than managers in a past era, are still fully integrated into the national political hierarchy. Their career lines lead back and forth across the government–enterprise divide, and successful careers lead upward into the state council, central committee, and perhaps eventually into the Politburo. The true owner of these firms is the Chinese Communist Party, even though foreign investors are permitted to buy minority stakes and even nominate representatives to boards of directors. The large corporations are a political project as much as an economic project, just as surely as Anshan Iron and Steel in the Mao era.

Perhaps most telling is the relationship of these large new corporations to China's financial system. China's state banks are little more than instruments for pouring investment and credits into sectors targeted as national priorities (Walter and Howie 2011). State corporations have been lavished with financing—especially since 2008—and similar credits are not available to domestic private firms. China's leaders have a strong political and economic stake in the success of these firms, and the leaders of these corporations have direct access to the halls of power. In some respects, this situation of "dual dependence" appears to re-create, on a much larger and more consequential scale, the same regime of bargaining and soft budget constraints that in the long run doomed socialist planned economies. It undermines competitive pressures, both from domestic private firms and from international peers. The growth of these large corporations has been spectacular, but the conditions that created this success may sow the seeds of future problems. Are these firms becoming "too big to fail"? Whether this will erode their performance in the long run and cause the current era to be viewed in retrospect as a kind of bubble era for which China will pay dearly in future years is a question well worth considering.

Notes

1 I am grateful to Dan Wang and Tianjue Luo for compiling the data presented in the figures and tables, and for permitting me to draw on our collaborative research to produce this paper.
2 Founded in China in 1999 by a foreign national, *Hurun Report* is a research service that compiles lists of China's high net worth individuals, similar to more familiar lists compiled by *Forbes* and *Fortune* magazines. The *Hurun Report* produces 20 issues a year, along with special online supplements.
3 They are, according to the World Steel Association, Hebei Iron and Steel (second), Baosteel (third), Wuhan (fourth), Jiangsu Shagang (eighth), Shandong (ninth), Ansteel (twelfth), Ma'anshan (eighteenth), Shougang (nineteenth), Valin (twenty-eighth), and Laiwu (thirtieth): www.worldsteel.org/?action=programs&id=73.
4 They are Baosteel, Hebei Iron and Steel, Shougang, Wuhan Iron and Steel, Sinosteel, and Jiangsu Shagang: http://money.cnn.com/magazines/fortune/global500/2011/ countries/China.html.

References

Anshan Steel Annals (1994) *Angang zhi (xia juan)* (Anshan Steel Annals (vol. 2)), Beijing: Renmin chubanshe.

Appel, Hilary (2004) *A New Capitalist Order: Privatization and Ideology in Russian and Eastern Europe*, Pittsburgh, PA: University of Pittsburgh Press.

Asia Times (2005) "Anben Merger a Watershed for Chinese Steel," *Asia Times*, August 18, available online: www.atimes.com/atimes/China/GH18Ad01.html (accessed July 18, 2013).

Åslund, Anders (2007) *How Capitalism Was Built: The Transformation of Central and Eastern Europe, Russia, and Central Asia*, Cambridge: Cambridge University Press.

Baosteel Group (2010) Baosteel Group corporate website, available online: www.baosteel.com/group_e/02about/ShowArticle.asp?ArticleID=1 (accessed July 22, 2012).

Blasi, Joseph R., Kroumova, Maya, and Kruse, Douglas (1997) *Kremlin Capitalism: The Privatization of the Russian Economy*, Ithaca, NY: Cornell University Press.

Brødsgaard, Kjeld Erik (2012) "Politics and Business Group Formation in China: The Party in Control?" *The China Quarterly* 212: 624–648.

Brown, J. David and Earle, John S. (2002) "Gross Job Flows in Russian Industry Before and After Reforms: Has Destruction Become More Creative?" *Journal of Comparative Economics* 30: 96–133.

Brown, J. David, Earle, John S., and Telegdy, Álmos (2010) "Employment and Wage Effects of Privatization: Evidence from Hungary, Romania, Russia, and Ukraine," *Economic Journal* 120: 638–708.

Cai, Yongshun (2002) "The Resistance of Chinese Laid-off Workers in the Reform Period," *China Quarterly* 170: 327–344.

Cai, Yongshun (2006) *State and Laid-off Workers in Reform China: The Silence and Collective Action of the Retrenched*, New York: Routledge.

Cai, Yongshun (2008) "Local Governments and the Suppression of Popular Resistance in China," *China Quarterly* 193: 24–42.

Chen, Feng (2000) "Subsistence Crises, Managerial Corruption, and Labour Protests in China," *China Journal* 44: 41–63.

Chen, Feng (2006) "Privatization and its Discontents in Chinese Factories," *China Quarterly* 185: 42–60.

China Agriculture Newsnet (2008) "2002 nian quanguo nongcun xinwen renwu—Wu Dongcai" (China Rural News Personality of 2002—Wu Dongcai), *Zhongguo nongye xinwen gang*, February 27, available online: http://union.china.com.cn/gaige/txt/2008-02/27/content_2084105.htm (accessed July 22, 2010).

China Daily (2008a) "Large Steel Group Emerges in Hebei," *China Daily*, June 6, available online: www.chinadaily.com.cn/bizchina/2008-06/12/ content_6756099.htm (accessed July 18, 2013).

China Daily (2008b) "Tender Heart, Steel Spirit," *China Daily*, August 18, available online: www.chinadaily.com.cn/bw/2008-08/18/content_6944557.htm (accessed July 18, 2013).

China Daily (2012) "Hunan Valin China Steel Group Ltd.," *China Daily*, available online: http://hn.chinadaily.com.cn/en/2012-01/29/content_14500827.htm (accessed January 7, 2014).

China Mining Association (2009) "China's Top Steel Producers in 2008," *China Mining Association*, February 19, available online: www.chinamining.org/News/2009-02-19/1235014000d21668.html (accessed July 20, 2010).

China Real Estate Statistics (2008) *Zhongguo fangdichan tongji nianjian 2008* (China Real Estate Statistics Yearbook 2008), Beijing: Zhongguo tongji chubanshe.

China Steel Statistics (1994) *Zhongguo gangtie tongji 1994* (China Steel Statistics 1994), Beijing: Yejin gongye bu fazhan guihua ju.

China Steel Statistics (2000) *Zhongguo gangtie tongji 2000* (China Steel Statistics 2000), Beijing: Guojia yejin gongye ju guihua fazhan si.

China Steel Statistics (2002) *Zhongguo gangtie tongji 2002* (China Steel Statistics 2002), Beijing: Zhongguo gangtie xiehui xinxi tongji bu.

China Steel Statistics (2008) *Zhongguo gangtie tongji 2008* (China Steel Statistics 2008), Beijing: Zhongguo gangtie gongye xiehui.

China Steel Yearbook (1996) *Zhongguo 1996 gangtie gongye nianjian* (China Steel Yearbook 1996), Beijing: Zhongguo gangtie gongye chubanshe.

China Steel Yearbook (1999) *Zhongguo 1999 gangtie gongye nianjian* (China Steel Yearbook 1999), Beijing: Zhongguo gangtie gongye chubanshe.

China Steel Yearbook (2002) *Zhongguo 2002 gangtie gongye nianjian* (China Steel Yearbook 2002), Beijing: Zhongguo gangtie gongye chubanshe.

China Steel Yearbook (2005) *Zhongguo 2005 gangtie gongye nianjian* (China Steel Yearbook 2005), Beijing: Zhongguo gangtie gongye chubanshe.

China Steel Yearbook (2007) *Zhongguo 2007 gangtie gongye nianjian* (China Steel Yearbook 2007), Beijing: Zhongguo gangtie gongye chubanshe.

China Steel Yearbook (2008) *Zhongguo 2008 gangtie gongye nianjian* (China Steel Yearbook 2008), Beijing: Zhongguo gangtie gongye chubanshe.

China Steel Yearbook (2009) *Zhongguo 2009 gangtie gongye nianjian* (China Steel Yearbook 2009), Beijing: Zhongguo gangtie gongye chubanshe.

China.org (2008) "Merger Yields New Iron-Steel Group in Shandong," China.org.cn, 27 March, available online: www.china.org.cn/business/2008-03/27/ content_13700076. htm (accessed July 20, 2010).

Chiu, Becky and Lewis, Mervyn K. (2006) *Reforming China's State-Owned Enterprises and Banks*, Cheltenham: Edward Elgar.

Chongqing Steel Yearbook (1993) *Chonggang nianjian, 1986–1990* (Chongqing Steel Yearbook, 1986–1990), Chengdu: Sichuan kexue jishu chubanshe.

Gerber, Theodore P. (2002) "Structural Change and Post-Socialist Stratification: Labor Market Transitions in Contemporary Russia," *American Sociological Review* 67: 629–659.

Gerber, Theodore P. (2006) "Getting Paid: Wage Arrears and Stratification in Russia," *American Journal of Sociology* 111: 1816–1870.

Giles, John, Park, Albert, and Cai, Fang (2006) "How has Economic Restructuring Affected China's Urban Workers?" *China Quarterly* 185: 61–95.

Gimpelson, Vladimir and Kapeliushnikov, Rostislav (2011) "Labor Market Adjustment: Is Russia Different? Discussion Paper No. 5588," Bonn: Institute for the Study of Labor.

Hanley, Eric, King, Lawrence, and János, István Tóth (2002) "The State, International Agencies, and Property Transformation in Postcommunist Hungary," *American Journal of Sociology* 108: 129–167.

Hurst, William and O'Brien, Kevin (2002) "China's Contentious Pensioners," *China Quarterly* 170: 345–360.

Hurun Report (2008) "Hurun Rich List 2008," available online: www.hurun.net/ usen/ HRRL.aspx?nid=2008 (accessed January 7, 2014).

Hurun Report (2009) "Hurun Rich List 2009," available online: www.hurun.net/ usen/ HRRL.aspx?nid=2009 (accessed January 7, 2014).

Hurun Report (2010) "Zhang Zhixiang yu Ningbo Jianlong" (Zhang Zhixiang and Ningbo's Jianlong), formerly available online: www.hurun.net/ shownews1350.aspx (last accessed July 20, 2010).

Jung, Joo-Youn (2011) "Reinvented Intervention: The Chinese Central State and State-owned Enterprise Reform in the WTO Era," in Jean C. Oi (ed.) *Going Private in China: The Politics of Corporate Restructuring and System Reform*, Stanford, CA: Stanford University, The Walter H. Shorenstein Pacific Research Center, pp. 119–134.

King, Lawrence P. and Sznajder, Aleksandra (2006) "The State-Led Transition to Liberal Capitalism: Neoliberal, Organizational, World-Systems, and Social Structural Explanations of Poland's Economic Success," *American Journal of Sociology* 112: 751–801.

Kornai, Janos (1980) *Economics of Shortage*, Amsterdam: North-Holland.

Kornai, Janos (1986) "The Hungarian Reform Process: Visions, Hopes, and Reality," *Journal of Economic Literature* 24: 1687–1737.

Kornai, Janos (1990) *The Road to a Free Economy: Shifting from a Socialist System, The Case of Hungary*, New York: Norton.

Kornai, Janos (1992) *The Socialist System: The Political Economy of Communism*, Princeton, NJ: Princeton University Press.

Lee, Ching Kwan (2007) *Against the Law: Labor Protests in China's Rustbelt and Sunbelt*, Berkeley, CA: University of California Press.

Leng, Jing (2009) *Corporate Governance and Financial Reforms in China's Transition Economy*, Hong Kong: University of Hong Kong Press.

Liu, Yu, Pan, Wei, Shen, Mingming, Song, Guojun, Bertrand, Vivian, Child, Mary, and Shapiro, Judith (2006) "The Politics and Ethics of Going Green in China: Air Pollution Control in Benxi City and Wetland Preservation in Sanjiang Plain," in J. R. Bauer (ed.) *Forging Environmentalism: Justice, Livelihood, and Contested Environments*, Armonk, NY: M. E. Sharpe, pp. 31–102.

McFaul, Michael (1995) "State Power, Institutional Change, and the Politics of Privatization in Russia," *World Politics* 47: 210–243.

New York Times (2009a) "China Steel Executive Killed as Workers and Police Clash," *New York Times*, 26 July, A10.

New York Times (2009b) "Bowing to Protests, China Halts Sale of Steel Mill," *New York Times*, 16 August, B3.

Oi, Jean C. (2011) "Politics in China's Corporate Restructuring," in J. C. Oi (ed.) *Going Private in China: The Politics of Corporate Restructuring and System Reform*, Stanford, CA: Stanford University, The Walter H. Shorenstein Pacific Research Center, pp. 1–18.

Oi, Jean C. and Han, Chaohua (2011) "China's Corporate Restructuring: A Multi-step Process," in J. C. Oi (ed.) *Going Private in China: The Politics of Corporate Restructuring and System Reform*, Stanford, CA: Stanford University, The Walter H. Shorenstein Pacific Research Center, pp. 19–37.

Price, Alan H., Brightbill, Timothy C., Weld, Christopher B., and Nance, D. Scott (2007) "Money for Metal: A Detailed Examination of Chinese Government Subsidies to its Steel Industry," *Wiley Rein LLP Report*, Washington, DC: Wiley Rein.

Reddaway, Peter and Glinski, Dimitri (2001) *The Tragedy of Russia's Reforms: Market Bolshevism Against Democracy*, Washington, DC: United States Institute of Peace Press.

Rizhao City Newsnet (2007) "Du Shuanghua—Rizhao gangtie jituan dongshizhang" (Du Shanghua: CEO of Rizhao Steel Group), Rizhao Information Website, January 1, available online: www.rz114.cn/manager/qyj107.html (accessed July 22, 2010).

Reuters (2008) "RPT-China's Rizhao, Shandong Steel Agree to Consolidate," November 5, available online: www.reuters.com/article/ idUSSHA2680120081106 (accessed July 20, 2010).

Sachs, Jeffrey D. (1993) *Poland's Jump to the Market Economy*, Cambridge, MA: MIT Press.

Shleifer, Andrei and Treisman, Daniel (2001) *Without a Map: Political Tactics and Economic Reform in Russia*, Cambridge, MA: MIT Press.

Steinfeld, Edward S. (1998) *Forging Reform in China: The Fate of State-Owned Industry*, New York: Cambridge University Press.

Tilly, Charles (1986) *The Contentious French*, Cambridge, MA: Harvard University Press.

Tilly, Charles, Tilly, Louise, and Tilly, Richard (1975) *The Rebellious Century, 1830–1930*, Cambridge, MA: Harvard University Press.

Treisman, Daniel (2007) "Putin's Silovarchs," *Orbis* 51: 141–153.

Walder, Andrew G. (1986) *Communist Neo-Traditionalism: Work and Authority in Chinese Industry*, Berkeley, CA: University of California Press.

Walder, Andrew G. (1992a) "Local Bargaining Relationships and Urban Industrial Finance," in K. Lieberthal and D. M. Lampton (eds.) *Bureaucracy, Politics, and*

Decision-Making in Post-Mao China, Berkeley, CA: University of California Press, pp. 308–333.

Walder, Andrew G. (1992b) "Property Rights and Stratification in Socialist Redistributive Economies," *American Sociological Review* 57: 524–539.

Walter, Carl E. (2010) "The Struggle Over Ownership: How the Reform of State Enterprises Changed China," *Copenhagen Journal of Asian Studies* 28: 83–108.

Walter, Carl E. (2011) "Stock Markets and Corporate Reform: A Pandora's Box of Unintended Consequences," in J. C. Oi (ed.) *Going Private in China: The Politics of Corporate Restructuring and System Reform*, Stanford, CA: Stanford University, The Walter H. Shorenstein Pacific Research Center, pp. 203–239.

Walter, Carl E. and Howie, Fraser J. T. (2006) *Privatizing China: Inside China's Stock Markets*, 2nd ed., Singapore: John Wiley.

Walter, Carl E. and Howie, Fraser J. T. (2011) *Red Capitalism: The Fragile Financial Foundation of China's Extraordinary Rise*, Singapore: John Wiley.

World Steel Association (2009) *Steel Statistical Yearbook 2008*, Brussels: Worldsteel Committee on Economic Studies.

10 Public sector units in China and India

Inefficient producers or creators of crucial knowledge assets?

Jayan Jose Thomas

Introduction

India and China, two of world's fastest growing economies, face similar policy challenges in relation to their respective public sectors. A view that has gained much influence is that the public sectors are a weak link in these countries' otherwise exciting growth stories, and therefore they must be reduced in size. This chapter, reviewing the relation between public sector and economic growth in India and China over a long period, contests the above opinion. Public sector units in India and China are frequently portrayed as 'inefficient' producers, causing a drain on the national economies. On the other hand, this paper highlights that public sector units are also creators of knowledge assets that are so crucial to these countries' future growth and competitiveness.

This chapter is organized as follows. The major objective of public sector investments in India and China from the 1950s was to speed up the industrialization programme in these countries. Even in 2009–10, the share of industrial sector (manufacturing, electricity and mining) in real investments by central government public sector enterprises was 74.4 per cent in India (GOI 2011a). The next section of this chapter makes a broad review of the state of industrial and especially manufacturing sector in India, making comparisons with China wherever possible. Next is a review of the various stages in the evolution of India's policies towards the public sector from the 1950s until the 1980s, and the following section analyses the policy changes in India after the beginning of economic reforms in 1991–92. Then I review the various phases in China's economic transition and the role played by the public sector in each. The next section discusses the role of the public sector as a creator of crucial knowledge assets, followed by concluding remarks.

Development of the industrial sector: India compared with China

The diversification of GDP in India occurred largely from agriculture to services, not from agriculture to industry—in a notable contrast with the experiences of China and other East Asian countries. In India, the contribution of manufacturing to GDP was only 16 per cent in 2009–10, while the combined share of services and construction was 65 per cent (see Figure 10.1 and Table 10.1). In comparison, manufacturing contributed 31 per cent to China's GDP (in 2006). Per capita manufacturing value added (at constant 2000 US$) was $91 in India in 2006; the corresponding figures were $530 for China and $4,131 for South Korea (World Bank 2011) (see Table 10.2 and Thomas 2010).

The slow expansion of the manufacturing sector has stunted the diversification of India's occupational structure. Even in 2009–10, of the total working population of 459 million in India, 238 million (52 per cent) were engaged in agriculture and allied activities. The slow progress in occupational diversification has also resulted in a relatively low labour participation rate—the proportion of population (15 years and above) who are economically active—in India. According to ILO (International Labour Organization) data for 2008, labour participation rate was only 56 per cent in India compared to 74 per cent in China and 71 per cent in Brazil. Female labour participation rates have been particularly low in India: only 33 per cent compared to China's 68 per cent (both in 2008). Informal sector workers form more than 90 per cent of India's total employment (Thomas 2011a).

In the late 2000s, the manufacturing sector provided employment to 52 million, or 11.4 per cent of India's total workforce (see Table 10.1). Within manufacturing, the factory sector, which broadly represents organized manufacturing, employed 12 million workers (in 2004–05). The rest of the manufacturing workers were engaged in small, informal enterprises in the unregistered sector. In India, registered factories comprise all factories that employ more than ten workers and operate with the aid of electric power as well as factories that employ more than 20 workers without the aid of electric power.

From 1978, China's labour market began to be liberalized, and the process picked up speed from the mid-1990s. As part of the reforms since the mid-1990s, lifetime tenures for workers began to be replaced by contracted tenures, large state-owned enterprises began to lay off workers, and workers began to migrate in large numbers from rural to urban areas (Ghose 2008). Despite such changes, China is distinctly ahead of India in terms of the actual numbers and quality of jobs generated.

In China, regular employment refers largely to salaried employment in formal enterprises, whereas irregular employment refers to casual wage employment and self-employment in both non-formal and formal enterprises. We do not have enough information to examine how far regular employment in China is comparable to formal or organized employment in India. Yet it is notable that in 2004/05, regular employment in manufacturing in China was 104 million (when Indian manufacturing employed a total of 56 million with only 12 million of them in the organized sector) (see Tables 10.2 and 10.3). Ghose (2008) notes that in China since the mid-1990s, labour incomes from all types of employment increased substantially even though the proportion of employed persons enjoying job security and non-wage benefits declined. On the other hand, growth of workers' wages and labour productivity decelerated in India during 1999–2005 (Thomas 2011a).

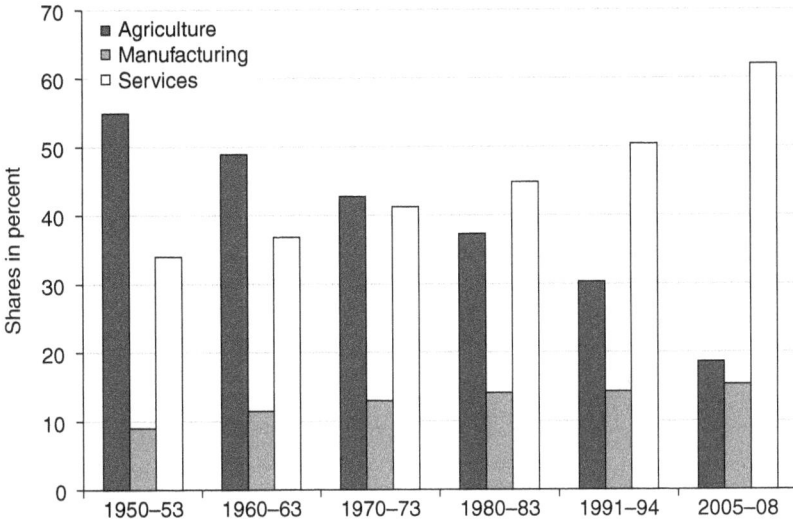

Figure 10.1 The shares of different sectors in India's GDP (at factor cost at 1999–2000 prices), 1950–53 to 2005–08, shares in percentages (source: *National Accounts Statistics*, various years).

Note
Construction is included within the service sector. The figures reported in this graph under 'agriculture' pertain to agriculture and allied activities such as fishing and forestry.

Long-term trends in India's manufacturing growth

Examining a plot of gross value added by India's organised manufacturing (using Annual Survey of Industries data) for the period 1959–60 to 2007–08, one can identify seven distinct growth phases. Growth rates for the different growth phases have been estimated using semi-logarithmic regression (see Figure 10.2 and Table 10.4).

The seven growth phases include a period of relatively fast growth of manufacturing from 1959–60 to 1964–65, followed by a period of much slower growth during 1965–66 to 1972–73. Within the second growth phase, manufacturing growth was statistically zero during the four-year period 1965–66 to 1968–69. Manufacturing growth picked up speed again from the mid-1970s but dropped to exceptionally low levels in the two years 1979–80 and 1980–81. India's manufacturing sector resumed faster growth from 1981–82 onwards. The six-year period from the mid- to late-1980s was one of particularly fast growth, but this phase too came to a close by 1991–92, a year in which India also faced a major balance of payments crisis.

Industrial growth in India has exhibited wide fluctuations after 1991. According to the Annual Survey of Industries (ASI), India's industrial sector expanded at relatively fast rates for four years after the start of economic reforms in

Table 10.1 Sector-wise distribution of India's GDP and employment[1]

Sectors	Shares in GDP, %		Shares in employment, %		Employment in millions
	1982–93	2009–10	1983	2009–10	2009–10
1. Agriculture and allied activities	35.1	14.6	68.2	51.8	238
2. Mining and quarrying	2.8	2.4	0.6	0.6	3
3. Manufacturing	14.3	16.1	10.6	11.4	52
4. Electricity, gas and water	1.5	2.0	0.3	0.3	1
5. Services and construction	45.0	64.9	19.9	35.8	165
5a. Construction	7.7	7.9	2.3	9.6	44
5b. Trade, hotels, transport and communication	16.7	26.5	8.8	15.7	72
5c. Financing, insurance, real estate and business service	8.3	17.2	0.7	2.2	10
Of which, IT[2] sector	–	4.1	–	–	2.2[3]
5d. Community, social and personal service	12.4	13.1	8.1	8.3	38
GDP/Total employment	100.0	100.0	100.0	100.0	459

Source: based on Thomas (2012); National Association of Software and Service Companies (2011) for data on the IT sector.

Notes
1 Totals may not tally because of rounding.
2 Information technology sector refers to the IT industry (mainly software production), engineering and research and development services, and IT-enabled services.
3 Figures for 2008–09; GDP at factor cost at 2004–05 constant prices.

Table 10.2 Manufacturing sectors of India and China: a comparison

	India[1]	China
Manufacturing value added as % of GDP, 2006	16.1	30.9
Manufacturing employment, in millions, 2005[2]	56	104
of which organized sector employment, in millions, 2005	12	–
Per capita manufacturing value added, in constant 2000 US$, 2006	91	530

Source: World Bank (2011); Ghose (2008); Thomas (2011a).

Notes
1 The employment figures for India correspond to the year 2004–05.
2 Refers to regular employment in manufacturing in China and to total (the sum of organized and unorganized) employment in India.

1991–92. But, subsequently, output growth decelerated and jobs were lost in most industries in India between 1996–97 and 2001–02. The severity of industrial recession in India during 1996–97 to 2001–02 was probably more than during any other periods of slow growth since 1959–60. The worst phase of industrial stagnation since the mid-1960s lasted for only four years compared to the six years of statistically zero growth since the mid-1990s.

India's industrial growth revived again from the second quarter of 2002–03. A surge in exports was a key feature of this growth revival. However, the revival of industrial growth in India since 2002–03 appeared to have lasted less than five years. The growth of IIP (index of industrial production) in India was on a downhill from April 2007 onwards—notably, months before the financial crisis began in the US, not to speak of its global spread since August 2008. The onset of the global financial and economic meltdown in August–September 2008 has

Table 10.3 The structure of employment and GDP of China, various years

		1991	1995	2000	2006
Shares in GDP, %	Primary[1]	17.5	12.3	9.5	6.7
	Secondary	52.6	60.6	62.8	65.6
	Tertiary	29.9	27.1	27.7	27.7
Shares in employment, %	Primary	59.7	52.2	50.0	42.7
	Secondary	21.4	23	22.5	25.1
	Tertiary	18.5	24.8	27.5	32.2
Employment in millions	Primary	391	355	360	326
	Secondary	140	157	162	192
	Tertiary	124	169	198	246
	Total	655	681	721	764

Source: based on Prasad (2009).

Note
1 Primary sector covers farming, forestry, animal husbandry and fishing. Secondary sector covers industry (mining, manufacturing and energy production) and construction. Tertiary sector covers the rest.

compounded the problems faced by Indian industry. Export-oriented industries such as garments, textiles, leather and engineering have suffered a sharp fall in the demand for their products from Western countries. Year-on-year growth of India's exports was negative for 11 continuous months from October 2008 to August 2009 (Thomas 2009b).

Clearly, the overall trends in manufacturing growth do not suggest any revival during the post-1990 years (Thomas 2011b). The latest ASI data available is for the year 2008–09. ASI data suggest a slowdown in growth between 2007–08 and 2008–09. More importantly, estimates of employment from National Sample Surveys show a fall of 3.7 million jobs in total manufacturing in India between 2004–05 and 2009–10.

Growth of manufacturing, by industries

Further, manufacturing growth in India has been polarizing—between different industries, between the registered and unregistered sectors, and between different regions. Between 1990–91 and 2008–09, the growth of GDP from unregistered manufacturing fell behind the growth of GDP from the registered sector (or broadly, the factory sector) (National Accounts Statistics data). Within the factory sector, ASI data on value added for the period 1991–2006 show that the

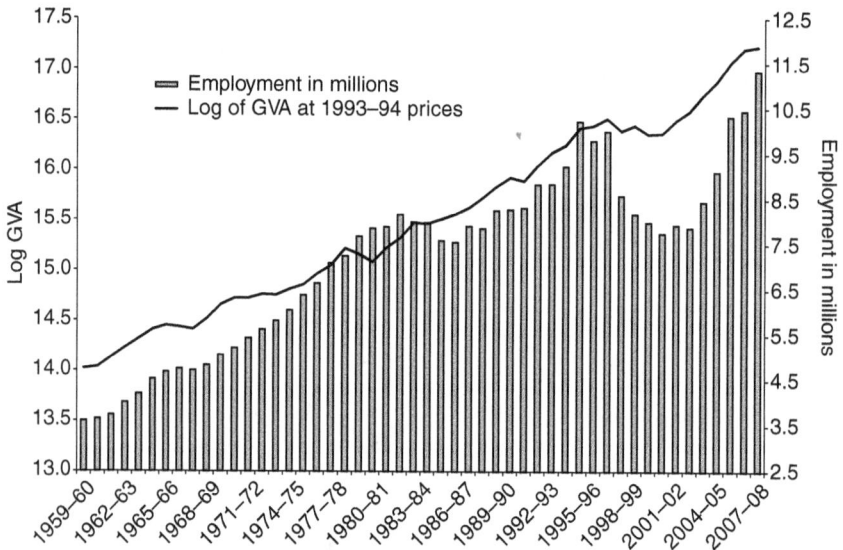

Figure 10.2 Employment in millions and log of gross value (GVA) added in India's factory sector, 1959–60 to 2007–08 (source: *Annual Survey of Industries*, various years).

Note
A part of the sharp fall in employment and value added in the late 1990s observed in this graph is due to certain changes in ASI coverage introduced during the 1998–2000 period.

Table 10.4 Sub-periods of growth in gross value added, organized manufacturing, 1959–60 to 2007–08

Sl. No.	Sub-periods	Rate of growth %	No. of years of growth
1	1959–60 to 1964–65	8.6	6
2	1965–66 to 1972–73	5.7	8
3	1973–74 to 1978–79	9.4	6
4	1981–82 to 1990–91	7.3	10
5	1992–93 to 1995–96	12.6	4
6	1996–97 to 2001–02	2.1[1]	6
7	2002–03 to 2007–08	15.8	6

Source: *Annual Survey of Industries*, compiled partly by Economic and Political Weekly Research Foundation (EPWRF).

Note
1 Not statistically significantly different from zero even at 10% level. All other growth rates are statistically significant at less than 5%. Growth rates are calculated using semi-logarithmic regression.

growth of capital-intensive industries, especially petroleum refining, was faster than the growth of labour-absorbing industries such as textiles and food.

In 2005–08, industries manufacturing chemicals, petrochemicals, rubber and refined petroleum products accounted for 24.2 per cent of the total value added by India's organized manufacturing sector. However, the combined share of these industries in total manufacturing employment in the country was only 4.9 per cent. On the other hand, textiles, garments and leather, together, accounted for a 33.5 per cent share in India's manufacturing employment, but the share of these industries in organized sector manufacturing value added was only 12.3 per cent (see Table 10.5).

Table 10.5 Manufacturing sector in India: shares of different industries in total employment and gross value added, percentages

	Organized manufacturing (ASI), 2005–08		Total manufacturing (NSS), 2009–10
	GVA	*Employment*	*Employment*
Food, beverages, tobacco	9.5	19.8	18.6
Textiles, garments, leather	12.3	24.0	33.5
Wood, furniture	1.4	2.8	15.5
Paper, printing	2.8	3.6	3.5
Chemicals and petroleum products	24.2	13.5	4.9
Metals, minerals, metal products	23.0	19.0	15.4
Machinery and equipment	16.4	10.8	5.8
Motor, transport equipment	10.4	6.5	3.0
Manufacturing	100	100	100

Source: NSSO (2011); *Annual Survey of Industries*, various years.

Employment generation in manufacturing

The National Sample Survey (NSS) provides data on employment in the whole of manufacturing, organized and unorganized combined. According to NSS data, 13.5 million manufacturing jobs were generated in India between 1993–94 and 2004–05; of these, 9.6 million were added during the period 1999–2000 to 2004–05 (see Table 10.6).

Export-oriented industries such as garment manufacturing (2.3 million new jobs), diamond cutting and polishing (0.7 million new jobs) and the textile industry were significant generators of employment in India during the 1999–2005 period. Another significant source of employment generation in India during these years were industries linked to construction, including the manufacture of bricks, cement and other non-metallic mineral products (1.1 million new jobs); manufacture of wood and wood products (0.64 million); and manufacture of furniture (0.5 million) (Thomas 2011b).

On the other hand, between 2004–05 and 2009–10, employment in Indian manufacturing declined by 3.7 million. There was significant decline in employment in industries manufacturing textiles, garments, leather and wood products. These were the very industries which had recorded good performance in employment generation during 1999–2005. But, by 2009–10, employment in these industries was hit by the global economic problems (see Table 10.6).

More worrying for the overall health of India's manufacturing sector was the somewhat stunted growth in employment between 1999–2000 and 2004–05 of two industries that are crucial to providing further growth linkages: chemicals and machinery equipment manufacturing. In both these industries, employment increase during the 16-year period after 1993–94 was less than the employment increase during the 10-year period of 1983 to 1993–94 (see Table 10.6).

Finally, at the global level India is still a small player in most industries even as China has dramatically increased its shares in global production in recent years. For instance, in the manufacture of electrical machinery, China's share increased from 12.2 per cent to 30.8 per cent between 2000 and 2007; India's share in this industry increased only marginally, from 1.6 per cent to 3.1 per cent (see Table 10.7).

The public sector and the evolution of political economy in India

After winning independence from British colonialism, India began a path of state-led development from the 1950s onwards, with the public sector playing a crucial role. The glorious years of Indian planning were from 1950 to the mid-1960s, roughly corresponding to the First, Second and Third Five-Year Plan periods. Guided by Jawaharlal Nehru's vision, the young republic assiduously set about the task of building industrial and technological capabilities.

Table 10.6 Net increase in employment in Indian manufacturing, 1983 to 2009–10, persons in 100,000 numbers

Industries	1983 to 1993–94	1993–94 to 1999–2000	1999–2000 to 2004–05	2004–05 to 2009–10
Food products, beverages, and tobacco products (15, 16)[1]	23.2	11.6	−2.5	−3.4
Textiles, apparel and leather products (17, 18, 19)	−2.8	−9.6	52.3	−16.4
Wood and paper products; printing, publishing (20, 21, 22)	9.4	13.3	13.4	−16.1
Chemical, rubber, plastics; petroleum, coal (23, 24, 25)	12.1	6.0	−0.5	−4.8
Non-metallic mineral products (26)	3.0	3.6	9.4	−1.5
Metals and metal products (27, 28)	4.2	8.8	2.5	0.7
Machinery and equipment other than transport equipment (29, 30, 31, 32)	6.6	0.2	1.0	4.9
Transport equipment and parts (34, 35)	0.2	−0.8	6.3	5.0
Other manufacturing industries[2] (33, 36)	7.9	1.1	13.1	0.8
Manufacturing	75.9	33.5	95.6	−36.9

Source: estimates based on NSSO (1987, 1997, 2001, 2006, 2011).

Notes
1 Figures given in brackets are the National Industrial Classification 1998 codes of the corresponding industries.
2 'Other manufacturing industries' include mainly the manufacture of furniture (361) and the manufacture of jewellery, diamond and gem cutting and polishing (369).

Table 10.7 Shares of India and China in total value added globally in selected industries, percentages, 2000 and 2007

		2000	2007
Textiles	India	3.4	4.2
	China	17.2	36.7
Coke, refined petroleum products, nuclear fuel	India	1.7	1.8
	China	7.6	15.7
Chemicals & chemical products	India	2.6	3.5
	China	5.8	12.5
Electrical machinery & apparatus	India	1.6	3.1
	China	12.2	30.8

Source: UNIDO (2009).

Public sector as an agent of resource mobilization and structural transformation

It may be noted that, even before 1947, the importance of the public sector and of planned development was recognized by the leaders of India's anti-imperial struggle as well as by the champions of domestic industry. In 1944, leading members of India's domestic industry drafted the Bombay Plan, which envisaged a major role for the government in the future economic path planned for India. India's Second Five-Year Plan, the implementation of which began in 1956, laid the foundations of a heavy industrialization strategy for the country. The Second Five-Year Plan accorded the highest priority to the building of a capital goods sector in India

The preference to investments in the capital goods sector in India that began with the Second Five-Year Plan was based on a two-sector model by Professor P.C. Mahalanobis. According to Mahalanobis' formulation, savings rate is a rigid function of structural features of the economy such as the capacity of the capital goods sector and capital–output ratios. A higher allocation of investment to the capital goods sector will result in a higher marginal savings rate, and thereby, faster rate of growth of output or consumption in the economy (Bhagwati and Chakravarty 1969; Chakravarty 1987).

India's heavy industrialization strategy was drawn up at a time when the basic constraint to development in third world countries was conceived to be the low levels of savings and capital formation in these countries. Arthur Lewis famously described the problem of transforming a country which saves 5 per cent of its income to a country which saves 20 per cent of its income (Chakravarty 1987). In India, the public sector was envisaged to become the active agent of resource mobilization for development (Balakrishnan 2010). Jawaharlal Nehru himself had made this clear through his writings and speeches. For instance, while inaugurating the second Hindustan Machine Tools Factory at Bangalore in 1961, he said: 'this factory has been made out of the profits or the surplus of the older

HMT factory and, rightly, therefore, it is called a gift to the nation by those who have been working in the old factory' (Nehru 1961 cited in Balakrishnan 2010).

India's planned development was able to achieve its stated objectives to a remarkable degree during the first 15 years, that is, from 1950 to the mid-1960s (Balakrishnan 2010). The Indian economy, especially the industrial sector, registered impressive rates of growth during these years, thus achieving a clear break from the stagnation of the colonial period. More importantly, there has been an impressive improvement in public sector savings and investment during these years (see Figure 10.3).

Inadequacies of India's state-led industrialization

After recording relatively fast rates of growth during the first 15 years, there was a sharp slowdown in India's industrial growth from the mid-1960s. This industrial growth slowdown provided the context for an important debate on Indian planning (Nayyar 1994). Some economists argued that the government should have intervened less in the economy given the inefficiencies that came to be associated with planned development. There were several criticisms on the country's industrial policy framework, particularly on the regime of licensing (Bhagwati and Desai 1970).

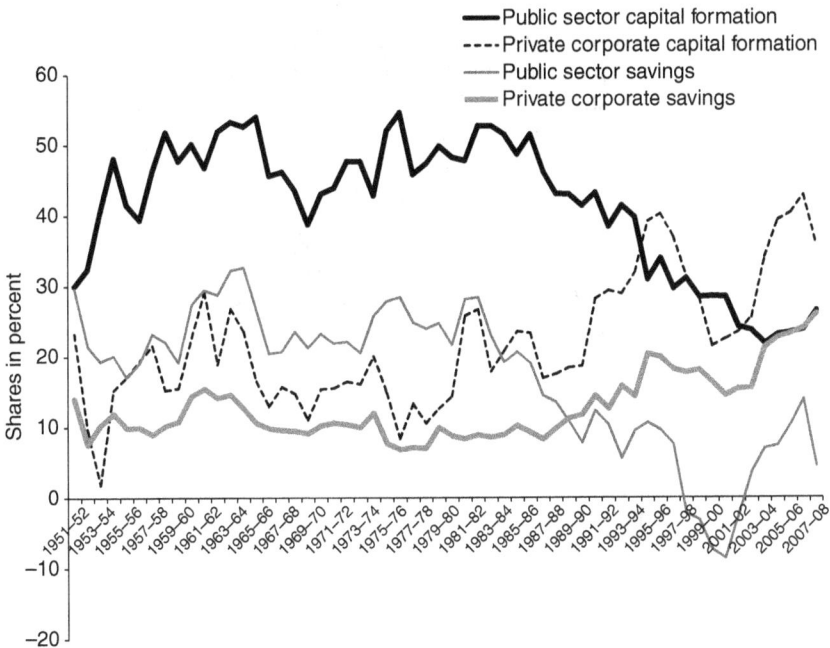

Figure 10.3 Shares of public sector and private corporate sector in total savings and capital formation in India, 1951–52 to 2008–09, percentages (source: *National Accounts Statistics*, various years).

However, another influential opinion in the academic debate was that the government ought to have intervened more in the economy, particularly to eradicate inequalities in the distribution of land and other assets (Bagchi 1970). The Indian state's planned intervention in economic growth was only modestly successful because of some of the inherent limitations of the societal and political conditions in the country on which the plan strategy was imposed. The state in post-1950 India attempted capitalist transformation through the instrument of planning without, however, transforming pre-capitalist agrarian relations—in other words, without effectively implementing land reforms or other measures to empower the vast sections of the under-privileged in the country.

As a consequence of the unequal income distribution and the slow growth of agricultural incomes, the expansion of domestic demand was slow. In turn, this was a major hindrance to India's industrial progress.

Indian industrialization was particularly unsuccessful with respect to generating employment opportunities to counter the massive levels of disguised and open unemployment in the country. According to Bhagwati and Chakravarty (1969), India's Five-Year plan models focused attention on scarce resources—that is, capital and foreign exchange—but assumed that labour was free. In the pattern of planned industrial development based on this assumption, it was not possible to make use of unemployed labour in the creation of extra social overhead capital (which could have helped in the redistribution of aggregate consumption).

It appears that a clear strategy on the small-scale sector was absent during the early years of Indian planning; this became another hindrance to employment expansion in the industrial sector. Plan models envisaged that the small-scale sector would produce consumer goods and generate the savings required to sustain the growth of the capital goods sector. However, there were ambiguities regarding the question of modernization of the small-scale sector. More often, advanced production techniques were discouraged—as in the case of the textile industry—for fear of creating unemployment. Overall investment levels in the small-scale sector remained low, and previous studies have identified the absence of credit facilities as the most important problem facing small firms in India.

Public sector as a source of employment and welfare

There was considerable political turmoil in India between the mid-1960s and the late 1970s. Prime Minister Indira Gandhi faced stiff opposition from within her ruling party as well as from outside; internal emergency was declared during 1975–77; and the non-Congress government that took office in 1977 lasted less than three years.

Given the continuance of large societal inequalities and the slow expansion of industrial employment (as discussed above), the public sector in India had to take on an important mantle, especially during the politically turbulent 1970s. The public sector became the single largest source of quality jobs and a major dispenser of welfare measures for the government. Total employment in central government public sector enterprises rose sharply from 0.7 million in 1971–72 to 2 million in 1982–83 (see Figures 10.4 and 10.5).

At the same time, however, public investment declined sharply in India after the mid-1960s (see Figure 10.3). Per capita availability of food grains and essential commodities declined to very low levels, especially in the drought year of 1965. The United States Congress refused to renew the Public Law 480 under which food grains were imported to India on concessional terms. With the suspension of American aid, the government's ability to import raw material and machinery for industrial development was greatly impaired (Frankel 2005: 293–295). In 1965, India and Pakistan were also engaged in a border war and this further added to the economic difficulties.

Public investment was (and continues to be) an important source of demand for capital goods and basic goods. Therefore, the decline in public investment growth after the mid-1960s resulted in a slowdown in the growth of demand for these goods (Patnaik and Rao 1977). The public sector is also the major source of investments in the creation of basic inputs (such as steel, petroleum, minerals) and infrastructures (such as railways, electricity, mining) for industrial expansion. The stagnation in public investments slowed down infrastructure expansion in the country, especially of railways and power (Ahluwalia 1985; Chandrasekhar 1988). Growth in infrastructure investment was at the rate of 17 per cent per annum in the first half of the 1960s, but this growth fell to 2 per cent per annum in the period between the mid-1960s and mid-1970s (Ahluwalia 1985: 76). It can be seen that the decline in public investment also resulted in a stagnation in investments by the private corporate sector (see Figure 10.3).

Bardhan (1984) attributed the high capital-output ratio and the low capacity utilization in the public sector to the 'politics of patronage' in the country. He notes:

> Senior appointments in the public sector are sometimes made more on the basis of political patronage than of merit.... Expensive projects are hastily initiated on grounds of political expediency or regional favouritism.... Irresponsibilities at the managerial, technical and worker levels thus feed on each other, creating a general atmosphere of demoralization and parasitism on the state
>
> (Bardhan 1984: 69–70)

There were several positive aspects, too, about the economic policies initiated in India between the mid-1960s and late 1970s. Indeed many of these policies were marked by a yearning for self-sufficiency and a rhetorical commitment to socialism. India inaugurated the 'Green Revolution' in agriculture in 1965 and 14 large commercial banks in the country were nationalized in 1969. These measures helped to revive savings and created a new class of capitalists and entrepreneurs in the Indian countryside. Policy measures such as the Indian Patent Act of 1970 and Foreign Exchange Regulation Act of 1973 contributed in some measure to the building of India's indigenous manufacturing capabilities.

Revival of public sector investments and industrial growth during the 1980s

The 1980s were a decade of gradual economic reforms in India—a period of transition between state-directed socialism and fast-paced market reforms. The industrial regulatory framework in the country began to be liberalized, and government policies displayed a favourable attitude towards private business enterprises. After a long phase of stagnation, India's industrial growth revived from the early 1980s (Raj 1984; Chandrasekhar 1988; Ahluwalia 1991).

Several economists argued that the rise in public investment in India during the 1980s was a factor behind the revival of industrial growth. Nagaraj (1990) found that the rate of gross fixed capital formation and the share of public sector investment in domestic capital formation rose during the 1980s. There was also an increase in the share of 'machinery and equipment' in gross fixed capital, and an acceleration in investment in railways, electricity and petroleum. Further, there was a distinct improvement in performance and output growth of public sector enterprises during the 1980s. Plant Load Factor of thermal power plants, which was on a course of decline in the late 1970s, increased steadily from 1980–81. Deficits in the power sector came down from 16 per cent in 1979–80 to 6.7 per cent in 1984–85. In railways, the revival of investment was followed by a streamlining of its operations and improvement in efficiency in the use of railway wagons. Studies have further shown that the growth of total factor productivity in Indian manufacturing accelerated to 3.4 per cent per annum during the first half of the 1980s, compared to the negative growth rate (−0.3 percent per annum) during the preceding 15 years of industrial stagnation (Ahluwalia 1991).

It was during the 1980s that the early stirrings of the information technology (IT) and telecom revolutions occurred in India. With more income in the hands of the Indian middle class, there was an explosion in the demand for consumer goods, from passenger cars to toothpaste. More significant were the rapid expansion of rural non-agricultural employment opportunities and the substantial reduction of poverty during this decade.

The public sector in India during the period of economic reforms

In 1991–92, in the wake of a balance of payments crisis, India initiated wide-ranging measures for economic liberalization. The country's policies relating to the macroeconomy, trade, industry, foreign investment, public sector enterprises (PSEs), agriculture and the social sector have been recast, thus marking a clear transition to a market-led model of economic growth.

The disinvestment of government equity in public sector enterprises has been an important objective of economic reforms in India from 1991–92. In the interim budget of 1991–92, the government announced its intention to divest a maximum of 20 per cent of its equity in selected central government PSEs. Since the 1990s, there has been a clear stagnation or even decline in the numbers of

PSEs and public sector employees. The shares of the public sector in total invest-ment and savings in the country were on a downward trend too (see Figures 10.3, 10.4 and 10.5).

The programme of disinvestment received further impetus towards the end of the 1990s. The budget speech of 1998–99 announced that, in general, the gov-ernment shareholding in non-strategic PSEs could be brought down to a low of 26 per cent, even as the government would continue to retain majority holding in strategically important units. Defence, atomic energy and railway transport were identified as areas of strategic importance. In other, non-strategic sectors, the government would go ahead with privatization only after installing proper mech-anisms for regulation and for avoiding concentration of private power. The budget speech of 2000–01 announced that the ownership share of government in PSEs operating in non-strategic sectors could be reduced even lower than 26 per cent. The strategic sale route to disinvestment would be given greater import-ance (GOI 2011a).

The government policy on disinvestment during the early 2000s is well sum-marized in the President of India's address to the joint sitting of Parliament in February 2002:

> disinvestment in public enterprises is no longer a matter of choice, but an imperative. The prolonged fiscal haemorrhage from the majority of these enterprises cannot be sustained any longer.... [T]he shift in emphasis from disinvestment of minority shares to strategic sale has yielded excellent results.
>
> (cited in Muralidharan 2003)

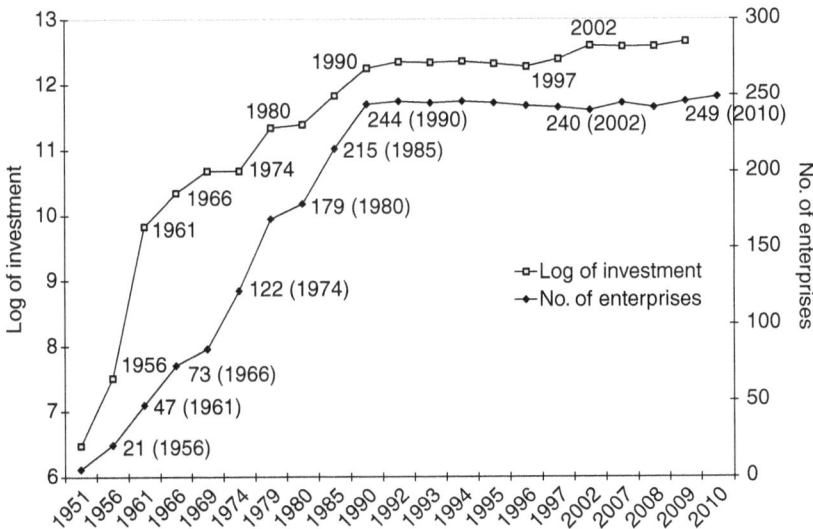

Figure 10.4 Central public sector enterprises in India: actual numbers and log of invest-ment, 1951 to 2010 (source: 'Public Enterprises Survey', various issues).

The government announced that the proceeds from disinvestment would be utilized for investments in the social sector, for restructuring of PSUs, and for clearing of public debts.

The reality, however, was that the major PSUs that were disinvested or sold to strategic partners during the early 2000s were profit-making ones. In fact, many of the disinvestment deals during these years amounted to handing over profitable PSUs operating in strategic areas to private monopolies. Thus, Videsh Sanchar Nigam Limited (VSNL), which was the sole international long-distance telecom provider and also the largest Internet service provider in India in the late 1990s, was sold to the Tata Group. The government abandoned a move for the acquisition of Indian Petrochemicals Ltd (IPCL) by the publicly owned Indian Oil Corporation Ltd, which would have created a major oil and petrochemical giant in the public sector. Instead, the government allowed IPCL to be taken over by the Reliance Group, one of the largest private sector companies in the country (Sridhar 2006).

Serious allegations of irregularity have been raised about several disinvestment deals that occurred during the early 2000s. The report of the Comptroller and Auditor General of India pointed out that the value of 'surplus land' amounting to 773 acres was not reckoned while determining the value of VSNL during its strategic sale. The Comptroller and Auditor General report also raised questions regarding the valuation of assets of Bharat Aluminium Company (BALCO)

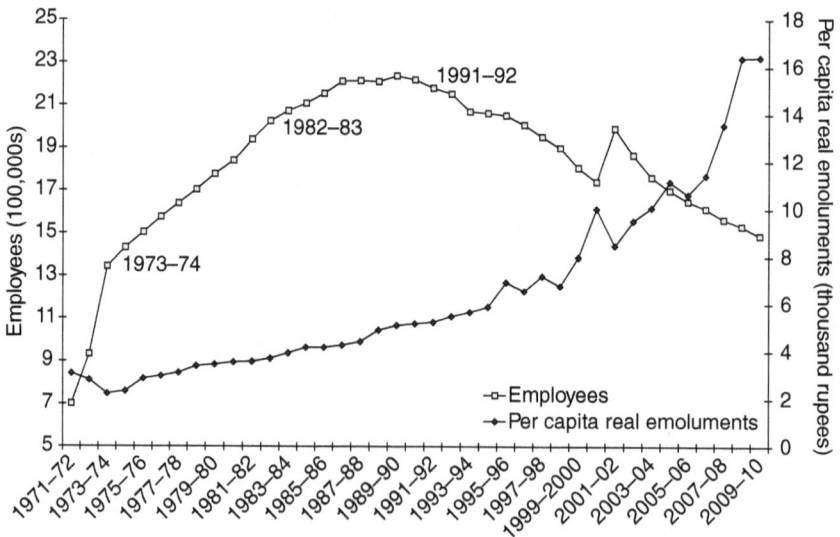

Figure 10.5 Central public sector enterprises in India: employees and annual per capita real emoluments (source: data reported in GOI 2011b).

Note
Emoluments deflated by Consumer Price Index for India (1960 = 100).

and Modern Food Industries Ltd (MFIL). Some of the enterprises turned 'sick' and substantially reduced their workforce after privatization. The post-adjustment claims made by the strategic partners were, in some instances, more than the amount that the government received through the privatization process (Sridhar 2006).

The government's plans for disinvestment met with considerable political opposition. In the general elections held in May 2004, the ruling alliance led by Bharatiya Janata Party was defeated, and a new United Progressive Alliance government led by the Congress Party and supported by left political parties came to power in India. The new government proceeded much more cautiously on disinvestment, to a large extent because of the pressure exerted on it by the left. In January 2005, the government indicated its intention to list large, profitable PSEs on the domestic stock exchanges and to selectively sell a minority stake in listed, profitable PSEs. At the same time, it was also decided that the government would retain at least 51 per cent shares as well as full management control of these enterprises (GOI 2011a). The Indian government has announced its intention to speed up the disinvestment programme again in the 2011–12 Union Budget.

A major casualty of the sharp slowdown in public sector investments in India since the 1990s is the state of the country's infrastructure, especially the power sector. As shown in Table 10.8, average yearly rates of growth of energy generation in India have slowed considerably during the post-1991 years. The comparison with China with respect to the growth of energy generation capacity is particularly instructive (Table 10.9). As power generation has lagged far behind economic growth, power deficits have become quite frequent in several regions of India.

It is important to note that the impact of power shortages has been severest on small-scale industrial enterprises. Reports indicate that power shortages have crippled the growth of small-scale industrial units, especially in textiles and engineering, in major industrial towns in the country including Ludhiana in Punjab and Coimbatore in Tamil Nadu. Thomas (2009b) reported that several textile and engineering firms in Tamil Nadu were operating at 50 per cent or even less of their production capacities between November 2008 and May 2009, when the state government imposed severe restrictions on the use of power. Notably, micro and small firms in Coimbatore were paying Rs.4.30 or more per

Table 10.8 Rates of growth of energy generation in India, percentages, different periods[1]

Period	Rate of growth
1977–78 to 1990–91	8.6
1991–92 to 1999–2000	6.8
2000–01 to 2009–10	5.7

Source: data from Ministry of Power reported in GOI (2011b).

Note
1 Energy generated by utilities and non-utilities from hydroelectric, thermal, renewable-energy and nuclear sources. Rates of growth calculated using semi-logarithmic regression.

Table 10.9 Energy generation in India and China in billion KWh, various years

Year	Energy generation in billion KWh		China/India
	China	India	
1990	621	289	2.1
1995	1,008	418	2.4
2000	1,356	555	2.4
2005	2,500	697	3.6
2008	3,467	840	4.1

Source: GOI (2011b), A. 27 and www.stats.gov.cn/tjsj/ndsj/2010/indexeh.htm (Table 7.6).

unit (or per kilowatt hour) of electricity and still suffering power interruptions. At the same time, the production facilities of multinational companies, such as Hyundai located in Chennai, were offered uninterrupted power supply at cheaper rates as part of the Memorandum of Understanding signed by these companies with the Tamil Nadu government (Thomas 2009b).

The transition from state to market in China

After the establishment of the People's Republic of China in 1949, the Chinese leadership under Mao Zedong set out on a socialist path of development for the country. The prominent features of this development transition included huge investments in heavy industries and tight government control over market forces. Investment as a share of China's GDP jumped to 26 per cent as early as 1954. Between 1952 and 1978, China's industrial output grew at an exceptionally fast rate of 11.5 per cent annually, and industry's share in GDP climbed from 18 per cent to 44 per cent (Naughton 2007: 56).

State-owned enterprises played a key role in China's industrial transition during the Maoist era (Nolan and Wang 1999). After the collectivization of agriculture in 1956, the Chinese government initiated compulsory procurement of agricultural products from farmers at low fixed prices. While relatively low food prices ensured low and stable industrial wages, the prices of industrial goods were fixed at relatively high levels by the government. It is argued that such artificially set prices benefited China's state-owned industrial enterprises, which recorded very high profits even when they were not very efficient (Naughton 2007: 55–77).

China's economic reforms had been a highly gradual process for most of the 1980s. The reform measures were first initiated in the agricultural sector. Food grain procurement prices were raised, and procurement targets were stabilized. These measures greatly eased the pressure exerted on farmers during the Maoist years. Rural collectives were eventually allowed to contract individual pieces of land to farm households, and this led to a surge in agricultural production.

Another important reform measure was the setting up of township and village enterprises (TVEs). The number of TVEs in China expanded at extremely fast rates between 1978 and the mid-1990s. During the period 1978 to 1996, employment in TVEs increased from 28 million to 135 million, and output from TVEs as a share of China's GDP increased from 6 per cent to 26 per cent. TVEs produced a significant impact on employment generation in China, especially in its rural areas. TVEs were also a source of competition to China's state-owned enterprises (SOEs) (Naughton 2007: 274–275). As part of the reform process, there was considerable decentralization of power from the central government to the local levels, and local governments became major supporters of the growth of TVEs.

During the early years of reforms, i.e. between 1978 and 1984, SOEs were given managerial autonomy. Managers of these enterprises were allowed to make profits out of their surplus (after meeting their planned quotas) production. In the mid-1980s, the 'contract responsibility system' was introduced in SOEs, in an attempt to separate ownership and management and thereby transform SOEs into truly independent economic entities. However, while managers of these enterprises could take credit for the profits made, they could not be held responsible for any losses. Therefore, it is argued that this phase of restructuring of SOEs was only partially successful (Xiao *et al.* 2010; Shiyi *et al.* 2011). At the same time, Nolan and Wang (1999: 187), point out that 'many fast-growing and fast-modernising large SOEs emerged under the contract system'.

Since the mid-1990s, the Chinese policy on SOEs has been that the government retains direct control over the large SOEs in strategically important industries, while smaller SOEs in non-strategic sectors are privatized. This policy is best characterized as one of 'grasping the big and letting go of the small'. Several SOEs were converted into joint stock corporations. SOEs also directed their investments into areas with large economies of scale and with strategic importance such as energy, petroleum refining and telecommunications.

The number of SOEs declined sharply after 1998. At the same time, however, SOEs continued to retain a domineering presence in the case of large enterprises. In 2005, 3,999 SOEs accounted for a 25 per cent share in the total numbers of large and medium-sized industrial enterprises in China, but their share in the total assets of these large and medium-sized enterprises was 58 per cent. In 2007, of the top-500 Chinese enterprises, 69.8 percent were SOEs and they accounted for 94 per cent of the total assets of these top-500 enterprises (Xiao *et al.* 2010) (see Table 10.10).

The Chinese record in employment and inequality: a key difference with the Indian experience

Compared to India, China had made remarkable achievements in social spheres during the Maoist period, before the country set out on a path of market-led economic reforms in 1978. Drèze and Sen (2002) highlight that China's much better record compared to India in human development indicators at the end of the 1970s was not on account of faster economic growth, but a result of extensive

Table 10.10 Performance of top-500 Chinese enterprises by type of ownership, 2007

	Distribution by ownership, %					Return on assets, %
	No. of enterprises	Assets	Profits	Employees	Taxes	
State-owned	69.8	93.6	87.9	89.3	92.7	1.4
Collective	5.8	4.2	2.2	2.4	1.7	0.8
Private	17.8	1.7	7.1	7	3.9	6.1
Foreign	6.6	0.5	2.8	1.3	1.7	8.5
	100	100	100	100	100	

Source: 'A Report on the Development of China's Enterprises 2007'. Beijing: Enterprise Management Publishing House: 88 (cited in Xiao *et al.* 2010).

state action, including public redistributive policies and policies for nutritional support and health care (Drèze and Sen 2002: 121). Carl Riskin (1987) writes that during the Cultural Revolution decade of 1966–76, Mao advanced principles that were aimed at self-reliance and egalitarianism. These principles tried to reduce 'the three great differences'—between 'city and countryside, worker and peasant and mental and manual labour' (Riskin 1987: 201–202). According to Riskin (1987: 250), 'China's poor emerged from the Maoist era significantly better off than the poor in most other developing countries' although poverty continued to remain in China. The overall Gini coefficient estimated for China declined to 0.33 in 1979, indicating less inequality compared to India (0.38 in 1975–76) and Indonesia (0.44 in 1976) (Riskin 1987: 250).

It may be noted that at the end of the Maoist phase of development, although China was egalitarian, it was also dualistic. There existed major gaps in income levels *between* the urban and rural sectors, while, at the same time, there was a great degree of equality *within* each of these sectors. The early years of economic reforms in China helped to bring down the country's rural–urban disparities considerably. Decollectivization of agriculture, higher agricultural output and higher prices for agricultural products gave a boost to rural incomes in China. China became less dualistic, in addition to retaining its earlier achievement of low levels of inequality within the rural and urban sectors. As a result, by the early 1980s, overall inequality levels in China were reduced to the lowest ever levels. In 1983, China's overall Gini coefficient, measured on income, was 0.28 (Naughton 2007). It is claimed that China was one of the most egalitarian societies in the world in the early 1980s (Naughton 2007: 217–222).

State employment had been a major source of employment in China's urban areas. Publicly owned enterprises, which comprise SOEs, urban collectives and TVEs, accounted for 24 per cent of the total employment in the country even in 1996, almost two decades after the reform process (Naughton 2007: 183). However, from the mid-1990s, workers in publicly owned enterprises were laid off in large numbers. Solinger (2002) showed that the number of workers laid off from SOEs in China (*xiagang* workers) ranged between 40 and 46 million.

The fast growth of the non-state sector after the mid-1990s could compensate, to a great extent, the job losses in SOEs (Shiyi *et al.* 2011).

It is to be noted that, after the mid-1990s, along with China's greater integration into the world economy, there had been a worsening of inequalities in the country. Not only peasants in rural areas but large sections of urban residents as well saw their incomes falling in China after the mid-1990s. Solinger's (2002) study on workers laid off from China's SOEs (*xiagang* workers) point to their deteriorating living conditions. Many of these laid-off workers were middle-aged, under-educated and unskilled, and they were unable to find new employment opportunities in the private sector, especially in sectors such as information technology and financial services. At the same time, for new job opportunities requiring only less skills and education, displaced urban workers had to compete with large numbers of poor migrants from China's interior regions (Solinger 2002).

From low wage competition to innovation: how easy is the transition for India and China?

The current phase of growth in India and China is, to a large extent, based on the availability and low costs of labour, be it factory workers or call-centre operators. However, advantages arising from low wages are likely to be short-lived.[1] Therefore, the challenge for firms in India and China is to move up the value chain and become leaders in innovation.

MNCs in the United States and Western Europe continue to reign supreme in high-technology industries. For instance, R&D spending by Pfizer of the United States in 2002 was US$4.8 billion, which was more than the national R&D expenditure of India (of $3.7 billion in 2001) (UNCTAD 2005: 120). At the same time, firms in India and China also suffer from several limitations. Lardy (2002) and Steinfeld (2004) argue that China's integration with the global economy remains a shallow one. Steinfeld's study, which is based on a survey of 1,500 enterprises across five major Chinese cities, showed that Chinese firms play a major role in a process of modularization of global manufacturing, in which component manufacturing processes are spread out across locations and firms all over the globe. However, Chinese firms engaged in modularized manufacturing are competing on the basis of low costs and high volumes, and they continuously face the risk of being eliminated by the next low-cost producer. Even in the case of its high-technology exports, China is largely an assembler of high value added components. It is estimated that 80 per cent of the value added by high-technology firms in China is created elsewhere (Steinfeld 2004).

Based on an analysis of firms in the aerospace, oil and pharmaceuticals industries, Nolan and Zhang (2002) found that China's leading firms face stiff challenges. In many sectors of global business, especially after the 1980s, there has been a growing concentration at the top, with a few leading, often oligopolistic firms, emerging as core 'systems integrators', and they control the entire sector. It was found that in terms of competitive ability, Chinese firms were weak vis-à-vis these global giants, despite over two decades of economic reforms in China. The relative weakness of Chinese firms was more marked in high-technology firms (Nolan and Zhang 2002).

D'Costa (2004) argues that India's software industry is overly dependent on the US export market and that this has locked the industry into a low innovation trajectory. It is also argued that India's IT industry comprises a large number of small, undifferentiated firms engaged in intense price-based competition in low-end activities (D'Costa 2009).

Recognizing the importance of publicly created knowledge assets

India and China still possess some advantages in innovation-based or knowledge-based industries. First is the advantage of human capital. In 2000–01, the total numbers of students enrolled for tertiary education were approximately 12 million in China and ten million in India (UNCTAD 2005: 162). Approximately 350,000 engineering graduates enter India's labour market every year. In 2004, China awarded 23,500 PhDs, 70 per cent of which were in science-related subjects (Altenburg *et al.* 2008). Second, both India and China have made huge public investments in science and technology over the past decades, and this is a strong base for future growth.

Since the 1990s, India has been a increasingly important player in high-technology services, especially software services. It is not adequately appreciated that this success is built largely on a foundation of public sector investments in the country in a range of high-technology areas. According to a senior employee of one of the first multinational giants to have set up an R&D centre in Bangalore (India) in the mid-1980s, 'one reason [for the investment] was the science and engineering institutions [in Bangalore]'. Further, 'We also wanted to collaborate with public sector units.... The depth of public sector companies in Bangalore was great.... We worked very closely with them, and many of them have over time launched very sophisticated and innovative systems.'[2]

Government's efforts in the innovation economy: China ahead of India

Given the growing challenges in the global innovation economy, it is impotent that PSUs in India and China continue to play an important role as generators of crucial knowledge assets in these countries. It appears that in recent times, China has clearly recognized the above-referred strategic importance of the public sector, whereas India has not.

In China, the government recently announced plans to raise the shares of seven 'new strategic industries' in the economy from the current 2 per cent to 15 per cent by 2020. These new industries, which include alternative fuel cars, biotechnology, environment and energy saving technologies, alternate energy, advanced materials, new generation IT and high-end manufacturing, are expected to transform China into a more advanced economy (Rabinovitch 2011). China has made rapid advances in the fields of health and agricultural biotechnology. Reports suggest that the government under Premier Zhu Rongji was highly concerned about the growing dominance of US biotechnology firms in Chinese agriculture and, therefore, the government stepped up funding for research on GM crops that are highly suited to local growing conditions (Chen 1999). In 1999, government expenditure on agricultural biotechnology research in China was nearly ten times the agricultural biotechnology research budgets of India and Brazil in the same year (Karplus 2003 cited in Thomas 2009a).

SOEs have received a substantial part of the stimulus packages unveiled by the Chinese government during 2008–09. Government majority firms such as China Mobile, Baoshan Steel and China National Petroleum Corporation are growing in size and stature.

With respect to making advances in research and development, India is falling significantly behind even China, not to speak of advanced Western countries (see Table 10.11). During 1999–2003, there were only 119 researchers in R&D per million people in India compared to 663 in China and 4,484 in the US (see Table 10.11). Despite the fact that India has a few world-class educational and research institutions, only 10 per cent of those belonging to the relevant age group get enrolled in institutes of higher education in India compared to 40–50 per cent in developed countries.[3] At the same time, China is aggressively promoting a programme of 'reverse brain drain'; the Chinese Academy of Sciences has many attractive schemes to woo returnee researchers (Zweig 2006).

Despite the advances made in the software industry, India has made only limited gains in high-technology manufacturing, such as the production of electrical systems. Bharat Heavy Electricals Limited (BHEL), the public sector unit which is India's premier producer of heavy electrical equipment, reported during the early 1990s that it could match its multinational rivals in product quality, price and delivery schedules. Yet it often lost out in securing contracts even in the domestic market because it was not able to offer long-term credit to its customers (Chakravarty 1990). Today, even as BHEL continues to be a profitable

Table 10.11 Indicators of performance in R&D: India, China and selected countries

Country	R&D expenditures as % of gross domestic product	Researchers in R&D	Patents granted to residents
	2000–03	1990–2003 per million people	2004 per million people
India	0.8	119	1.0
China	1.3	663	–
Brazil	1.0	344	–
South Korea	2.6	3,187	738
United States	2.6	4,484	281

Source: UNDP (2006: 327–330).

unit in the public sector, India's record in the manufacture of electrical and non-electrical machinery remains poor, especially in comparison with China. As Table 10.12 shows, there has been a sharp rise in recent years in the ratio of imports to output in the case of industries manufacturing machinery and equipment in India.

The case of India's pharmaceutical industry further illustrates a lack of commitment in the country to making advances in innovative industries. India's domestic pharmaceutical industry has benefited greatly from state intervention, notably in the form of the Indian Patent Act of 1970, which allowed only process patents on drugs and food products. The share of Indian firms in India's pharmaceuticals market (by sales) increased from 32 per cent in 1970 to 77 per cent in 2004 (Thomas 2009a). More importantly, domestic pharmaceutical firms manufacture and sell generic drugs at relatively low prices in India. Indian firms have been major exporters of active pharmaceutical ingredients (APIs) and pharmaceutical formulations of several medicines, including vaccines and anti-retrovirals (ARVs) (Thomas 2009a).

However, for all these the introduction of product patenting in India since 1 January 2005, as part of the country's commitments to the World Trade Organization's Trade Related Aspects of Intellectual Property Rights (TRIPS), has posed major challenges to the generic drug industry in India. Indian drug firms are no longer able to manufacture generic versions of patented drugs. For some years, India's leading drug producers have been trying to enter the highly competitive market for generic drugs in Western countries, but they face many challenges from global pharmaceutical giants, especially in the form of patent-related litigations. For instance, in 2007, Ranbaxy's legal and professional expenses were more than one-third of its R&D expenditures. This Indian drug company was later (in June 2008) taken over by Daiichi Sankyo

Table 10.12 Imports as a percentage share of domestic manufacturing output of machinery and equipment industries in India, 1996–97 to 2007–08

Years	Import as % of domestic manufacturing output of machine tools, machinery, electronic and computer goods, and transport-equipment industries
1996–97	26.1
1998–99	27.6
2000–01	23.6
2001–02	26.0
2002–03	30.1
2003–04	34.2
2004–05	31.1
2005–06	41.8
2006–07	43.6
2007–08	50.4

Sources: output figures from Annual Survey of Industries, various issues; import figures from Export Import Data Bank (2011).

of Japan. In recent years, MNCs have increased their presence in India, conducting contract research and clinical trials on global diseases, eyeing the market of rich patients in India and abroad (Thomas 2009a; Chaudhuri 2005). The biggest losers of these developments are the poor patients in India and other less developed countries, who are denied the supply of affordable, generic drugs.

Conclusions

Public sector units in India and China are frequently portrayed as 'inefficient' producers, causing a drain on the national economies. This chapter, reviewing the relation between public sector and economic growth in India and China over a long period, contests that opinion.

In India, during the early 1950s, the public sector was envisaged to become the active agent of resource mobilization for development. Between 1950 and the mid-1960s, India did record impressive expansion in public sector savings and investment. There was also a revival in overall industrial and economic growth of the country during this period, thus achieving a break from the economic stagnation during the colonial period.

However, the state-led industrialization in India was not successful in transforming either the pre-capitalist agrarian relations or the unequal income distribution in the country. More importantly, it failed to generate employment opportunities in manufacturing and non-agricultural sectors in sufficiently large numbers. Given these circumstances, the public sector became the single largest source of quality jobs and a major dispenser of welfare measures in India. During the politically turbulent 1970s, employment in public sector enterprises increased rapidly even as public investment declined sharply in India. Subsequently, however, there was a remarkable revival in public sector investment and an improvement in the performance and output of public sector enterprises in the country during the 1980s.

The disinvestment of government equity in PSEs has been an important objective of economic reforms in India from 1991–92, but the process was particularly fast for a few years during the early 2000s. While the stated objective of reforms was to privatize loss-making units, some of the major PSUs that were disinvested or sold to strategic partners in India were indeed profit-making ones. In fact, many of the disinvestment deals in India during the early 2000s amounted to handing over profitable PSEs operating in strategic areas to private monopolies. The sharp slowdown in public sector investments in India since the 1990s has worsened the state of the country's infrastructure, especially the power sector. Today power shortages are a major constraint to the growth of India's industrial sector, especially micro and small industries.

Compared to India, China has made remarkable achievements in reducing societal inequalities and in generating massive numbers of non-agricultural jobs during the Maoist period and during the early years of economic reforms. It appears that this has given greater freedom to the Chinese government while restructuring the country's SOEs. Since the mid-1990s, the Chinese policy on SOEs is best characterized as one of 'grasping the big and letting go of the small': i.e. the government retains direct control over the large SOEs in strategically important industries, while smaller SOEs in non-strategic sectors are privatized.

The crucial challenge of the future for India and China is to move up the value chain, from being low-cost producers to becoming leaders in innovation. But given the dominance of Western MNCs in the global innovation economy, it is important that PSUs in India and China emerge as generators of crucial knowledge assets in these countries. The public sector can help generate new innovations in agriculture and labour-absorbing industries that can transform the lives of millions of poor in these and other developing nations (for instance, biotechnological innovations that drastically enhance value addition in the jute industry).

The Chinese state's carefully planned investments in new areas such as biotechnology and alternative fuel cars indicate a clear recognition of the above-referred strategic importance of the public sector in that country. India had very well recognized the importance of the public sector as knowledge creators during the early decades of its planned development, but recent trends point to an absence of such commitment from the Indian state.

Notes

1 Reports indicate that average wages in China's coastal cities have already risen above the corresponding wages in major south-east Asian cities. In 2005, average monthly wages for a factory worker, including social security costs, was almost $350 in Shanghai and almost $250 in Shenzhen. By comparison, monthly wages of a factory worker were approximately $200 in Manila, $150 in Bangkok and $100 in Batam in Indonesia. See *The Economist* (2007).
2 See: http://timesofindia.indiatimes.com/business/international-business/Texas-Instrumental-in-getting-tech-MNCs-here/articleshow/6533555.cms#ixzz0zBv5yBSa (accessed 5 October 2010). [*Times of India* 'Texas "Instrumental" in Getting Tech MNCs Here', *Times of India*, 11 September 2010.]
3 See the report '30 New Universities to Expand Access to Quality Education' (2007).

References

'30 New Universities to Expand Access to Quality Education' (2007) *The Hindu*, 25 June, available online: www.hindu.com/2007/06/25/stories/ 2007062551480900.htm (accessed 5 October 2010).

Ahluwalia, I.J. (1985) *Industrial Growth in India—Stagnation since the Mid-Sixties*, Delhi: Oxford University Press.

Ahluwalia, I.J. (1991) *Productivity and Growth in Indian Manufacturing*, Delhi: Oxford University Press.

Altenburg, Tilman, Schmitz, Hubert and Stamm, Andreas (2008) 'Breakthrough? China's and India's Transition from Production to Innovation', *World Development*, 36(2): 325–344.

Bagchi, Amiya Kumar (1970) 'Long-Term Constraints on India's Industrial Growth 1951–1968', in E.A.G. Robinson and Michael Kidron (eds) *Economic Development in South Asia*, London: Macmillan, pp. 170–198.

Balakrishnan, Pulapre (2010) *Economic Growth in India: History and Prospect*, New Delhi: Oxford University Press.

Bardhan, Pranab (1984) *The Political Economy of Development in India*, New Delhi: Oxford University Press.

Bhagwati, Jagdish and Desai, Padma (1970) *India: Planning for Industrialization*, London: Oxford University Press.

Bhagwati, Jagdish N. and Chakravarty, Sukhamoy (1969) 'Contributions to Indian Economic Analysis: A Survey', *The American Economic Review* 59(4): part 2 (Supplement) (September): 1–73.

Chakravarty, Nitish (1990) 'Heavy Electrical Equipment: BHEL Progresses Despite Odds', *Survey of Indian Industry 1990*, Chennai: Hindu Group of Publishers.

Chakravarty, Sukhamoy (1987) *Development Planning: The Indian Experience*, New Delhi: Oxford University Press.

Chandrasekhar, C.P. (1988) 'Aspects of Growth and Structural Change in Indian Industry', *Economic and Political Weekly* 23(45/47): 2359–2370.

Chaudhuri, Sudip (2005) *The WTO and India's Pharmaceuticals Industry: Patent Protection, TRIPS, and Developing Countries*, New Delhi: Oxford University Press.

Chen, Zhangliang (1999) 'Unlimited Prospects for Biotechnology', interview with Chen Zhangliang, *Knowledge Economy* [*Zhishi Jingji*], December: 22–28, available online: www.usembassy-china.org.cn/sandt/biotechch.html (accessed 15 March 2006).

D'Costa, Anthony P. (2004) 'Export Growth and Path-Dependence: The Locking-in of Innovation in the Software Industry', in Anthony P. D'Costa and E. Sridharan (eds) *India in the Global Software Industry: Innovation, Firm Strategies and Development*, Basingstoke: Palgrave Macmillan, pp. 51–82.

D'Costa, Anthony P. (2009) 'Extensive Growth and Innovation Challenges in (Bangalore) India', in Govindan Parayil and Anthony P. D'Costa (eds) *The New Asian Innovation Dynamics: China and India in Perspective*, Basingstoke: Palgrave Macmillan, pp. 79–109.

Drèze, Jean and Sen, Amartya (2002) *India: Development and Participation*, New Delhi: Oxford University Press.

Export Import Data Bank (2011) Government of India, Department of Commerce, Government of India, available online: http://commerce.nic.in/eidb/default.asp (accessed 20 April 2011).

Frankel, Francine R. (2005) *India's Political Economy 1947–2004*, 2nd edition, New Delhi: Oxford University Press.

Ghose, Ajit K. (2008) 'The Growth Miracle, Institutional Reforms and Employment in China', *Economic and Political Weekly* 43(22): 47–56.

GOI (2011a) 'Public Enterprises Survey 2009–10', Volume I, New Delhi: Government of India, Ministry of Industry, Department of Public Enterprises.

GOI (2011b) *Economic Survey 2010–11*, New Delhi: Government of India, available online: http://indiabudget.nic.in/budget2011-2012/survey.asp (accessed 8 January 2014).

Karplus, Valerie (2003) 'Global Anti-GM Sentiment Slows China's Biotech Agenda', *YaleGlobal*, 26 September, available from: http://yaleglobal.yale.edu/content/ global-anti-gm-sentiment-slows-chinas-biotech-agenda (accessed 8 January 2014).

Lardy, Nicholas R. (2002) *Integrating China into the World Economy*, Washington DC: Brookings Institution Press.

Muralidharan, Sukumar (2003) 'Disinvestment Discord' *Frontline* 20(1): 18–31, available on: www.frontline.in/navigation/?type=static&page=archiveSearch& aid=200301 17005800400&ais=01&avol=20 (accessed 15 July 2011).

Nagaraj, R. (1990) 'Industrial Growth—Further Evidence and towards an Explanation and Issues', *Economic and Political Weekly* 25(41): 2313–2332.

National Association of Software and Service Companies (2011) Available online: www. nasscom.org (accessed 20 July 2011).

Naughton, Barry (2007) *The Chinese Economy: Transitions and Growth*. Cambridge, MA: The MIT Press.

Nayyar, Deepak (ed.) (1994) *Industrial Growth and Stagnation—The Debate in India*, Delhi: Oxford University Press.

Nehru, Jawaharlal (1961) 'A Gift to the Nation', speech at the inauguration of the Second Hindustan Machine Tools Factory at Bangalore. Reprinted in *Jawaharlal Nehru's Speeches Volume 4*, 1965, Publications Division, Ministry of Information and Broadcasting, Government of India, New Delhi.

Nolan, Peter and Wang, Xiaoqiang (1999) 'Beyond Privatization: Institutional Innovation and Growth in China's Large State-Owned Enterprises', *World Development* 27(1): 169–200.

Nolan, Peter and Zhang, Jin (2002) 'The Challenge of Globalization for Large Chinese Firms', *World Development* 30(12): 2089–2107.

NSSO (National Sample Survey Organization) (1987) Report on the Third Quinquennial Survey on Employment and Unemployment (Thirty Eighth Round, January–December 1983), New Delhi: Government of India, Department of Statistics, National Sample Survey Organization, Report No. 341.

NSSO (National Sample Survey Organization) (1997) Report on Employment and Unemployment in India, 1993–94 (Fiftieth Round, July 1993–June 1994), New Delhi: Government of India, Department of Statistics, National Sample Survey Organization, Report No. 409.

NSSO (National Sample Survey Organization) (2001) Report on Employment and Unemployment Situation in India 1999–2000, Parts I & II (Fifty Fifth Round, July 1999–June 2000), New Delhi: Government of India, Ministry of Statistics and Programme Implementation, National Sample Survey Organization, Report No. 458.

NSSO (National Sample Survey Organization) (2006) Report on Employment and Unemployment Situation in India 2004–05 Parts I & II (Sixty First Round, July 2004–June 2005), New Delhi: Government of India, Ministry of Statistics and Programme Implementation, National Sample Survey Organization, Report No. 515.

NSSO (National Sample Survey Organization) (2011) Key Indicators of Employment and Unemployment in India 2009–10 (Sixty Sixth Round, July 2009–June 2010).

Patnaik, Prabhat and Rao, S.K. (1977) 'Towards an Explanation of a Crisis in a Mixed Underdeveloped Economy', *Economic and Political Weekly* 1(6/8): 205–218.

Prasad, Eswar S. (2009) 'Is the Chinese Growth Miracle Built to Last?' *China Economic Review* 20: 103–123.

Rabinovitch, Simon (2011) 'China Outlines Strategic Industries', *Financial Times*, 4 August.

Raj, K.N. (1984) 'Some Observations on Economic Growth in India, 1952–53 to 1982–83', *Economic and Political Weekly* 19(41): 1801–1804.

Riskin, Carl (1987) *China's Political Economy: The Quest for Development since 1949*, New York: Oxford University Press.

Shiyi Chen, Jefferson, Gary H. and Zhang, Jun (2011) 'Structural Change, Productivity

Growth and Industrial Transformation in China', *China Economic Review* 22: 133–150.

Solinger, Dorothy J. (2002) 'Labour Market Reform and the Plight of the Laid-off Proletariat', *The China Quarterly* (170): 304–326.

Sridhar, V. (2006) 'Disinvestment: Scam Accounts', *Frontline* 6 October.

Steinfeld, Edward S. (2004) 'China's Shallow Integration: Networked Production and the New Challenges for Late Industrialization', *World Development* 32(11): 1971–1987.

The Economist (2007) 'The Problem with Made in China: Manufacturing in Asia', 13 January.

Thomas, Jayan Jose (2009a) 'Innovation in India and China: Challenges and Prospects in Pharmaceuticals and Biotechnology', in Govindan Parayil and Anthony P. D'Costa (eds) *The New Asian Innovation Dynamics: China and India in Perspective*, Basingstoke: Palgrave Macmillan, pp. 110–137.

Thomas, Jayan Jose (2009b) 'Industry: Hurdles to Growth', *Frontline* 23 October, available online: www.frontline.in/static/html/fl2621/stories/ 20091023262104700.htm (accessed 8 January 2014).

Thomas, Jayan Jose (2010) 'An Uneasy Coexistence: The New and the Old in Indian Industry and Services', in Anthony D'Costa (ed.) *A New India: Critical Reflections in the Long Twentieth Century*, London: Anthem Press, pp. 71–98.

Thomas, Jayan Jose (2011a) 'Locked in a Low-skill Equilibrium? Trends in Labour Supply and Demand in India', *Indian Journal of Labour Economics* 54(2): 195–218.

Thomas, Jayan Jose (2011b) 'Manufacturing in India: Has there been a Revival since the 1990s?' Paper presented at the Workshop on Economic Reforms and the Evolution of Productivity in Indian Manufacturing, Indian Institute of Technology Bombay, 18–19 March 2011.

Thomas, Jayan Jose (2012) 'India's Labour Market During the 2000s: Surveying the Changes', *Economic and Political Weekly* 47(51): 39–51.

UNCTAD (United Nations Conference of Trade and Development) (2005) *World Investment Report 2005: Transnational Corporations and the Internationalization of R&D*, New York: UNCTAD, available online: http://unctad.org/ SearchCenter/Pages/Results.aspx?k=world%20investment%20report%202005 (accessed 8 January 2014).

UNDP (United Nations Development Programme) (2006) *Human Development Report 2006: Beyond Scarcity: Power, Poverty and the Global Water Crisis*. New York: UNDP, available online: http://hdr.undp.org/en/content/human-development-report-2006 (accessed 8 January 2014).

UNIDO (United Nations Industrial Development Organization) (2009) *International Year Book of Industrial Statistics 2009*, Cheltenham: Edward Elgar Publishing.

World Bank (2011) *World Development Indicators*, available online: http://data.worldbank.org/data-catalog/world-development-indicators/wdi-2011 (accessed 8 January 2014).

Xiao, Geng, Yang, Xiuke and Janus, Anna (2010) 'State Owned Enterprises in China: Reform Dynamics and Impacts', available online: http://globalcenters.columbia.edu/ eastasia/files/beijing/content/pdf/2009-SOEs_in_China-Reform_dynamics_and_ impacts_Chinas_New_Place_in_a_ World_in_Crisis_2009_0.pdf (accessed 7 January 2014).

Zweig, David (2006) 'Learning to Compete: China's Efforts to Encourage a "Reverse Brain Drain"', in Christiane Kuptsch and Eng Fong Pang (eds) *Competing for Global Talent*, Geneva: International institute for Labour Studies, International Labour Organization, pp. 187–214.

Serial publications

Annual Survey of Industries, Central Statistical Organization, Ministry of Statistics and Programme Implementation, Government of India (annual publication). Available online: http://mospi.nic.in/.

National Accounts Statistics, Central Statistical Organization, Ministry of Statistics and Programme Implementation, Government of India (annual publication). Available online: http://mospi.nic.in/.

Public Enterprises Survey, Department of Public Enterprises, Ministry of Heavy Industries and Public Enterprises, Government of India (annual publication). Available online: http://dpe.nic.in/.

11 Public sector reforms and political discourse in India and China

Manoranjan Mohanty

The experience of public sector reforms and the discourses accompanying this process in India and China challenge some basic categories and beliefs that have dominated development thinking in the contemporary world. This chapter takes up some comparable as well as distinct examples from both countries to argue that the future course of reforms in general and public sector reforms in particular, is likely to be on new and creative lines rather than following the neo-liberal script that has been advocated by the forces of globalization. The attempt to deride the role of the state in directing a country's development process, equate the notion of state with bureaucratic, inefficient, authoritarian, and corrupt machinery and discredit public action in general has failed to carry conviction despite massive campaigns to that end by the votaries of globalization and liberalization. That is partly because of the debates and contestations over paths of development and consequences of policies raised by political parties and social movements in India and the policy debates within the Chinese Communist Party (CCP) as well as issues raised by protest movements and active social groups in China. What is remarkable is that the totality of the Indian and Chinese experiences encompassing both state policies as well as social dynamics contributes many fresh ideas on the critical issues in development theory overcoming many dichotomies reinforced by the neo-liberal discourse.

It is important to locate this discussion not only in the 20- to 30-year perspective of India's and China's reforms, but also in the broader span of their post-independence history of 60 and more years as also the debates during the freedom struggle and the revolutionary movement about the vision of the future of their societies. At the same time we have to keep in view the global history of industrial revolution and the role of state, capital, and community in that process and the experiences during the crisis periods such as the 1929 Great Depression, the Asian financial crisis of 1997 and the global economic crisis of 2007–2009 and subsequently. When put in a longer historical perspective the neo-liberal premises undermining the significance of state and public action do not get vindicated.

At the same time, this discourse brings out the need for an inquiry into such questions as the social character of the state and the nature of the state apparatus. One had to investigate as to whether state power was exercised to benefit upper classes, upper castes, and dominant ethnic groups or common people, whether it was a political system of centralized and authoritarian power or of decentralized and participatory decision-making structures, whether it was an agency of foreign capital or serving interests of the national republic and its constituent units and citizens. At a time when an information and communication explosion had engulfed the whole world and media played a crucial role in influencing the processes of legitimacy of institutions and leaders of society and state, the character of what is called "public action" needed to be probed. This is not to ignore the fact that the state is the aggregate power structure of society and reflected the interests of dominant sections. But the modern state is also an arena of struggle and people used the electoral process and social movements to pressurize the state to respond to their interests. Therefore, during the early decades of independence most post-colonial states were activist states directing social process and economic growth towards egalitarian ends. When these states faced crisis situations in the 1970s and 1980s the initiatives were launched from the West to discredit public action by attributing the causes of the crisis to the role of the state. In fact, the neo-liberal attack was meant to reappropriate the state apparatus mainly to serve the interest of capital while people's movements were engaged in transforming the social and functional character of the state to serve the interest of the vast masses of the population (Mohanty 1998).

Keeping this broad perspective in mind, we will first discuss the theoretical formulations made in the course of the reform process in India and China, then take up a few conceptual issues arising from these debates regarding public sector reforms and finally conclude by reflecting upon the possible developments in the near future.

Theoretical premises of the reform ideology

Before taking up some of the specific issues let us briefly look at the way the ideological line on reforms was sought to be projected during the past three decades in China and India. In both cases, prevailing models of economic development were frontally challenged. In China, Mao Zedong's economic ideas propounded during the Cultural Revolution (1966–1976) which focused on egalitarianism were repudiated in toto when the Third Plenum of the Eleventh Central Committee announced its strategy of Reform and Open Door in December 1978. In India, the reforms were launched in 1991 in the wake of a severe foreign exchange crisis when the World Bank advised India to depart from the Nehru model. The central role assigned to the public sector during the regimes of Nehru and Indira Gandhi now came under sharp challenge. It should be noted that in case of China the new line was formulated in terms of gradual development of a market economy guided by the CCP and the state.

In case of India ideological debate was joined in full steam and it often took the form of a strident offensive by the votaries of neo-liberalism against as they put it, "socialists of all varieties" which included Nehru. But in both cases the campaigns aimed at discrediting public initiatives and celebrating private enterprise, discrediting the state as an agency of transformation and social man-agement though in differing degrees (Patnaik *et al.* 2004). Strong efforts were made to promote the philosophy of individualism with stress on acquisitive and competitive values as most desirable for human beings. This perspective pre-sented the relationship between the individual and the collective as one mainly of conflict and confrontation. What is noteworthy was that in countries like India the media, print and electronic, now having themselves emerged as cartels and monopolies, promoted these ideas as unchallengeable and universal truths. In China the official media itself contributed to this line of thought.[1] A new body of social science writings linked to academic institutions and groups backed by massively funded research projects subscribing to neo-liberal ideology came out and dominated the scene to argue the logic and empirical validity of these formu-lations. In China this formed a part of the justification of "socialist market economy" (Xue 1985) while in India much of it passed for new modern social science of economic growth in the phase of globalization (Patnaik 2003; Acharya and Mohan 2010). After the steadily high growth rate of the economies of China and India became part of the global political discourse, there were comparative studies of India and China not only justifying the neo-liberal paths of develop-ment but also demanding how they should do even more of the same.[2]

Fortunately, the dynamics of the world process and the conflicts and tensions arising out of the social situation in many countries and especially in India and China did not permit this ideological offensive to go uncontested. So the debates in both countries remained alive.[3] After the global economic crisis of 2007–2009 when many of the neo-liberal assumptions crumbled, the confidence in the neo-liberal faith considerably waned.

In India, when the economic reforms were launched in 1991 the common refrain of the pro-reform elite was the attack on what was called "license raj" referring to the restrictions imposed on the entrepreneurs by the government. Decades earlier, Ram Manohar Lohia had coined the term "license-permit raj" in the early 1960s to criticize bureaucratic control over many activities (Lohia 1963). But it should be pointed out that he was not against state initiative, he was only against a centralized state. He was for decentralized, participatory public action together with private enterprise with a commitment to promoting egalitarianism.[4] In the 1990s targeting "license-permit raj" became the common parlance of the reformists demanding liberalization of the economy by denigrat-ing governmental regulation in general. Under the earlier system, the priority sectors and areas for private entrepreneurs set out by the government were regarded as too constrictive for business initiatives (Rao 2011).

One of the major intellectual articulations of the neo-liberal drive to dismantle public sector in India was by Arun Shourie, India's Minister of Disinvestment in 2001. While the Congress government at the time of launching the reforms in 1991 had set up a Disinvestment Committee, later a Commission and a Depart-ment of the Government of India, the BJP-led NDA government had a full-fledged Minister of Disinvestment. On November 6, 2001, Shourie addressed a letter to the members of parliament making a case for disinvestment in public sector units. Besides the familiar arguments about the inefficiency, he argued that the annual income from the public sector was less than the interest that the sales of the equity shares would earn from a bank. Such a statement made out of context made little sense. It did not take into account the value of the public service that the public enterprise entailed. But this became a much quoted statement. The other quote from Shourie was his slanderous assertion that the Navaratnas (literally meaning nine jewels referring to the nine leading public sector undertakings of India) were "bleeding cancers" incurring large-scale losses from the public exchequer.[5] This was an attack on the public sector enterprises of India in steel, petroleum, power, cement, and heavy machineries which were designed during the Nehru era to function as the commanding heights of the Indian economy and perform the role of catalysts for building a new, democratic, egalitarian India.

The neo-liberal ideology had its package of doctrines consisting of building civil society organizations or NGOs as agencies of public welfare rather than relying on the state agencies. That was considered to be a central part of the process of democratization in the developing countries. "Empowerment" was yet another concept popularized by the forces of globalization which often meant formal participation even without structural changes in power relations. So dismantling the public sector was projected as a part of the new wave of promoting liberty of individuals seen as entrepreneurs whose freedoms had been curtailed thus far by the state (Mishra and Kiranmai 2011).

In China, the discourse on the reforms evolved in course of the inner-Party debates even before the World Bank promoted the neo-liberal agenda for the developing countries. The critique of the development path symbolized by the Great Leap Forward and the Cultural Revolution unfolded the reforms discourse[6] (Xue 1985; Deng 1987). It started with the dismantling of the rural communes and introducing the Household Responsibility System giving the village-owned land on contract to households for farming. This came with the sharp critique of what was called the policy of "Eating from the Iron Bowl," which meant practicing equalitarianism. This doctrine implied that everyone got the same wages irrespective of how much or what quality of work they did. It was pointed out that unless workers got material incentives for their work and that on a differential basis on the quality and quantity of performance they would not give their best. Earlier in the Maoist framework of "red and expert," every worker was expected to be imbued with revolutionary zeal to work to the best of their ability for building socialism. That was considered too idealistic a condition. This also started the wave of debates questioning the superiority of the collective ownership of production. Gradually, the reforms in the urban and industrial sector allowed setting up of private enterprises ultimately leading to the emergence of a major private sector in the Chinese economy (White 1998). Setting up Special Economic Zones (SEZs) and launching Joint ventures with capitalists from within the country and abroad was the route through which the private economy expanded fast. When the collectively owned township and village enterprises (TVEs) could not compete with the bigger enterprises and faced bankruptcy, most of them were taken over by the private entrepreneurs while some were closed down. The decision to admit capitalists into the Party under Jiang Zemin's framework of Three Represents legitimized this development (Mohanty 2003).

Another statement that became popular in the 1980s and was attributed to Deng Xiaoping was "To be rich is glorious." [7] Hoardings displaying Deng's picture with this saying were visible all over China for many years during the 1980s. After the Tiananmen Square demonstrations in 1989 there was a short period of internal debates on ideological and policy issues again, but this phase of debates ended with Deng's speeches during his southern tour of SEZ areas in February 1992. He gave a call to boldly go ahead with reform and open door and "never be afraid of the phenomenon of capitalism." After that China saw an accelerated development of capitalist enterprises and a steady trend of high rates of economic growth.

During the 1990s the attack on the ideology of socialist ownership was very common in several of the popular publications. The reforms in the state-owned enterprises were pushed forward in the 1990s. The CCP, however, carefully formulated its position on the subject. The announcement of its path of pursuing "reform and open door" while building a "socialist market economy" at the Fourteenth Party Congress in 1992 ensured that the Party and the state under its leadership would maintain overall control over the economy (Jiang 2002). As China made swift transition to a rapidly developing market economy, the line was further amplified in 1997 as "Deng Xiaoping's Theory of building socialism with Chinese characteristics." The Asian financial crisis and later developments in the global economy as well as problems of inflation and an overheated economy, besides the socio-political considerations, made it further incumbent upon the central government to retain the right to exercise macro-economic coordination and control. That in fact remained as a special feature or a "Chinese characteristic" of China's socialist market economy. As a result, the official policy of the CCP has remained one of maintaining the dominant role of the public ownership system while developing multiple forms of ownership including private, cooperative and many other forms (Li 2011).[8]

Yet, in the popular discourse in China the skepticism on the role and capacity of the government and public enterprises has grown in the recent years just as in India. The media and academia are extremely critical of the nature of the decision-making and the inefficiency of government procedures (Chi 2004). The neo-liberal ideology has acquired a substantial base among the Chinese middle class and the class of entrepreneurs who are well integrated with the global political economy (Redding and Witt 2007). Among the rural population, the migrant workers in the cities, and the unemployed youth there is still a different perception of the state as a welfare agency. But their disaffection has also grown in the recent years as evident in the rising trend of social protest. The number of "mass protest incidents" reached 180,000 according to one estimate in 2010.[9]

In India too, we see a similar phenomenon. There is great expectation from the state as a source of welfare in such areas as poverty eradication, expanding public health and education, and employment opportunities. Besides the active role of the state during the Nehru years in promoting public education and public health systems, even during the height of the reform period the UPA government took a number of state initiatives after it came to power in 2004. The Mahatma Gandhi National Rural Employment Guarantee Act 2005 (MNREGA) providing assured employment to rural poor for 100 days to the passage of Right to Free and Compulsory Education of 2009 (RTE) meant to educate all children in the age group of six and fourteen symbolized the perspective of those who believed in the positive role of the state. But these were grudgingly accepted by the top policy-makers as necessary concessions in electoral politics rather than essential requirements to build an equitable society. While accepting these as "populist measures" by leaders operating in a competitive party system the middle class and the entrepreneur class are engaged in extracting more and more autonomy for themselves by limiting the role of the government. This situation has meant that these welfare measures remain in the margins of the growth strategy and not integral to its core. Even though these measures are welcome interventions, they are not accompanied by the required structural measures to provide long-term solutions to these problems. These have essentially turned out to be destitution relief programs to manage tensions in rural and tribal areas. In recent years, resistance to the state has grown among tribal areas and the state authorities have come down heavily with police and paramilitary repression to clear ground for mining industries.

So behind the successful growth stories of China and India the contestations over the role of state have also grown. The common people see the state abandoning its welfare and the pro-people activist role for a role to facilitate and promote the welfare of the elite in both the countries. There are other important aspects of the discourse on the state which also have a bearing on its economic role. State power is not only to be seen as the centralized power but has many layers of territoriality. Both in China and India the provincial or state governments exercise considerable power mainly due to the political and economic status they enjoy. The Indian constitution guarantees a federal division of powers between the Union and the States. But it is the political influence that a regional party or government enjoys which determines the extent of its autonomy. In China, which is a unitary state according to the constitution, the political influence of a region largely flows from its resources and economic performance. The system of appointment of regional Party secretaries and governors by the central party leadership ensures central control and a degree of coordination. But in both countries, the local situation determines the kind of role the state plays by way of economic initiatives and welfare measures. In both countries, the regional and local governments play a crucial role in both spheres. With the introduction of Panchayati Raj (rural local self-government) and a host of rural development measures in India and village elections and the program of building "a socialist countryside" in China, the state's welfare role is once again more visible (Mohanty and Selden 2007). But as mentioned earlier these measures are often seen by the neo-liberals as wastage of valuable resources (Ahluwalia 2011).

Thus even though the reform discourse in both countries sought to project a negative picture on the role of the state decrying its interventionist role and limiting it in the name of promoting growth through private initiative, in actual practice its role remained far more complex, effective in many respects and limited in others (Nagaraj 2006). Keeping this general picture in mind let us now take up a few critical issues which have dominated the discourse on public sector reforms and see how the Indian and the Chinese experiences have actually presented new insights into understanding these issues. These are by no means an exhaustive list of issues, but they illustrate the dimensions which have been blurred in the course of the dichotomous formulations which dominate the prevailing discourse. It is the nuanced and complex, even creative understanding of these issues that is likely to decisively impact the future of economic activity in the coming decades not only in China and India, but perhaps globally.

State vs. market

Contrary to the assertion that market operation is always superior to the state's, the Chinese and the Indian experiences show a wide spectrum of practices where macro-economic planning and coordination have been most effective in operating various kinds of market mechanisms. Public sector enterprises have been given effective autonomy as market actors and have taken many innovative operational steps. Many assumptions that state activity is necessarily inefficient, corrupt and unprofitable have been questioned. What is more, the notion of the state has been much differentiated as layers of collectivities and their functions and powers have varied.

Deng Xiaoping set the theoretical frame for the reforms by suggesting that there were three instruments of transformation of a traditional society into the modern age. They were: market, technology, and management, which according to Deng were independent catalysts affecting all societies, all classes and all other social formations everywhere in the world (Deng 1987). It was argued that the emergence of the market—the arena of buying and selling, the realm of commodity exchange—involved the most efficient allocation of resources. This line of thought was the subject of heated debates during the Cultural Revolution and the Shanghai Group on Political Economy had come out with a number of critical publications arguing that market was always uneven and class-related and socialism had to curb the market economy through state control.[10] During the early years of reforms a series of theoretical publications came out in China spelling out the Deng perspective on the universality of market principle (Xue 1985). However, ultimately, when the Deng theory on building socialism with Chinese characteristics was announced, a highly nuanced formulation on the market was accepted. Even though this was passed as one of the "Chinese characteristics," the implicit claim of the general or universal relevance of this formulation was evident.

The formulation on the market principle had three components. First, all actors in the production sphere were to behave as actors in the market, taking rational decisions to allocate resources to maximize their gain. Second, there were many actors in the market, not only the state and the collectives, but individual producers, entrepreneurs, new entities of many kinds of joint, cooperative, corporate organizations with property rights and entitlements. Third, the state had to play the role of the coordinator, balancer, final arbiter in crisis and conflicts to maintain the desired direction of development while respecting the autonomy and rights of all the market actors.

This is how the China's Twelfth Five-Year Plan puts it in Part XI, Chapter 45 on "Reform in Difficult Area, Improving Socialist Market Economy":

> Uphold and improve the basic economic system, with public ownership playing a dominant role and diverse forms of ownership developing side by side, and create an institutional environment under which economic entities under all forms of ownership use factors of production equally in accordance with the law, engage in fair competition in the market, and enjoy equal legal protection.
>
> (China's Twelfth Five-Year Plan 2011)

This theoretical formulation allows a great variety of production relations and ownership systems prevailing in China which cannot be reduced to just the two opposite forms of state ownership and private ownership. Interestingly, the Indian experience contributes to the same line of thought even though it is located in a liberal democratic set up. Despite the critiques by the neo-liberals of the Nehru period, the framework of a mixed economy laid the basic structure of Indian political economy. The public sector constituted the "commanding heights" of the economy developing critical infrastructure in sectors such as steel, cement, petroleum, electricity, and heavy machinery besides a high commitment to public education, public health, and world-class technology and management education. All these arenas of public investment and public management have paid off enormously in the past two or more decades with India emerging as a high-growth economy with a globally spread middle class and professional elite. The Nehru model did allow adequate incentives for private capital to operate heavy and light industries in such crucial sectors as steel, textiles, cement, and other sectors. The infrastructure that was laid out was highly subsidized for use by private capital. Thus it was said that India's public sector subsidized India's capitalist development. In fact, there is a whole body of literature on the experiences of state-led capitalist development during 1960s and 1970s, on "rentier state" and "developmental state." It analyzed how the political and bureaucratic state apparatus used state resources mainly to promote a capitalist class, often monopoly capitalism in many emerging countries such as South Korea (Kim 2003).

But such an active role by the state had a long-term value as well. Just as the infrastructure in rural China, the achievements in land reforms, education and health, and heavy industries development in the Mao era provided a major base for the success of China's reforms after 1978, the achievements in the Nehru era have to be reckoned as major factors for India's successes in the reform period since 1991. At the same time the neglect of land reforms and the persistence of poverty in India, and the serious disruptions due to massive policy shifts in China during the first two decades, have to be recognized as responsible for many serious problems in India and China.

In India the significant role of the private sector in agriculture, rural crafts, and all forms of industries and commerce provided the general setting for development during the past six decades. Electoral politics demanded that the state provided support in various forms to enhance production and profit to entrepreneurs. Policies such as those related to Green Revolution in agriculture and the various industrial policy resolutions are just two of many policy instruments through which the Indian state regulated these sectors. Ensuring minimum support prices for certain agricultural products, procuring grains for public distribution purposes, and imposing restrictions on domestic or foreign trade have been some of the policy practices in both countries in order to manage uneven supplies and fluctuating production. The five-year plans were major frameworks for state guidance of the economy as a whole. However, their centrality in resource allocation underwent a significant change with the onset of reforms, though they continued to set priorities. In the Indian development discourse there also exists an important Gandhian strand for the promotion of khadi and village industries, through individual, cooperative, and community ownership for which the state had specific policies of support for technology innovation and marketing. Besides the prevalence of a wide variety of cooperatives all over India which is protected under the Indian constitution, cooperatives of a capitalist kind flourished in Maharashtra and some other places and are a significant part of the Indian economy. Then there are community-owned forests, land, and water resources in many parts of India which have been legalized in many of the recent legislations such as the Forest Rights Act of 2006. Thus the multiple forms of ownership under guidance of the state are functioning both in India and China. The question is about the direction of change in the course of the recent reforms and the politics guiding that process. Paradoxically in both cases the overall trend is that of development of a capitalist-oriented market economy which is responsible for growing tensions in society and therefore being contested at various levels.[11]

While it is important to reconceptualize the state–market dichotomy, it is extremely important to note how efforts are being made in both India and China to reorganize the state apparatus and re-examine its functions in response to the challenges of a new situation of increasing people's consciousness. "Remaking the administrative state" in China by downsizing and streamlining the government agencies (Yang 2004: 55) and "reform of the excessively dictatorial state" by promoting decentralization and evolving new and more effective forms (Shue 1988: 152) have been on the agenda of political reforms during the reform period. Yet as Wen Jiabao warned in a press conference as premier in March 2012, the progress on it had been too slow and unless significant progress was achieved in this there would be more "cultural revolutions." At the Eighteenth

Party Congress of the CCP in November 2012 in his political report Hu Jintao focused on both tasks, namely promoting participatory democracy and fighting corruption which his successor Xi Jinping picked up as the main agenda of the new regime to realize what he calls the Chinese dream of rejuvenation of the Chinese nation (Mohanty 2012).

From the rising trend of rural protests in both India and China we find an interesting comparative insight on the nature of the state in the two apparently contrasting political models. Both have demonstrated their ability to "prevent the emergence of a horizontal movement that would challenge the state beyond the locality or enterprise whether in the form of mass protest or new political parties" (Mohanty and Selden 2007: 473). In other words, while promoting a market economy, both states resort to a variety of legitimation and coercive measures to keep discontent limited to localities. This is how state and market forge partnerships in the interest of class, ethnic, and regional interests. In the same way the public and private discourse too should dispel many superficial assertions.

Public vs. private

Making a sharp distinction between the old European categories of public and the private has steadily broken down as private domains become subject to public norms, and the areas of autonomy and the boundary of each "private" sphere get constantly redefined. Yet defense of the "private" is often regarded as a part of the creed of a host of ideologies. They range from conservatism to liberalism either in the name of protection of individual rights or as a signifier of the modern era that identified boundaries of the propertied classes. In the context of globalization there is a paradoxical trend. On the one hand there is a neo-liberal stress on the leading role of the private enterprise[12] in promoting economic growth. On the other hand, the reality is that there are even less discrete, separate, antagonistic spheres of activity as public and private in the era of information technology, mass communications, and consumerism, and the emerging challenges of democratic citizenship (Mahajan and Reifield 2003). Creation of SEZs in the reform period in both countries was an assertion of the rights of the private entrepreneurs legally excluded from much of public regulation by the state. At the same time those islands of autonomy act as economic and social catalysts, both in positive and negative ways.

If we look at the forms of ownership in various countries we find that they have become complex combinations of many types in every country. The emergence of joint enterprises and many other kinds both in India and China has gone much beyond what neo-liberal theory calls "public–private partnerships." The issues of ownership and management of individual, collective, cooperative, worker-owned and shareholder systems have carried many unique features. The assumption of early European capitalism was that individual liberty and right to property allowed the individual to fully utilize his/her entrepreneurial ability. That became the basis of building the capitalist system. But gradually it became clear that society and the state provided not only the law and order environment but a whole range of infrastructure and other facilities to enable the entrepreneur to produce, market, profit, and grow. The economic realm was never a private realm. In practice the claim to private enterprise, the right to autonomous decision-making, was an assertion of power of the bourgeoisie which it exercised through its agency of the state. The social contradictions which manifested gradually made the hollowness of this privacy claim abundantly clear. Tenants became peasants claiming land rights over the land they tilled which the landlord had claimed under the old system as his private right. The workers brought to the open the dynamics of the capitalist system and exposed its link with the state that protected it.

The feminist movement has contributed significantly to this discourse by asserting that "personal is political." The fortress of the patriarchal family whether in Britain or in India and China was thrown open when the types and the magnitude of male oppression were gradually brought to light. When we apply that perspective to the contemporary debates on private and public in all other spheres of life and activity many new issues come to the open. In the name of private enterprise and their commitment to efficiency, the corporate firms have refused to accept norms of social justice. The demand for reservation for disadvantaged sections of society such as the scheduled castes, scheduled tribes, OBCs (Other Backward Classes), and women in the corporate sector have been continuously turned down by the industrial management in India. Thus far the Indian government has refrained from making it legally binding for them. However, a time may come when the corporate sector will have to respond to these demands. In China, reservation for minorities and women is yet to acquire any political acceptance even in the state sector. In fact in many enterprises, when there is an upgrading of technology and production process, it is the women workers who get retrenched to begin with.[13] Thus the entrepreneurs in the private sector refuse to accept the demand for reservation or even affirmative action for the historically disadvantaged sections of society on the plea that it would compromise efficiency. Even public enterprises seeking competitive advantage try to make similar claims. But gradually such notions are being challenged in all the countries. Norms of social justice that require protective discrimination for the disadvantaged are slowly getting currency and defense of the private realm of the enterprise is being shaken up.

In both China and India, the tendency to treat all public enterprises as autonomous market players is so strong that the ideology of the private enterprise has taken hold. The fact is that they are all public entities using public resources and functioning in the public realm, but due to the prevailing power structures the enterprises are operating as private domains. As such even as they make profit as economic entities, they structurally serve the interest of the male, upper class and—in India—also upper caste sections of society. As social movements make headway this private realm will be further challenged. Social justice norms demand the breakup of the private/public demarcation. It is becoming increasingly clear that all human activity is public activity with spaces of autonomy, horizontal and vertical, that are constantly renegotiated and commonly agreed upon for mutual benefit by various layers of society.

This distinction between public and private is nowhere challenged more head-on than in the context of the environmental perspective on development. Much of the history of capitalism was about the right of the entrepreneur to discover raw materials and use it to earn maximum profit. Even today, the neo-liberal tide has enabled many big corporations to go to mineral rich areas in India and elsewhere on the invitation of the central and state governments. They have the capital and technology to explore the minerals and set up processing industries. The deforestation and global warming that the people of the world have suffered due to this pattern of industrialization during the past hundred or so years is incalculable. Now the environmental movements have acquired some strength, and consequently environmental clearance is a required condition in most countries. The environmental movements and the campaigns against mega-mining projects in contemporary India have shown how important is it for people to organize themselves and ensure that the state implements environmental norms along with respecting the land rights of affected people.[14] In case of China the danger of an authoritarian government deciding to go ahead with a project irrespective of its environmental and social effects is no doubt there. But in recent years the people's pressures on government have yielded results and many projects have been shelved or relocated.[15] It is also true that in India the media and parties are mobilized to support projects, often frustrating the demands of people's movements. The global trend of green ideology is a welcome phenomenon and "green socialism" has many supporters in India and China. There is also a trend of "green capitalism" with many Western firms claiming to promote green technology. But at the moment that seems to be another method of developing specialized technology to capture the markets in developing countries.

Thus the social justice and environmental demands make every production activity a public activity that affects the whole society and that, too, for generations. The claim of a private sphere of autonomous decision-making for reasons of efficiency and profit can no longer avoid public audit on equity and sustainability.

Yet the reasons for efficient production irrespective of their social and ecological consequences are often cited to advocate big size firms for "economies of scale." Hence the neo-liberal era has witnessed a strong obsession with size leading to a spate of mergers and acquisitions on a global scale.

Size obsession

The dictum that the bigger the scale the more efficient and productive it is—"too big to fail"—is one of the principal strategies of market economy under globalization. Yet this too is not accepted uncritically in India and China. Even though there have been mergers of public sector companies in both countries, some have been also split to encourage competition and efficient management. Besides the arguments of promoting a competitive economy under the macro-economic coordination of the state, the debate on TVEs in China and cottage and small industries in India throws some interesting light on this issue.

There was a time when monopoly was considered an economically irrational phenomenon by theorists of capitalism as it thwarted healthy competition. All capitalist countries had regulatory mechanisms to prevent the development of monopolies. In India the Monopoly and Restrictive Practices Commission was an active agency for many decades. During the past two decades however, the clock has turned full circle and purchases and mergers are considered a norm. Until the shock of the 2008–2009 when once again the severe risks embodied in monopolies became a subject of discussion this line of thinking was not questioned. In both India and China the trend of merger has continued in recent years. Foreign companies have been allowed to enter the Indian market and Indian companies have also bought foreign companies. In China, too, mergers and groupings have continued during the reform period.

The philosophy underlying this perspective needs scrutiny. Mahatma Gandhi had presented a critique of Western capitalism in *Hind Swaraj* in 1909 showing how that type of industrialization had destroyed rural artisans in India (Parel 1997). The *charkha* or the spinning wheel to spin and weave one's own cloth on a handloom, was a symbolic assertion of that view by Gandhi and his followers. E. F. Schumacher (1973) reconstructed that view in the 1960s in his "Small is beautiful" statement. Herbert Marcuse's powerful argument that this type of industrialized society created a "One Dimensional Man" governed by capital and technology and causing human alienation in life and society was yet another landmark statement (Marcuse 1964). Today when issues of social justice, environment, and self-determination have come to the center, it is important to engage in a new discourse on scale and size. Just as it may not be realistic to insist on everything small, it is equally unjustifiable to defend the doctrine of the big.

Neo-liberals were engaged in a sustained campaign for accelerated reforms in India, to go for a "second generation of reforms" in which merger was a big item on the agenda. In China's Twelfth Plan a commitment has been made to

> guide the merger process to enable the enterprises to develop further as market players and eliminate the institutional barriers … to help the advantaged enterprises to carry out alliances by cross-regional merger and reorganization … and develop larger enterprises and become world famous brand.
>
> (China's Twelfth Five-Year Plan 2011: Part III, Chapter 9, Section 4)

Both in India and China small and medium industries do figure in the planned economy and get special mention in the Twelfth Five-Year Plan documents. But the experience with the TVEs in China and cottage industries in India show that when they are asked to be competitive in the emerging market, many of them are not able to compete and just close down. They require a structural position in the economy where they are not dismissed as "petty producers" but a legitimate part of the total economy. If direct participation by the labor in the production process and in its management is a democratic value and if that system is more capable of moving towards equity and sustainability then small-scale production has a critical place in the political economy. Unfortunately, the industrial revolution ideology has reached such a stage in the contemporary phase of globalization that the alternative perspective on decentralized production has been a subject of ridicule. The debates, however, will continue as to what is the desirable combination of various sizes and forms of production units. But the neoliberal faith in the big needs re-examination.

It is thus argued that large-size firms under private ownership unhindered by state regulation will ensure production on such a scale and of such a quality that it would automatically generate conditions of welfare of all. Therefore, the argument goes, production should not be tied up to welfare considerations. This is an assertion unsubstantiated by history, either colonial or post-colonial.

Production vs. welfare

The idea that production should be left to the private sector while government should be in charge of welfare programs is seriously debated in India and China. In Western countries the critics of "big government" even advocate privatization of health, education, and other social services which, according to them, the consumers should buy in the market. The alternative mode of thinking is to see both production and welfare processes together in state, private, and all other spheres of production. Reduction of public investment in health, education, research, and infrastructure development under the spell of globalization for a certain period created havoc in both countries. Collapse of the public health system in China was evident during the outbreak of SARS there in 2003. Thereafter, many remedial steps were initiated, but never was the earlier situation of public health for the rural population restored. The Indian story was equally disturbing. Public health facilities continued to deteriorate during the first two decades of reforms while private hospital facilities sprang up all over catering to the rich—a phenomenon paralleled in China. The allocation for health in Indian Five-Year Plans never reached the promised 3 percent and remained at less than 1.5 percent, which is slightly better in China. This was in contrast to the commitment of the state and all enterprises public and private to support health needs of the population. In both countries the Twelfth Five-Year Plan allocated more resources for health. But the logic of the market economy had already generated so much momentum that the public health programs will be difficult to implement.

A kind of production that can lead to socially just and environmentally sustainable development can only be ensured by a democratic, participatory, and responsive state (Bhaduri 2005). The more centralized and bureaucratized it is the more likely is it to be pushed in one direction or the other as was the case in both countries during the 1990s when the neo-liberal ideology was at its peak in both China and India.

During the 1990s the inadequacy of public investment in health, education, and other welfare activities was evident both in India and China. Rural areas in China suffered especially because the TVEs whose income was a major source of support for the village welfare became weaker or bankrupt. In India investment in school education was directed towards special programs such as universalizing literacy rather than strengthening the government school system as a whole. Privatization of education and health became a general policy in both countries. As a result the goal of universalizing primary health care and primary education to a minimum standard remained on paper.[16] The state of education and health both in India and China remains highly unequal between rural and urban areas, between the rich and the poor people, and among different caste and ethnic groups. The condition of the girl child remains most deplorable with the alarming trend of falling proportion of the female child in the age group of birth to six years. The Chinese census data of 2010 showed an alarming trend of falling sex ratio among children compared to that of 2000. It is only slightly better in India but depressing nevertheless. In 2001 for every 100 female children in the age group of birth to six years there were 108 male children in India. By 2011 the sex ratio worsened and the gap widened further with 109 male children for every 100 female children. In China it was even worse. In 2000 for every 100 female children there were 116 males whereas in 2010 for every female children there were 118 male children. This is a general indication of economic, social, and cultural trends adversely affecting women in both countries. Thus both in education and health common people suffered in course of the reforms. The claim that state should withdraw from economic activities to pay more attention to social welfare proved to be false as it privatized the social sector as well. And its capacity to garner resources for welfare through taxation and other means was constrained due to the neo-liberal economic strategy.

The argument that if everyone gets employment and earns a reasonable income, he/she can buy health insurance, can pay the fees to send the children to school, can pay the rent or the mortgage on housing has been tested again and again in Western countries. President Obama's Affordable Healthcare Act passed by the US Congress in 2010 provided yet another occasion to stage this debate with the Tea Party forces organizing strong opposition. In the 2012 presidential elections in the US this became one of the heated issues of debate between Obama and Romney.

But one message clearly emerges from history. The state has to so regulate industry that it not only provides employment but also contributes to the public fund for ensuring education, health, and other welfare services to the common people. In the modern history of Europe the state took an active role in promoting public health and education as a result of which the foundations of democracy and capitalism were laid. The idea of socialism built further upon that experience. In populous developing countries such as China and India where social inequality existed in huge proportions, this role of the state is of special significance. But the neo-liberal strategy puts the mantra of controlling fiscal deficit on such a high pedestal that welfare spending is regarded as uneconomic.

Fortunately, both in India and China people's movements have ensured that the state launch right-based initiatives. MNREGA, RTE and the National Rural Health Mission are some of the measures implemented by the political leadership despite the grudging acquiescence of the reform economists. In China too, the nearly universal health insurance program has made steady progress in recent years.

Thus the neo-liberal attempt to separate the realms of production and welfare has not stood its ground despite the fact that this view has its votaries among the decision-makers and planners in both countries.

Possibilities in the near future

The contestation over the ideas was bound to continue in the near future in both countries. The elite's determination to achieve high growth, which has driven the reform process in India and China, sought to promote a particular discourse on state, the public, the scale of economy, and the relationship between production and welfare. But the problems arising out of that experience had to be tackled keeping in view the objectives and goals of the political past of both countries which had gone through revolution and freedom struggle. Even though the visions were reinterpreted during the reform years, the growing inequalities, regional disparities, corruption, and alienation weakened the claims of success of the two rising economies. The global economic crisis of recent years further challenged the legitimacy of the neo-liberal approach. Therefore, both countries were engaged in achieving several goals simultaneously growth with equity and sustainability. This is evident in the way the Twelfth Five-Year Plans had been formulated in China and India.

The Approach Paper for India's Twelfth Five-Year Plan announced the goal as "faster, sustainable and more inclusive growth" adding "sustainable" to the formulation of the title of the Eleventh Plan (Planning Commission 2012). It has also mentioned its focus on health, education and skill development, natural resources, and infrastructure development. The official development discourse in India replaced "equity and social justice" with "inclusive" as a part of the neo-liberal dictum. Still it would appear from many formulations in the approach paper on achieving "inclusiveness" as if the planners were responding to the issues raised by the social movements. But the overall strategy remained the same—one of achieving a high rate of growth by continuing the process of globalization, liberalization, and privatization and pushing for the next generation of reforms along the neo-liberal path. The Chinese Twelfth Five-Year Plan document has committed China to achieving what it calls "pattern transformation" so as to achieve balanced, coordinated development according to the "outlook on scientific development." CCP's Eighteenth Congress, too, affirmed its commitment to change the growth model, mainly implying a shift from an export-oriented economy to promoting domestic consumption.

In the Chinese plan there is an appearance of bold initiatives for addressing issues of social inequity and environmental concerns. But the preoccupation with high growth, with the continuation of the same strategy, persists because it has achieved tremendous success in economic growth, building infrastructure, and raising people's livelihood condition. But the experience with the Hu Jintao regime since 2002 shows that despite the attempts for equitable development, inequalities, corruption, and social discontent have grown.[17]

In a way China has landed in a "success trap" which does not allow it to change its reform strategy because of strong domestic and global commitments and structures already built up.[18] Therefore, one can see diverse pulls in both countries. For both, the neo-liberal strand is a powerful factor in economic development. But the totality of the social process presents many innovative and creative dimensions of development and alternative policies and practices. The next decade in both countries will likely see continuation of a high or a moderately high growth rate but with great deal of turbulence arising from the consequences of such a growth strategy. These would continue to be the issues taken up by the social movements. There is enough evidence that the neo-liberal political discourse has encountered effective contestation. The notion that an active economic role of the state and a dominant public sector are features only of the early phase of nation-building and development in the newly independent countries or countries inspired by the then Soviet Union is sharply contested in view of the experiences of India and China. They represent innovative paths that break down some of the traditional dichotomies. Undoubtedly, there are strong forces of neo-liberal thought in both countries, but there are also fairly powerful forces of alternative thought arising out of their historical processes. The implementation of the Twelfth Five-Year Plans of India and China are poised to be more innovative in this respect even though both countries have to go a long way developing their models—China's "socialist market economy" and India's "inclusive and sustainable development." With a high rate of growth, improved living standards, and large-scale infrastructure development, China has achieved tremendous success following this path, but it can avoid falling into a "success trap" only by handling these dichotomies more creatively and overcoming the enormous pressures for following the neo-liberal dictum. In the case of China, even though there is a consensus among the CCP leadership on "reform and the open door," the inner Party struggle over development policies has been the main method of carrying on the political discourse even though the academic debates within the country and internationally, and in public forums, have acquired momentum in the recent years. In India, people's movements and the left parties are the main source of policy challenge as there is a consensus among the dominant parties over the neo-liberal path. The coming years therefore are bound to see increasing contestation over policies as people's consciousness grows in both countries making demands for realization of their basic socio-economic and political rights.

Conclusion

The discourse on public sector reforms in India and China has to be seen at three levels. First, the theoretical and ideological debates were no doubt wider in scale in India than in China, but by the turn of the century both countries had a large number of severe critics of state action in the economic sphere. Second, the ruling parties in both countries never accepted full-scale privatization as their dominant policy. In India both the NDA and UPA continued to maintain critical sectors in the public sphere while continuing economic reforms to promote private initiative and efficient management. Third at the level of intellectual discourse and social practice a process of serious questioning had unfolded to critique the dichotomous notions such as those of state vs. market and private vs. public. The issues that had emerged as crucial in the emerging development discourse both in India and China were about how to orient economic growth towards the promotion of social justice, equality, and environmental sustainability with participatory, transparent, and accountable political process. Rather than uncritically accepting the idea that private enterprise alone was the panacea for all problems, the new development thought saw social action in many forms including state, collective, and cooperative at levels starting from the village or town to the national, which could go hand in hand with forms of private enterprise but all of them subjected to the tests of justice, equity, sustainability, and democracy. Such a trend in development discourse was not confined to India and China, but was increasingly acquiring global proportions.

Notes

1 A campaign to "emancipate thought" (*jiefang sixiang*) was launched in China in 1979 to get rid of the Maoist ideas on economic development, and shift the focus of work from class struggle to economic construction.

2 There were three trends in the Dragon–Elephant comparative studies. One showed how authoritarian China was more efficient in achieving high growth rates than democratic India (Guruswamy and Singh 2010). Another was to counter this view and show how India was able to accomplish high growth rate in the first decade of the twenty-first century (Bahl 2010). A third line of analysis showed serious weaknesses in both systems despite the hype over high rates of growth (Bardhan 2010). It also emphasized the fact that democracy in fact had advantages over authoritarianism in economic development. Arguing along these lines, another study shows how both countries pursued sometimes divergent and sometimes similar paths of transformation, thus having a great deal to learn from one another (Tan 2008). However, the neo-liberal thesis that China and India represented the unfolding process of privatization, liberalization and globalization in world scale and thus "world was becoming flat" gained much ground in public consciousness (Friedman 2005).

3 Amit Bhaduri described the economic theory of neo-liberal market economy as "a failed world view" which in India has caused "growing inequality and lack of employment opportunities ... coupled with an output composition oriented towards a rich minority" (Bhaduri 2009: 39–40).

4 Lohia was for nationalizing industries while allowing private enterprises to operate. Trying to integrate many elements of Gandhian economics with Marxian socialism he formulated many original ideas to promote social, economic, and political equality. Several essays in the special number of *Economic and Political Weekly* (2010) devoted to Politics and Ideas of Ram Manohar Lohia bring this out.

5 The letter is discussed in detail by Chandrasekhar (2001). Shourie (2004) elaborates his perspective on disinvestment.

6 Hu Jintao (2007: 10) puts it thus:

> the second generation … made a scientific appraisal of comrade Mao Zedong and Mao Zedong Thought, thoroughly repudiated the erroneous theory and practice of "taking class struggle as a key link" and made the historic policy decision to shift the focus of work of the party and the state onto economic development and introduce reform and opening up. It sounded the clarion call … for taking our own road and building socialism with Chinese characteristics.

7 In 2010 there was a search in China about the exact source of this statement of Deng Xiaoping on "to be rich is glorious"; but no one could trace it. It was most probably attributed to Deng. Obviously Deng had not questioned this slogan.

8 Li (2011: x) explains the transformation of the "highly centralized planned economy to socialist market economy" by identifying the unique features of the market economy pursued in China which were different from the traditional market economy. He describes them as "structural breakthrough and innovation."

9 For a discussion on the negative consequences of the Chinese economic policies and explaining them in terms of Marxist theory see Hart-Landsberg and Burkett (2005) and a further set of reflections on its formulations in *Critical Perspectives on China's Economic Transformation* (2007).

10 Many of these debates resurfaced in the evaluation of the Chinese reforms in China and abroad on the occasion of the 30 years of reforms in 2008 and thereabout. Hart-Landsberg and Burkett (2005) reconstruct many of those arguments. See also Wang (2010).

11 Chi Fulin (2005: 3) pointed out that while the government-led mode of economic growth ensured rapid growth, with the onset of a market economy, social, and economic conflicts as well as other problems had arisen resulting from the previous mode.

12 Montek Singh Ahluwalia (2011: 94), Deputy Chairman, Planning Commission affirms that the XII Plan of India will be driven by the private sector.

13 There is much evidence of it reported by many studies. My own study in Wuxi confirms this (Mohanty 2010).

14 The global discourse breaking the claims of exclusive rights is aptly captured by Praful Bidwai (2011). The grass-roots movement against mega-mining projects in Odisha reaffirm this perspective (Sahu and Dash 2011).

15 For example, the dam in the Nu River in Yunnan Province was stalled because of the local people's movement. China's Eleventh Five-Year Plan had strict norms for environmental auditing and energy saving.

16 Ahluwalia (2011: 92) admits: "the picture of performance on inclusiveness is clearly mixed. Both the extent of poverty and the lack of access to essential services remain serious problems."

17 This is why Pranab Bardhan (2010) highlights the areas of serious weaknesses in both China and India.

18 Hu Jintao's "scientific outlook" policies trying to address the problems were intended to overcome the "success trap" Mohanty (2007).

References

Acharya, Shankar and Mohan, Rakesh (eds.) (2010) *India's Economy: Performances and challenges: Essays in Honour of Montek Singh Ahluwalia*, New Delhi: Oxford University Press.

Ahluwalia, Montek Singh (2011) "Prospects and Policy Challenges in the Twelfth Plan," *Economic and Political Weekly* 46(21).

Bahl, Raghav (2010) *The Amazing Race Between China's Hare and India's Tortoise*, New Delhi: Penguin.

Bardhan, Pranab (2010) *Awakening Giants: Feet of Clay: Assessing the Economic Rise of China and India*, New Delhi: Oxford University Press.

Bhaduri, Amit (2005) *Development with Dignity*, New Delhi: National Book Trust.

Bhaduri, Amit (2009) *The Face You were Afraid to See*, New Delhi: Penguin.

Bidwai, Praful (2011) *The Politics of Climate Change and the Global Crisis: Mortgaging our Future*, Hyderabad: Orient Blackswan.

Chandrasekhar, C. P. (2001) "The Disingenuous Minister", *Frontline* 18(25), available online: www.frontline.in/static/html/fl1825/18251160.htm (accessed January 8, 2014).

Chi, Fulin (2004) *China: The New Stage of Reform*, Beijing: Foreign Languages Press.

Chi, Fulin (2005) *Evaluation Report on China's Reform*, Beijing: Foreign Languages Press.

"China's Twelfth Five Year Plan" (2011) Full English version, available online: http://cbi.typepad.com/china_direct/2011/05/chinas-twelfth-five-new-plan-the-full-english-version.html (accessed January 8, 2014).

Critical Perspectives on China's Economic Transformation (2007) New Delhi: Daanish Books.

Economic and Political Weekly (2010) 45(40) (October 2), available online: www.epw.in/ejournal/show/1/_/2075 (accessed January 8, 2014).

Deng, Xiaoping (1987) *Fundamental Issues in Present-Day China*, Beijing: Foreign Languages Press.

Friedman, Thomas L. (2005) *The World is Flat: A Brief History of the Twenty First Century*, New York: Farrar, Straus and Giroux.

Guruswamy, Mohan and Singh, Zorawar Daulat (2010) *Chasing the Dragon: Will India catch up with China?* New Delhi: Pearson Education.

Hart-Landsberg, Martin and Burkett, Paul (2005) *China and Socialism: Market Reforms and class Struggle*, New York: Monthly Review Press.

Jintao, Hu (2007) "Report to the Seventeenth Congress", *Documents of the 17th National Congress of the Communist Party of China*, Beijing: Foreign Languages Press.

Jiang, Zemin (2002) *Three Represents*, Beijing: Foreign Languages Press.

Kim, Samuel S. (2003) *Korea's Democratization*, New York: Cambridge University Press.

Li, Tieying (ed.) (2011) *Reforming China: International Comparisons and Reference*, Singapore: Enrich Professional Publishing (original Chinese edition published by China Renmin University Press, 2008).

Lohia, Rammanohar (1963) *Marx, Gandhi and Socialism*, Hyderabad: Nava Hind Publications.

Mahajan, Gurpreet and Reifield, Helmut (eds.) (2003) *The Public and the Private: Democratic Citizenship in Comparative Perspective*, New Delhi: Sage.

Marcuse, Herbert (1964) *One-Dimensional Man: Studies in the Ideology of Advanced Industrial Society*, London: Routledge.

Mishra, R. K. and Kiranmai, J. (2011) "Disinvestment in Public Enterprises in India: A Critical Analysis", *Alternative Economic Survey, India: Two Decades of Neoliberalism*, New Delhi: Daanish: 287–304.

Mohanty, Manoranjan (1998) "Social Movements in Creative Society," in Manoranjan Mohanty, Partha Mukherji with Olle Tornquist (eds.) *People's Rights*, New Delhi: Sage, pp. 68–81.

Mohanty, Manoranjan (2003) "CPC's Fourth Generation Ideology," *Economic and Political Weekly* 38(14): 1365–1369.

Mohanty, Manoranjan (2007) "Grappling with the 'Success Trap' in China," *Economic and Political Weekly* 42(44): 17–19.

Mohanty, Manoranjan (2010) "China's Reforms: The Wuxi Story," in *China after 1978: Craters in the Moon—Essays from Economic and Political Weekly*, Hyderabad: Orient Blackswan, pp. 89–122.

Mohanty, Manoranjan (2012) "Harmonious Society: Hu Jintao's Vision and the Chinese Party Congress," *Economic and Political Weekly* 47(50): 12–16.

Mohanty, Manoranjan and Selden, Mark (2007) "Reconceptualising Local Democracy," in Manoranjan Mohanty, Richard Baum, Rong Ma, and George Mathew (eds.) *Grassroots Democracy in India and China: The Right to Participate*, New Delhi: Sage, pp. 459–477.

Nagaraj, R. (2006) "Public Sector Performance in India Since 1950: A Fresh Look", *Economic and Political Weekly*, June 24: 2251–2257.

Parel, Anthony J. (ed.) (1997) *Gandhi: Hind Swaraj and Other Writings*, Cambridge: Cambridge University Press.

Patnaik, Prabhat (2003) *Retreat to Unfreedom*, New Delhi: Tulika.

Patnaik, Prabhat, Chandrasekhar, C. P., and Ghosh, Jayati (2004) "The Political Economy of the Reform Strategy: The Role of the Capitalist Class," in Manoranjan Mohanty (ed.) *Class, Caste, Gender*, New Delhi: Sage, pp. 89–105.

Planning Commission, Government of India (2012) "Approach Paper to the Twelfth Five Year Plan," available online: http://planningcommission.gov.in/plans/ planrel/12appdrft/ approach_12plan.pdf (accessed January 8, 2014).

Rao, Ashok (2011) "The Political Economy of Disinvestment: Are We Recolonizing India?" in *Alternative Economic Survey, India: Two Decades of Neoliberalism*, New Delhi: Daanish, pp. 305–320.

Redding, Gordon and Witt, Michael A. (2007) *The Future of Chinese Capitalism: Choices and Chances*, New York: Oxford University Press.

Sahu, Subrat Kumar and Dash, Mamata (2011) "Expropriation of Land and Cultures: The Odisha Story and Beyond," *Social Change* 41(2): 251–270.

Schumacher, E. F. (1973) *Small is Beautiful: Economics as if People Mattered*, London: Hartley and Mark.

Shourie, Arun (2004) *Governance and the Sclerosis That Has Set In*, New Delhi: Rupa and Co.

Shue, Vivienne (1988) *The Reach of the State: Sketches of the Chinese Body Politic*, Stanford, CA: Stanford University Press.

Tan, Chung (2008) *Rise of the Asian Giants: The Dragon–Elephant Tango*, Kolkata: Anthem Press.

Wang, Shuaguang (2010) "Double Movement in China," in *China after 1978: Craters in the Moon—Essays from Economic and Political Weekly*, Hyderabad: Orient Blackswan, pp. 65–88.

White, Lynn T. III (1998) *Unstately Power: Local Causes of China's Economic Reforms*, Armonk: M. E Sharpe.

Xue Muqiao (1985) *China's Socialist Economy: An Outline History (1949–1984)*, Beijing: Foreign Languages Press.

Yang, Dali Y. (2004) *Remaking the Chinese Leviathan: Market Transition and the Politics of Governance in China*, Stanford, CA: Stanford University Press.

Zheng, Yongnian (2004) *Globalization and State Transformation in China*, Cambridge: Cambridge University Press.

Index

Page numbers in *italics* denote tables, those in **bold** denote figures.

For Product Safety Concerns and Information please contact our EU
representative GPSR@taylorandfrancis.com
Taylor & Francis Verlag GmbH, Kaufingerstraße 24, 80331 München, Germany